Four Eyes

A Memoir
of a Millennial Caregiver

ALISHA BASHAW

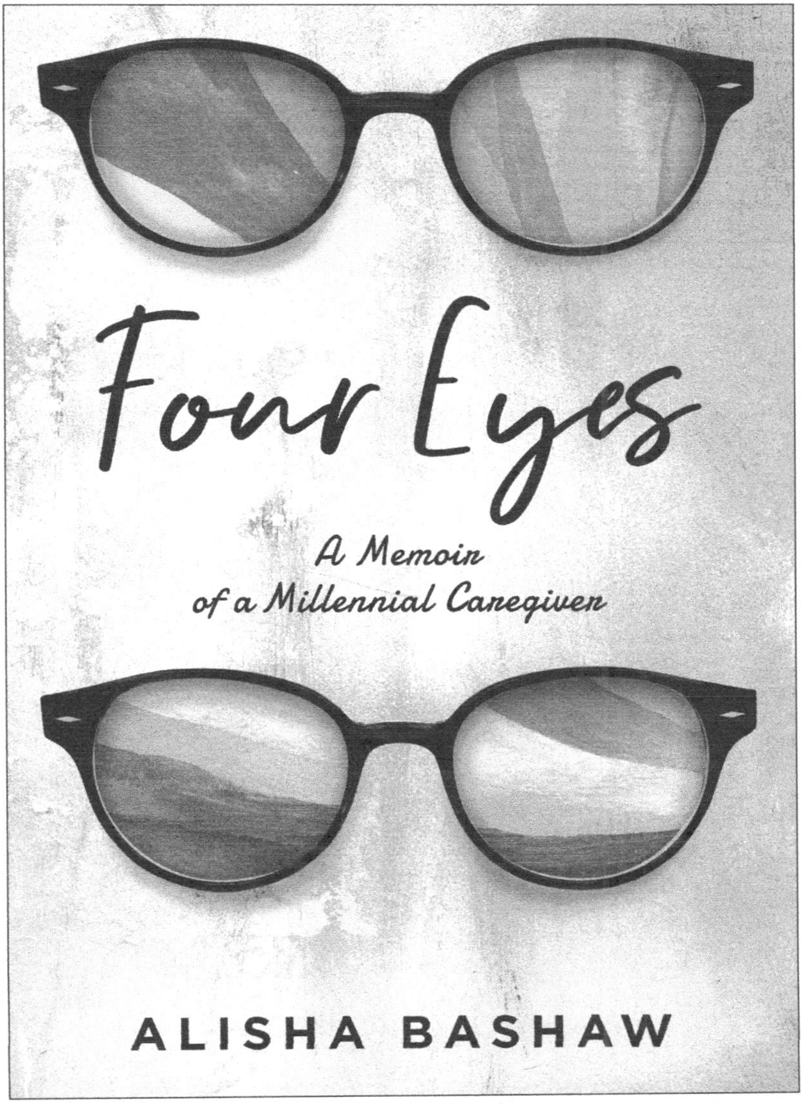

Woodhall Press
Norwalk, CT

FOUR EYES

A Memoir of a Millennial Caregiver

ALISHA BASHAW

Woodhall Press
Norwalk, CT

woodhall press

Woodhall Press, 81 Old Saugatuck Road, Norwalk, CT 06855
WoodhallPress.com

Cover design: Asha Hossain
Layout artist: Wendy Bowes

Library of Congress Cataloging-in-Publication Data available

ISBN 978-1-949116-71-7 (paper: alk paper)
ISBN 978-1-949116-72-4 (electronic)

First Edition

Distributed by Independent Publishers Group
(800) 888-4741

Printed in the United States of America

*for all organ donors, everywhere,
especially my mom and dad*

CHAPTER 1

November 26, 2016, 10:31 A.M.

I LOOKED AROUND the room. It was mostly the same as they all were, minus the mind-numbing beeps of machines and mazes of tubes in the ICU that constantly reminded me that everything was not okay. Hospice was different. It was bland, ordinary; not memorable or forgettable, just there. The walls held the disappointment of decline for millions of loved ones between the many layers of beige paint.

My brother, Mat, arrived with breakfast. I focused my attention on the Styrofoam "to-go" container he handed me, and pondered how I had become a card-carrying anti-environmentalist overnight.

The nurse was talking to us. Her makeup was patchy, and there was a bit of lipstick on one of her front teeth. I noticed every detail these days. All the details but my own. I was gone, melded deeply into the folds of my upbringing's "shoulds," functioning for others, despite my growth in recent history. Individuation had suffered one too many of Guilt's blows as I searched my hollowed insides for any trace of me remaining.

The nurse's blonde hair was perfectly—and unnaturally—set into a shoulder-length horseshoe around her head, and she was staring at us.

1

"Sorry, what?" I snapped out of it briefly.

"That's okay, honey. I asked what color? Purple or leopard print?"

Mat and I laughed out loud at the thought of leopard print.

"Purple," we said in unison.

The nurse began moving around again, still talking to us. I had no idea what she was saying. I looked at Mat. He was also vacant, afraid of what was to come. None of this made sense. My brain was foggy, and I was unsure if this was really happening. Lord, how I wished it weren't.

Moments ago in my dream, I was in the living room of my old ranch-style house in Michigan with Sniff, our beloved keeshond, and my dad. My dad was young, and healthy. He even had hair. We were talking about my mom. "Rivers and Roads" by the Head and the Heart was playing on repeat, and the chorus blared out "River and roads, rivers and roads, rivers 'til I meet you" with a knowing confidence. My dad had a light behind his eyes that illuminated him in a way that I had not seen in quite a while. I started to talk with him, and he kept telling me of the beauty of life, like he always did. He asked about my mom.

Reality jarred me from remembering more of my dream when another nurse entered the room. This one had pain medication. At the sight of the needle, I could feel myself float into the present, gather all the willpower I had left, and choose to enter this situation.

My mom was dying. She lay before Mat and me, shallowly breathing, unconscious. Her blood pressure was dropping by the minute. The nurses were now curling her shorter blondish-brown hair. She always wanted to look her best. They continued telling us how our mom had told them of her love for deep purple satin, affirming our color choice for the nightgown they had placed her in, despite it being a soft lavender. I nodded along with their assessment, though I had never once heard her utter such a preference. I studied her face, swollen from the fluid retention that renal failure brings. She was so beautiful, just like always, and began to breathe in increments of seconds. Mat and I held her hands, and began to cry.

"I love you, Mom," Mat said. "You are not alone. It's okay now." He kept going. My insides froze. Holding back tears made my face hot, and I wiped them away silently with my sleeve.

When he was done, we looked at each other, and our pain merged with the collective grief of the many others who had come before us and lost loved ones in this same room. The beige-painted walls were caked in layers of despondent defeat.

"I love you too, Mom," I uttered as I squeezed her hand and gave her permission, once again. Permission that I had given her several times throughout the past five years, but this time, it was for real. This time, I hated it the most. "I am going to live my life well, I promise. We will be okay," I said through a wall of tears. "You are so strong, you don't have to be scared."

My mom started to breathe the short bursts of little breaths we had been warned about.

I started to spill out my dream to her with urgent clarity. "Mom, I saw Dad, and he was okay. He was with Sniff, and he was in our old living room, and he was young and had hair and he asked about you. He's okay," I gushed.

In my dream, I had been confused at how my dad could exist in both a canister of ashes on my kitchen table and also in my old house on Bradford Street. Now, however, my understanding took a new shape as I envisioned him appearing in my dream to invite my mom to be with him and Sniff and to leave her long suffering behind.

"Mom, I think Dad is asking you to join him," I whisper-cried, wiping my wet face on the back of my hand. "Mat was in my dream too, and he said that Dad had been around. I know you will be too."

She was unresponsive. I looked at Mat's tear-stained face as he encouraged her to join my dad. We watched as my mom's breathing slowly moved from every two seconds to every five, then seven, and finally none. She slowly took her last breath and exhaled what looked like coffee grounds, which we were assured was "normal," ending a grueling five-year, knock-down, drag-out war with chronic illness, her body, and wholeness.

She was gone.

I took in this new reality as if concrete were slowly filling and hardening my lungs. Everything was fuzzy. Off-kilter. Wrong. My mom was dead.

My mind knew this moment was coming and tried to prepare for the tears, the chilled numbing, the sorrowful grief, and any other emotions tagging along, but my heart was the one talking. It was pumping fear through my veins with hot, angry beats. My skin was red and raised as my mind raced to catch up to it. What happens now? How could I have ever prepared to be a young adult orphan?

CHAPTER 2

November 26, 2016, 3:00 P.M.

THE REST OF that day was a blur. I couldn't focus on anything, and I felt like I was drunk. Immediately after my mom died, a different nurse entered the room and covered her eyes with saline and gauze, stating, "She had such beautiful blue eyes; we want to make sure to preserve them for donation, as she wanted."

Though I knew this was coming, I was not ready. I wondered if anyone was ever ready for this. I wanted to scream at the nurse to back away from my mom, to not touch her or her eyes. My own burned with the stinging truth that all she once was no longer existed. That her wish was to give her sight to others who needed it upon her death. That that would make her the happiest. It was beautiful. Reflective of my mom. And it hurt like hell. Organ donation was a part of the mystery.

We called the pastor of the local church she had attended; he arrived and hugged Mat and me tightly as we cried and talked about next steps.

Mat got the tall gene of the family at just over six feet, and whenever I stood next to him at five-foot-one, it was rather humorous. He was in the construction field and had been all over the corporate ladder, his latest job bringing him to Quality and Safety Assurance at jobsites. He had dark hair, now balding in his mid-thirties, and a kind smile. He was tanned and muscular, and was a great Mr. Fixit. I wished he could fix this. We both did.

The hospital placed a single white rose above the room number so the funeral home would know which room to enter. We sat with my mom's body, dressed in light purple, her eyes covered in gauze, and accepted condolences from moving mouths and compassionate eyes. I wondered if anyone could really see me. I felt as if I had been shattered into a million pieces and was floating into a different dimension. I didn't like this reality, my new truth.

Just two months ago, I had been crying on the phone to both my parents from Michigan, where Mat and I had traveled for my grandpa's funeral. I was distraught, and remembered my parents telling me, "It's okay to be a crying mess, Lish; it's really sad," as I told them I was hiding in a bathroom in my grandparents' condo, completely melting down as my sadness burst out of me and I was running out of breath. The condo was full of my childhood memories and irreplaceable sentiment that was hard to pack.

We had seen my grandma earlier that day in her nursing home, and it stung when she didn't remember who Mat and I were. My grandparents were always around as we grew up, and though my grandma was still alive, dementia had slowly taken her memories, one by one, over the past few years. I didn't know which kind of "gone" was worse.

My parents and I cried together on the phone, my mom not speaking much, as she had just begun to process the loss of her dad. "Call us later tonight, okay, honey?" they had asked. How was that only two months ago?

Carol, my mom's oldest friend, arrived to gather us and take us to her place to regroup and take a shower.

"It'll make you feel better," one of the nurses commented.

FOUR EYES

I had my doubts. No amount of scrubbing could take this stain away.

The funeral home folks arrived, shook our hands, and avoided eye contact with our red faces and puffy eyes. I wondered what I looked like. My eyes were so raw from crying, my face felt hot and swollen; my clothes were unmatched, and there was no way I wasn't giving off that "I've been living in hospice for the last ten days" vibe.

I heard myself say the words I needed to say in the moment—"Yes, nice to meet you; thank you for your condolences"—and then drift further and further from the room, my ears ringing. I watched myself gather my belongings, sort through my mom's remaining items, and pack them into generic plastic hospital bags. A whole life reduced into a plastic bag or two. I watched myself say goodbye to my mom one last time, and leave the room while they placed her body in a bag.

We waited outside her room, where I intricately studied the white rose above her door sign. Layered petals unfolded into the next and attached to a thick green stem covered in leaves, thorns and fine hairlike fibers. In a few minutes, they rolled my mom out of the room on a gurney; a tall, quiet man lifted the rose from its place and set it gently atop my mom's body bag. As if that made it better. We all walked in silence through the hospital to the hearse, where they loaded my mom inside; the men shook hands with us again, stating more polite condolences as they got into the car. I wondered how many times they had done this in this week alone. And how many more times I could politely accept them.

I stared at the car, recognizing in a sharp instant that this would be the last time I ever saw my mom. My insides lit on fire and burned and twisted and raged as my body temperature boiled, and I could feel my pulse thumping into my fingertips. My eyes were wet, my tears everywhere.

I watched the men drive my mom away.

I floated above myself into the next action, and got into Carol's car to return to her house. I felt my heart beat, but watched it continue to slowly bleed. I watched my familiar life churn, fight, and suffer a blow so big that it keeled over and began to writhe in pain. I couldn't breathe. I watched life disappear from all that I had ever known and resign to its own death, leaving my insides empty and hollow. My face scrunched up in pain. As we drove away from the hospital, I watched the old me grow smaller and smaller in the mirror until it was no more. I was no more.

CHAPTER 3

November 27, 2016, 10:00 A.M.

I WOKE UP the next morning standing in my broken heart. In its shards. Everywhere I looked, it was overwhelming. There were pieces strewn all around me, big and small, sharp and edgy, raw and wounded. I was lost in a sea of pulsating pain, slowly oozed out of a dream and steeped into the reality of a new day. It was a slow death of old me, and painful—unlike hers, thankfully. There was space all around me, begging to be filled. But it was vast, and the wasteland of death had moved in. Nothing hid its openness. Each moment was the same. Numb. My thoughts drifted to the hows that framed my current reality. This wasn't supposed to happen. I was only thirty-four. I thought back to the beginning and that first phone call.

CHAPTER 4
April 17, 2012, 5:30 P.M.

"**HAPPY BIRTHDAY TO** you, happy birthday to you, happy birthday dear Daaaaaaadddddddd," I sang theatrically as I answered his call.

"Lish . . . ," his voice was low.

"Happy birthday toooooo yoooouuuuuuuuu!" I dragged out the ending to be extra obnoxious, overexaggerating a jazz hand for emphasis.

"Lish," he began again. "I don't know how to say this, but Mom had a heart attack; you need to come home this weekend." My dad spoke flatly. My free-swaying jazz hand abruptly stopped, fingers wide apart, as I stood in disbelief.

"What?" I asked. I was at school, and class had just ended. I started to quickly gather my books and notebooks from my desk and toss them into my favorite thrift-store-find backpack, convinced I had misheard him.

It was my dad's sixtieth birthday, and my mom and I had been planning a surprise 1970s-themed party for my dad. It was their favorite decade. I was flying home the day after next. We had been planning this for months, and he had no idea I was coming home. My mom had been hiding all the decorations as they arrived and texting me about them in secret. The doorway beads, the lava lamp, the peace-sign

10

buttons, and the party hats were all hidden throughout the house, and we had a plan of decorating attack all set to begin tomorrow night, when I would arrive home from the airport. I lived for surprises, and my excitement was almost turning to restlessness in anticipation.

What I didn't know yet was that my mom was also surprising me with a thirtieth-birthday celebration, as my birthday had been two weeks prior. Many of my friends still in Colorado were planning on attending the party, and my mom had been in contact with them behind my back. She had been busy, and I had no idea. She also liked creative surprises.

"Seriously, Babes, I don't want to scare you, but we are in the hospital now." My dad's words came through the phone line across the country like a pitchfork.

"Oh, my God, you're serious. Um, what happened?" I stammered, trying to make sense of his words.

"Well, you know your mother," he began, letting the familiar phrase convey her fierce independence and desire to do everything all by herself, all at the same time. "She called me yesterday to help her carry her supplies into her new moms' class at the hospital because she was a little out of breath. She also had a backache all weekend."

"And that means she had a heart attack? How bad was it? Is she okay?" I wondered, my brain firing thoughts and questions almost faster than my mouth could deliver them.

"She had a doctor's appointment this morning; they drew some blood and sent us on our way. We were going to the Japanese place, you know, my favorite spot, for my birthday lunch, and Dr. Malloy called and told us to get to the hospital immediately. Some of her heart enzymes were elevated, and they were indicative of a possible heart attack or blood clot. And, well, you know your mother . . ." he trailed off.

"What did she do, Dad?"

"Well, she wanted to make sure my birthday was special, and asked if we could go after lunch. Dr. Malloy said absolutely not; she was upset, but I convinced her to just get it checked out. So we drove to MCR, and she walked herself into the hospital—and had a heart attack soon after, without even knowing or feeling it. The doctors said there was previous damage to her heart too, so she probably had one at home over the weekend too. She's getting a CAT scan now to check for blood clots."

The silence grew, and the cold chill of the Pittsburgh night air expanded inside of me. I was sitting in my car now, unable to speak, unable to move. My mind was whirring with possibilities and worst-case scenarios. Tears began to pool in the corners of my eyes.

"Babes? You there?"

"Yeah, I'm here," I sniffled.

"I think you'd better come home."

"Yeah. Well, some birthday, huh?"

"Yeah, it's a gift I'll never forget, that's for sure," he joked dryly.

"So, I don't know if Mom told you, but I was actually planning on coming home this weekend anyway. We were planning you a surprise party."

"She told me."

Well, shit, I thought to myself.

CHAPTER 5
April 19, 2012, 3:45 P.M.

I WALKED INTO the Medical Center of the Rockies for the first of what would become innumerable times. My dad was walking along next to me, and his bright white Reebok shoes were untied. For him, the undone laces meant that my mom was going to get better. For me, they meant he could fall over at any time. I went with his version.

"Second floor," the elevator announced, and we exited onto the Cardiac and Surgical ICU floor. I followed my dad left into the Cardiac ICU wing, and we walked down to her corner room, on the right. My dad was on the shorter side and was slightly stocky, with olive-toned skin and wire-framed glasses that sat atop his face 60 percent of the time. The other 40 percent, he spent looking for them.

My mom was lying flat on the bed, in an induced coma, and was breathing through a ventilator. I held my breath as I took in the sight of my very capable and independent mom exhibiting only her mortal humanity at this moment. Her hair was a mess, and her makeup was smudgy due to the oxygen tubing in her nose and around her ears. She would hate that.

"The doctors thought it was going to be triple-bypass

surgery, but when they got in there, it ended up being a quadruple bypass. Her heart was not doing what it needed to do on its own, so they had to put in a balloon pump to help it beat regularly," my dad caught me up quietly.

I nodded, not able to take my eyes off all the machines connected to her. I started counting the medications attached to her IV. One, two, three, four . . .

"There was no blood clot, but she had an angiogram yesterday; they found three blockages, so they prepped her for surgery today."

Five, six, seven. . . . In all my years, I had only seen my dad cry a handful of times; today was one of them. In an instant, he poured out his worst fear.

"My mom was on a ventilator," he spoke of my grandma, "I know what happens when the vent comes out," he said, alluding to my grandma's death within a few hours.

"We don't know that, Dad," I said, beginning my pattern of what was to become the eventual holding of hope for us all. I was, however, the eternal optimist.

For the next few days, I kept staring. The nurses taught us how to wet her lips with tiny sponges on sticks to prevent chapping, and they began to roll her onto alternating sides every few hours to prevent bedsores.

Bedsores, I thought. Aren't those for old people? She is going to be fine.

CHAPTER 6

April 21, 2012, 11:30 A.M.

"DAD," I SAID as I watched him begin to cry. "They are taking out the balloon pump. That's a good sign! Her heart can beat on its own again without any help."

"I know, sweetheart. I know," he said as he lay his head down on the bed, showing off his bald spot that had grown bigger over the years as his salt-and-pepper hair sprouted farther and farther away from the top. He had a small combover left.

He held my hand from across her hospital bed. Surely this will be over soon.

CHAPTER 7

April 23, 2012, 10:45 A.M.

THE LAST TWO days felt like thirty. "Hospital time," as we came to know it as, was a completely different existence. Before long, twelve hours would pass, and although having done nothing but talk to my mom hoping she could hear, wet her lips with the weird stick sponges every so often, and talk about all the what-ifs with my dad and Mat, who came after work daily, I was completely exhausted. I remembered driving the twenty minutes back to my parents' house to let Sniff out, but that felt like yesterday. Maybe it was?

The doctors had slowly been bringing my mom out of the induced coma, and she graced us with her shining bright blue eyes several times. She remained in and out of consciousness on the ventilator, but could look at us and communicate with her eyes, as the ventilator was still in place of any words she might muster. It was weird to see her that way, unable to communicate via her traditional means. A teacher of thirty years, she thrived on her words to leave impacts, imprints. This was new territory for us all.

Dr. Stevens entered my mom's room with his typical cheerful greeting: "Hey team, how we doing in here?"

My dad answered for us all and went right into the

questions. This was it, in his mind. The day she would either come back to us or pass on once they took her off the ventilator. He was still not convinced that she was not going to follow after his mom, and as I looked over, a single tear slipped from his eye.

Dr. Stevens explained the day's plan. They would slowly be waking her up to complete consciousness, and then they'd get her standing to walk to a chair to sit upright for a while.

"You guys ready?" he asked, mostly rhetorically.

Were we? I wondered to myself. Maybe my dad was right? I was getting more nervous, and I shoved my hands into my jeans pockets to stop them from shaking.

The team of nurses unhooked the tubing from the ventilator and turned off the machine. My mom's chest began to rise and fall gently on its own. We stared at her breath, as if our staring could make it continue. So far so good, I thought, eyeing my dad in the process.

A few hours later, she opened her kind blue eyes, as if for the first time. The nurses had been weaning her off the sedation drugs, and she came to like a dimmer switch, a little bit at a time.

My dad cried. Tears of joy this time, though, and grabbed her hand as she came into her new reality in a hospital bed, recovering from quadruple bypass surgery. When Mat got there after work, my mom greeted him with a faint smile, and a hug. She was weak, but still here. The doctors were able to get her up and walking four feet to a chair, where she spent twenty minutes sitting upright, the accomplishment for the day. After much cheering, they escorted her back to bed for more pain medication. Her rib cage was sewn together with wire, and it would take a bit to heal.

"Hon, it's so good to see you," my dad lovingly spoke, his tears long gone by now. "I can't wait to hear what you remember from all of this," he said, stroking her hair.

She stared back blankly from her slightly fuzzy blue eyes and slowly shook her head as if to say, "Nothing. I remember nothing."

I smiled. It was probably better that way.

CHAPTER 8

April 25, 2012, 3:30 P.M.

SNIFF'S NOSE WAS glued to the same part of the sidewalk in our cul-de-sac as it always was. Our neighbor's pug was barking a more ferocious hello than she could deliver, and Sniff knew it, lingering longer.

"Come on, Sniff, we get to go see Mom today!" I tried. She didn't budge.

"Sniff, want to go buh-bye?" I tried again. Her ears shot up instantly, and she ran to me and licked my hand. I chuckled to myself as we walked back to our house—and tried not to think about what she had just been sniffing, which was now, in part, on my hand.

I opened the door to the dark gray Ford Fusion, the latest installment in my parents' Ford lineage, and the one I always drove when I was home from grad school to visit. She hopped in and took her place in the passenger-side seat like an old pro. The drive to the hospital was rote, and uneventful. If only its internal experience could match the external. I parked in the lot I now knew pretty well, scoring a closer spot than usual. As soon as her leash was clipped on, Sniff was off on her mission: to find my mom and lie next to her while she healed.

It's funny that after a while, such a sterile place could offer some comfort in its tan walls and extravagant art pieces that aimed to get you to pretend you were anywhere but here. The elevator dinged its staccato "second floor," and we took to the familiar hallway with the purple carpet leading the way to my mom's room.

"Hi, Zoe!" a group of nurses exclaimed as we rounded the corner. It was always weird to hear Sniff's real name used, as Sniff fit her so much better in my mind, but she didn't care. She would take pets from anyone. She wagged her curlicue tail, which in turn wagged her whole body as we continued toward my mom's room. When we got to the door, we were not prepared for what we saw.

My mom was sitting upright in a chair about four feet from her hospital bed, and was talking to a friend on her cell phone. She was a small-framed woman with fair skin, and stood at average height. Her slender cheekbones no longer looked sunken in. The giant chair made her look like a kid. The nurse greeted me with an enormous smile and shared the daily update with me as my awe set in. This was her third time up in the chair today, to drain her chest and the wound from an upright position, and she had been taking phone calls . . . All. Day. Long.

Wow! This is amazing, I thought. Finally! We are through the worst of it!

"Okay, good to talk to you too," my mom ended her last call, her voice scratchy and fragile.

"Hi, hon," she turned her attention to me. "How are you?"

It took me a minute to register with reality, as I was not anticipating her coherence.

"I'm great now, Mom, especially to be able to talk with you!" I answered, still in shock, trying to catch my breath again after realizing I had been holding it. "How are you feeling?"

"Oh, pretty good," came her standard reply. She was

rarely less than that.

"Where's Dad?" I asked, finally scanning the room to realize he was not in his visitor position.

"Oh, Stu came to take him to lunch today," she said, her voice beginning to show its fatigue.

Stu and Lisa were our across-the-street neighbors. My parents had moved from Michigan in 2002, and had befriended most of the entire block. Mostly my mom's doing. Stu and Lisa were no exception, and had become my parents' closest friends. I was so happy that my dad was getting out of that 10 × 8 cell block for some air and to connect with a good friend.

"Awesome!" I said, noting a bit of light returning to my mom's eyes. I could see her in there, and I knew she was going to be okay.

Sniff finished inspecting the room for any alterations since she had been here twelve hours ago and lay down next to my mom's bed, sighing loudly for what felt like both of us.

The nurse was back. She had shoulder-length blonde hair that was half tied back and a warm presence. "Okay, Sherri, it doesn't look like we are close to weaning you off that last IV med just yet, but hang tight; we will get there," she offered in her singsong voice as she prepared my mom's bed for her to get back into it. "We can try again tomorrow, but for now your blood pressure is too low without it," she said, smiling at me. She turned back to my mom and said, "It's not much to worry about. You've come a long way!"

She moved over toward the chair my mom was in, and wrapped the off-white cloth gait belt with red and blue stripes down the middle around her for support. "Let's get you back in bed here to get some more rest."

My mom groaned. "Oh, already? I don't know, but I'll try," she offered hesitantly. With that, the nurse aided her in standing, guiding her along as she ever so slowly shuffled

21

the four steps back to her bed. Once in a seated position, it was another fifteen minutes before she was lying down.

It must be so painful to move up and down like that, I thought. What a trooper she is.

She was exhausted and had just begun to drift back off to sleep when my dad returned. He made his rounds of hellos to Sniff and me, pulled up a chair next to my mom's bed, and rested his own bright eyes for a post-lunch food-coma catnap. He accidentally bumped her foot as he sat, dislodging the sheet from atop a few toes. They looked slightly bluish. "Huh," I thought aloud, and pointed them out to my dad. "She must be cold," he responded. "She's always cold." I found some socks lying in a pile of clean laundry my dad had brought back from the house for her and put them on her feet. I looked at my dad, and he was already dozing. I sat on the floor with Sniff, petting her until the nurse's next check-in an hour later. It was the most peaceful hour I had had in more than a week.

CHAPTER 9

April 27, 2012, 1:47 P.M.

MY MOM'S DETERMINATION and faith pushed her forward into recovery. The doctors removed her catheter and placed her on a new medication to help her heart pump regularly. She received an echocardiogram, and I first learned what an ejection fraction was, which would soon become an active part of my vocabulary. I had grown up with words, books, and feelings, but never medical lingo—until now. My mom's ejection fraction, or percentage of oxygenated blood that flowed out of the left ventricle of her heart to the rest of her body, tested at 30 percent. A normal percentage, we all learned that day, is 55 to 60 percent and higher. In layman's terms, her heart was failing. No one knew what to make of this information as it slowly seeped into our psyches.

"She's crying again, Dad," I said, nodding toward my mom's room as we walked back from the hospital kitchenette down the hallway with purple carpet. The more I stared at the carpet, the more I saw the subtlety of the gold flecks embedded within it. "How am I just noticing this now?" I murmured out loud to no one in particular.

"Ow-ow-ow!" came her painful cries, floating down the

hallway and stopping at our hearts.

A small hand reached up for mine, snapping me back into the moment. My two-year-old nephew, Brooks, had recently discovered the freezer in said kitchenette and insisted that we take a group trip with my dad for "poxicles," as he called them. He liked the red ones best.

"One, two, three, swiiiiinnnnngg," my dad cheered as we simultaneously held Brooks's hands in ours and swung him high as he erupted into a fit of giggles.

"I know," my dad's delayed response came through the laughter in a steely monotone. "It's getting worse and worse lately. She's in so much pain; it's awful to watch."

"Poxicle, pwease?" Brooks asked through a goofy smile, looking up at us and pleading with his big brown eyes.

"Well of course, buddy," my dad replied as we got to the room and he handed Brooks one. I mentally noted his untied stark-white Reeboks.

"Dad, please be careful with those laces," I said for the hundredth time. He was really taking this "untied laces means she'll get better" thing seriously. And at this point, I would take anything.

Brooks, elated with his red poxicle, ran to show it off to his dad, who was standing next to my mom, trying to help.

"Mom, what is it? What hurts?" Mat asked, worried.

The tone of sadness in her anguished cry met our laughter like a brick wall. Immediately, the mood changed as nurses assisted in finding my mom a new, more comfortable position as she wailed in excruciating pain.

"My feet hurt," she cried as the nurses finished propping her up onto one side and moved down to investigate them. They removed the sheet and audibly gasped at what were no longer slightly bluish toes, but deeply plum-colored feet.

"This wasn't here two hours ago," one nurse exclaimed to the other. "We've been monitoring their bluish hue, but this is new. I'll go page the doctor," she exclaimed as she flew from the room.

We all shared the shock as my mom explained that she had woken up to pulsating feet that were hard as rocks and heavy to move. What was this? I thought, horrified at the sight of the unknown.

Dr. Stevens came in a few minutes later to assess. He raised his eyebrows at the nurse and ordered some tests. Raised eyebrows meant a whole lot in medical land. I wracked my brain, trying to decipher what this version of them meant as I watched the nurse pull out the supplies needed for a blood draw. My mom's cries were stable, but still present.

"I'm going to need to get some blood, Sherri, so we can figure out what is going on here, okay?" the nurse prodded gently. My mom began to cry harder again, and half-heartedly offered up her bruised right hand, as the veins in her arm had proven too hard to find since her admission ten days ago.

"Just do it fast, please," she begged the nurse.

"I'm so sorry, hon," the nurse empathized as she stuck a butterfly needle into my mom's hand and drew three vials of blood.

CHAPTER 10

April 28, 2012, 10:00 A.M.

I SIGHED A heavy sigh in an attempt to exhale exhaustion. Without any luck. I looked across the room at my dad, dozing. Again. My mom was snoring softly in her bed. A nurse came in and noticed the sleepy room before making eye contact with me. She had a clipboard and had come to report some test results.

"Hey, Alisha," she began. I listened for her intonation. Intonation could tell you quite a bit before anything was even said.

"Hi," I smiled back. "What's the scoop?" I asked, not deciphering anything.

"Well, as we discovered yesterday, she's having a very strong allergic reaction to the blood thinner heparin," she said, nodding at my snoring mom and her purple feet; the purple had begun to extend up her legs. "But we are going to run some more tests just to make sure everything is okay. She hasn't been eating too much, and has been sleeping a lot. She is in the extremely miniscule percentage of people who react to heparin this way, so we want to be extra cautious."

"Okay," I held my gaze steady. Nothing new, I trained

myself to think. Wait to react.

"I'm sure she's just catching up on rest," I weakly offered back. "She's been on the go for a long time before any of this, and the allergic reaction is taking a lot out of her. It doesn't shock me that she is taking longer to heal." I smiled for both of us as the nurse nodded politely and said she'd check back in later.

Time passed in beeps and buzzes until I couldn't take the monotony anymore. I started to pace the hallway and eventually did a full loop until my legs remembered they were part of my body. On my way back to my mom's room, I saw a doctor speeding up to talk with our nurse. I was alert, concerned.

"Got your page. What do you need?" the doc asked quickly.

Our nurse looked up and pointed at a room that wasn't my mom's. Phew, I thought.

"Room 2516 is struggling with their decision about organ donation. They are processing the news that she won't make it; Dad is in favor, but the son is really upset. I just wanted you to have a heads-up to what you are walking into."

I felt for them, the similarity of their situation to ours not lost on me. How does anyone begin to make sense of that process? I was so glad I wasn't in their shoes. Yet.

CHAPTER 11

April 29, 2012, 12:37 P.M.

WHEN MY MOM retired from teaching fourth- and fifth-grade science, she could finally relax. And relax she did . . . for a whole six months. My mom was a creative, a people person, a connector, and sitting at home relaxing was definitely not her style. She thrived in conversation with others, always finding a way to really get to know them, and they felt it. She loved connecting with others herself as well as using her weblike network to bring people together for mutual benefit. She was extremely likable, and people often sought her company. She was most at home as the hub of her collection of people from all walks of life. They were all welcome, and everyone could learn from one another. These connections fueled her fire to continue befriending people everywhere she went, and she was always on the go.

She soon began finding part-time jobs, seeking her doctorate in homeopathic studies at a school online, crafting and sewing any new thing she could dream of, teaching English grammar to a beloved neighbor from Germany, and trying to cure every ailment (literally every . . . single . . . ailment) with peppermint oil. I was skeptical that peppermint oil would do much for her current situation, but I tossed a blue glass bottle of it into my purse for my next trip to the hospital, just in case. Present reality was a stark contrast to my mom's nature.

The part-time job she found and loved best was working for the State of Colorado for an organization called Bright Beginnings, a program designed to help new moms become comfortable with caring for their child, get connected to resources in their community, and have access to developmental information and supports. Ironically, the classes she taught were all held in local hospitals, and MCR was no exception.

One of her bosses at the time had a daughter who was diagnosed with leukemia at the age of three and, at the age of eleven, was again fighting for her life. My mom wasted no time supporting her boss and daughter any way she could, including RSVPing to a fundraising event to be held in Jenna's honor the previous night. She had stubbornly insisted that she was feeling better, just needed more rest, and that my dad go without her.

"You have to go to represent us, please, Butch? I want her to know we are praying and pulling for her!" she coaxed him.

My dad, knowing what he was up against with years of experience with my mom's stubbornness, simply sighed and agreed to go. As I walked in, he was telling my mom how the event had been a wonderful success.

"How's it going today, Ma?" I asked lightheartedly. She hated when I called her "Ma." I was hoping for a smile.

"Ugh," she groaned at me. "I'm okay. Still hurting."

"The docs have given her something for the heparin reaction, and the plum color is slowly fading back to blue," my dad offered. "But they say it will probably take a while."

My mom was a fighter. And one with endurance. She was such an important figure in her world, in her community, and I couldn't imagine a situation other than her returning to her old self and resuming her life. This would all be over soon.

I sighed a big sigh, realizing that my plane back to Pittsburgh was leaving early tomorrow morning. I was both eager to get back to my house, my city, my school, and hesitant to leave while my mom was still hospitalized. This was the first of many times I became aware of just how not black and white this situation was. Gray was everywhere.

CHAPTER 12

May 11, 2012, 7:14 P.M.

LIFE, AS I knew it, had significantly changed. I had flown back to Pittsburgh to enormous support awaiting me from my friends and professors. The past eleven days had been a blur of wrapping up a semester's worth of classes, asking for extensions on certain assignments, trying to work at my AmeriCorps job for the allotted number of hours per week I owed them until summer break, and running a half-marathon a couple of friends from grad school and I had signed up for on a whim.

I had trained for half-marathons before and knew how much work they were. All of my high school cross-country training cycled through my mind as I took up running again. "Arms and knees, arms and knees, Lish," came the voice of my high school coach. And "If you can do these hills today, you can do anything," from Mat at practice one day when I was particularly struggling. I knew it was a mental battle, and one of endurance, not strength. My training this go-around, however, had taken a turn for the worse when a friend had died over my Christmas break home just four months ago. Grief felt like a vice in my chest when I ran, and I never seemed to get enough air. Each step on the pavement pounded a new truth of Liz's death into my being, and it was extremely overwhelming. I caved under its pressure and ended up walking or forgoing most of my training. Yet, come race day, we managed to make the 13.1 miles in mostly one piece.

Exhaustion transitioned from being my bane to my friend and eventually into my normal. I leaned on my fast school friends Courtney and Kelly a tremendous amount, and they listened and sat and experienced it all with me without expecting anything in return. It was uncomfortable. Rule number one of the evangelical social contract in which I was raised was to always place others before yourself, no questions. Second only to God. I came after these, but only when I had time, and often as a last resort. To have issues or problems of my own meant that I was becoming the word I hated the most: "selfish." And being selfish was the worst thing you could be in this contract. There was no in-between. That issues existed at all in my life was a commentary on how strong my faith was or, in this case, wasn't.

And yet, in my sad moments when I had not fulfilled my end of this social contract with these friends, they did not pull their relationship away from me as a consequence; in contrast, they were not put off by my feelings at all. Even more surprisingly, they seemed to come closer to me and to my experiences. It didn't make sense. They didn't seem to understand the contract at all. It made me begin to question my signature on said contract, and upon examination, it wasn't my name that I had used to close this deal at all. It was signed with approval-seeking behavior, dated with over-apologizing for potentially inconveniencing another.

I didn't know the rules of this new contract that rendered the old one void, yet I found such comfort in the ebb and flow of the support Courtney and Kelly and I were able to give one another. There was space for everyone, and it was a true give-and-take. I liked this new contract, despite wrestling with the old one's continuous voice telling me I had become the dreaded "s" word. Guilt was born in me, and I began to recognize my inherent pull toward believing it.

Yet, feeling truly seen as already enough just as I was became intoxicatingly new and refreshing. I started to believe that maybe I wasn't alone or responsible for how they felt as I told them more and more of the sordid medical details. I began to trust that they could care for themselves and ask for what they needed when they needed it. And though Guilt was present, this also created space for me to have my experience as just my own, and not in a ranked order of any kind. The rankings were obsolete. I could be however I needed to be without feeling judged. I proceeded in this new deal with cautious optimism.

The support system of my professors was an added bonus, and the more vulnerable I was with my emotional wreck-ness, the more authentic I became in speaking to my needs, not just the needs of others. Pretense was getting edged out, and I could feel Individuation wedging itself into my psyche. Behind Guilt, of course.

I was fortunate to fall asleep each night, very grateful for what I had while praying for strength for my mom to continue her fighting and healing. After all, deep inside, I just knew that she would be alright. Changed, but fine. Definitely still able to carry on. Our family would eventually reminisce about this in memory only. We would continue on, no matter the toll. We always had. She always had.

My gut intuition about life had always been eerily accurate, though I rarely spoke about it. It was my secret signal with God, my inner knowing, the foundation of my evangelically-rooted faith for as long as I could remember. I was taught that sometimes God spoke through this "inner knowing," and I leaned heavily on this when I couldn't hear an actual voice, despite my endless trying. It became my gauge of measuring my actions in accordance with God's will for me. If I just knew something was right in a way that was hard to explain, then it was God. If not, I was clearly out of sync with his will and being punished with silence until I corrected course. There was no way, no chance, no remote possibility that my mom's situation would be any different. My inner knowing was coming. Wasn't it?

My dad called every night with an update, none of them very good. I began to greatly despise my phone. He reported that my mom was not healing, that her blood pressure was so low at times, they were afraid that if they took her off the IV medication that boosted her blood pressure, she wouldn't make it. Her feet and legs were back to normal, though her toes remained dark black and would need to be amputated. Patients on IV medications cannot leave the ICU, so my mom's journey continued to be punctuated by beeps and drips and alarms. My dad sounded more and more haggard each night, dragging out his words, and sighing a lot. He was spending twelve-hour days at the hospital to be with her in the unfolding news of what was next, and I was certain he was not sleeping much, if at all. I was itching to get home. To do something—anything. To help in some way. There was something so helpful about presence, and if I were there, I could at least compute what was happening with my own perspective rather than secondhand through my dad's.

These calls threatened my carefully crafted universe revolving around papers, due dates, meetings, group projects, study sessions with friends, the third calendar I had recently acquired to keep track of my current life, and my seeming functionality. I could feel my grasp on my details slipping, and another calendar was sure to steer me back toward sanity. Right?

Occasionally I would celebrate small victories with my dad when he reported that my mom ate a full meal, or didn't wake up in pained tears, but overall, the mood was grim. I dug deep within whenever he would hand my mom the phone when she mustered strength to talk, and tried to bring my usual upbeat outlook into our conversations. I could feel my mom's depression through the phone, and it hit me square in the chest like a freight train. Her one- or two-word answers knocked the wind out of me and flattened my determination. Talking for long was becoming less of an option for us both.

The amputation of her toes had occurred, and all her toes, save her two big toes and a pinky toe, were gone. She was utterly devastated and embarrassed at her new "ugly feet," as she called them over and over again, despite what anyone told her.

"You should see them, Lish. I will never be able to wear flip-flops again," she said on repeat.

Due to her feet, it had become harder and harder for her to get up and participate fully in physical and occupational therapy, which made it harder for her to heal. She was declining, and fluid was beginning to build up in her lungs, eventually resulting in pneumonia. She wasn't eating much, and the latest report from my dad, last night, included a possible nasogastric tube being placed from her nose to her stomach to get her some nutrition. It was with this update that I told him I would be home at the end of the week. I bought my ticket immediately, hardly noticing the price.

That all sounds fixable. I thought after I hung up. Just a complex process of what will heal first, I told myself to soothe my sadness.

The next night, while I was doing my homework, my phone buzzed at me from my pocket. It was my dad. I looked around my basement room's beige-painted paneling for something to stare at that that would be better than answering another hard phone call from my dad. There was nothing. I closed my eyes and answered.

I lay back on my bed as I listened and began counting my ceiling tiles. My landlord had graciously built a third room in his two-bedroom listing to accommodate my roommates and me, and I ended up in the basement addition. The ceiling tiles reminded me of those in schools and office buildings, and I spent many nights counting them and imagining what could come out of a large hole in one of the metal-rimmed squares that was only filled with half a tile. My landlord painted the paneling walls beige to lighten it up, and put in carpet that reminded me of commercial sandpaper. I had my own entrance, was right next to the laundry room, and was so grateful to have this space, especially as a poor graduate student. I was less grateful for the house centipedes that also called my four walls home; regardless, it was a safe space in which I could light my candles, curl up on my bed, and brace for difficult conversations about what was happening to my family across the country.

My dad's update was worse than usual. The amputation of my mom's toes had taken a hard toll on her, and she was not handling it well. I couldn't imagine anyone who would. He reported that she had been placed on many additional pain medications, anti-nausea medication, and antibiotics for the pneumonia along with the continued blood pressure medication that left her stranded in the ICU. Her allergic reaction to heparin had resulted in the fear of blood clots forming in her feet and legs, and she had been given several pints of blood plasma to help boost her blood volume, which would help decrease clotting. She ended up with a nasogastric tube placed in her small intestine for five hours before it wriggled its way out, and she was getting weaker by the minute with no way to sustain nourishment. My dad's shoes remained untied.

Twenty-seven. There were twenty-seven ceiling tiles. Well, 26.5 if you counted the half-tile, half-hole situation. I liked to round up. There were twenty-seven ceiling tiles, and I was going home tomorrow.

CHAPTER 13

May 12, 2012, 5:02 P.M.

"CABIN CREW, PLEASE prepare for landing," the voice came over the plane's loudspeaker, making its abrupt way into my dream. We were gliding over the Rockies; gliding gently in a yellow life raft down the Amazon river; listening to the birds chirping, monkeys howling, and the paddling of the yellow life raft carrying a plane. We were arriving somewhere. The descent of the landing gear screeched me back into reality. I opened my eyes, groggily grasping for my whereabouts. They appeared slowly, tray table first. My iPod had been playing the same Sara Groves album on repeat, and one of the earbuds had fallen into my lap. As I picked it up and held it in my hand, it all came back, and the blurriness faded. All the memories were there—the plane, the airport, the urgency. I was back.

I deplaned and wandered around slowly, allowing the blood to flow again into lower extremities that had been cramped up for the three-hour flight. My phone buzzed in my pocket.

"Hey, kiddo." It was my dad. "You made it." His voice was less than cheery. "I am about ten minutes away."

"Okay," I replied. "Me too. I still have to get my bag."

"Meet you outside then. I'm in the car," he said, clearing up that our family van was not the chariot of choice for this trip.

"See you soon," I said as I hung up. I stopped walking and stretched as high as I could. It felt great. I felt the urgency begin to rise in me as I finished bending my legs repeatedly. It was time to hustle. We had made a plan before I got on the plane in Pittsburgh that we would go right to the hospital from the airport, as my mom wasn't doing well, though I didn't yet know all the details. I picked up my pace and rounded the corner to the baggage claim. The gold animals etched into the airport flooring caught my eye.

Interesting, I thought. I had never noticed them before, despite many trips to and from Denver International Airport. What is with the flooring and gold flecks in this state?

My dad met me outside, and got out to give me a big hug before lifting my bag into the trunk.

"Geez, what do you have in here, bricks?!?" he asked as I handed him my backpack full of school books and the latest DSM for my diagnosis class. I was working on my master's in Clinical Mental Health Counseling, and loving every minute of it.

"Pretty much," I joked back. "I didn't know how long I'd be here or what I would need, so I brought them all."

"I can tell," came his dry reply. "Well, you probably won't need them today or tomorrow," he said as he foreshadowed what was to come.

We made small talk on the hour-and-a-half drive up north to Loveland from the airport, and I could tell my dad was very disheartened, despite his untied shoe laces. His updates reflected such. I found every silver lining I could for the remainder of the drive, and we talked about nothing being certain, for good or bad. I think he almost believed it. I had to believe it.

The hospital loomed in the distance.

There it is, I thought. A new character in my life story.

FOUR EYES

My dad parked and we walked in together in silence. Everything in me screamed no, but my feet plodded dutifully onward.

"Second floor," the elevator announced loudly, and as I rounded the corner into the Cardiac ICU, it was like no time had passed at all.

Marni and Ryan, two of the nurses who took to caring for my mom and our family right away, greeted me with hugs.

"You're back!" they exclaimed. "It's nice to see you." Their hugs felt kind, and I felt like I was home.

They led us to my mom's new room, a few rooms over from her first one, and explained that my mom had requested a change of scenery, and this room had a much nicer view of the mountains out of its windows. I totally agreed, and took in the view from the doorway. The sun was beginning to set, and it was absolutely gorgeous. The Rockies were highlighted by a glowing backdrop of colors as the sun lowered, and the sky imitated a painting, swirling together rich hues of purples and pinks and yellows and oranges. It was breathtaking.

"Good choice of a room switch, Mom!" I offered in greeting as I moved closer to her and around the foot of the bed.

"Hi, Lish," she managed as she slowly opened her eyes. "How was your flight?" She coughed as she spoke.

Typical Mom, always asking about everyone else, no matter what. I smiled, recognizing the familiarity of that trick in my own life.

Chuckling, I filled her in on the uneventful nature of my flight home. She looked pale, and had lost a significant amount of weight in the eleven days I had been gone. Suddenly, all my dad's updates came to life in front of my eyes. I noticed her bandaged feet, swollen and covered in the cheap yellow "Totes" socks with rubber pads on the bottom they give you in hospitals. Yellow, I thought. She hasn't had a yellow pair yet.

She seemed weak, and was fragile to the touch. She couldn't breathe well, and coughed often. My dad's words came back to me: There was a huge fluid buildup in her lungs, and she had a bad case of pneumonia. I couldn't help but think about what an utter shock this must be to her—to leave work one day out of breath and then be ushered into a major health crisis lasting a month at this point. In the ICU no less. Her smile was faint as I bent down to give her a hug. She only raised one arm a few inches in return. Her usual bright blue eyes were half closed as she looked at the sunset.

"It's beautiful," she rallied to say before a coughing fit took over.

I looked around at the machines beeping and humming for my mom's life. A mixture of gratitude and anger stirred inside me. I closed my eyes briefly, and took it all in. This version of my mom was just so different from the one that had walked herself into the hospital a month ago, not even knowing she had suffered a heart attack.

The nurses came in with nighttime medication and rotated her off her back, where a small, dime-size bedsore had begun to form. They encouraged my dad and me to go home and get some rest too as they gestured toward my mom, who had fallen asleep soon after taking her meds.

"That's a great idea," I said, and led my dad out of the room. "Let's go home."

CHAPTER 14

May 13, 2012, 8:47 A.M.

"LET'S GO, ALISHA!" my dad roared from the garage. "Right now!"

"Dad, what's the deal?" I yelled back from my room-turned-office, annoyed.

"I didn't sleep all night, and I just can't shake the feeling that your mom isn't okay, so let's go!" he yelled.

"Why don't I meet you there, then? I need a shower," I responded, waking up slowly to the urgency. Again.

I heard the door slam and watched him pull out of the driveway and speed down the neighborhood street. I tried desperately to separate his anxiety from my own, to no avail. I quickly jumped in the shower, got dressed, and climbed into the family van to meet everyone at the hospital, grabbing the flowers on the way out. Mat was also on his way. As I put the Ford Econoline into gear, memories of family road trips across the country filled my brain. Whether it was this van or another, so much of my childhood had been lived inside those wonderful aluminum boxes.

At the start of each summer, after they were through teaching for the year, my parents would pack us all up and road-trip from Michigan all over the country. My parents had been mostly drawn west, specifically to Colorado, for as long as I could remember. Their lifelong dream of retiring there had become a reality, and though they really missed their friends back in Michigan, they had fallen deeply in love with the mountains and landscape of the West.

Memories of endless trips out west and down south filled my mind as I recalled the carefree nature of those adventures. Driving all through the night, waking up at 3:00 a.m. and piling out of the van to eat at a local Waffle House because my dad was tired and hungry. Visiting everything interesting along the way, my mom sifting through the copious packets of information she had gathered about different destinations as we approached each one. Mat and I taking turns on the couch bed in the back and laughing in hysterics after being stuck in the van for hours on end, playing the alphabet license plate game, listening to audiobooks, stopping at Cracker Barrels along the way to return and exchange new audiobooks. Making last-minute hotel reservations in the middle of the night, swimming in the hotel pool anytime there was one, and my parents' fierce determination to see the country and experience the freedom of the road.

My parents had a vision for their retired lifestyle that was full of adventure, gratitude, and exploration, and they passed the lens through which they saw life onto Mat and me from very young ages. We all had a lot of love for the road, for discovering new things, new ways of being in the world. Ways of being that were in stark opposition to what we were currently experiencing. None of us were nearly as excited about this "adventure."

I arrived at the hospital, and navigated parking as was the usual custom in the Bashaw family: to look for a "Jeff." Jeff was a friend of my dad's that, by some miracle, nearly always managed to find a parking spot close to any entrance. I swung around the front row; nothing. A smug smile crept onto my face as I rounded row two. There was a space waiting, just for me. "Jeff does it again," I muttered to myself as I made the seventeen-point turn required to park the beastly van. It was worth every crank of the steering wheel.

I walked inside, counting my steps: one, two, three, four; one, two, three, and four . . . getting lost in the rhythm all the way up to the second floor. The ICU was quiet today. So was I. I yawned as I rounded the corner, and the familiar beige counters greeted me with their bland yet calming mediocrity. I gathered all the internal optimism I could grasp as I walked into my mom's room.

"Happy Mother's Day, Mom!" I brightly sang, surveying the room and instantly choking on the fear hanging in the air. My dad was at her side, holding her left hand, and a CNA was folding a cold washcloth in half to place on her forehead. I met my mom's glassy gaze and twitched as I felt my heart drop to my stomach. I nervously glanced up at my dad. He was fixed on her.

The CNA awkwardly stumbled around the head of the bed to shut off a beeping alarm. A nurse poked her head in, alarmed as well at the machine alerting us that my mom's blood pressure was dropping. She looked peaked and helpless as she half-smiled in my direction and began to cough.

Suddenly, my shower seemed selfish, and I instantly regretted not hurrying with my dad to get here before now. My mind whirred. What is happening? Why is she so pale? What's the plan? Why am I still holding these damn flowers?

A doctor I had not met before swiftly entered the room, messed with an IV bag, and began talking to my mom.

"Sherri, let's breathe." His voice was calm yet firm, and his strong hands began illustrating a perfect square in tandem with his words "in two three four, out two three—" He was interrupted by her cough. She sounded as though she was underwater. I began to wonder what it was like to drown, to not be able to sustain breath, terrifyingly gasping for air. A shiver up my spine drew me back into my body. I didn't want to find out, and I didn't want to watch my mom find out either.

"Sherri, you're okay, you can do this; calm down and breathe with me." The doctor kept talking to her, this time peering directly into her wide, blue, scared eyes.

He began the counting again, and I watched as she watched him, desperate to stop coughing, gasping for air. My dad was laser focused on the scene as if he were grading it, studying her response for any signs of calm that he could share with her. She began to regulate her breaths to the doctor's counting, very slowly, never losing eye contact with him. Finally the doctor relaxed his stare and stepped back a foot. My mom blinked and turned her head to my dad, who was affirming her ability to keep breathing calmly. She continued inhaling and exhaling to the counting that was no longer audible except in my head, as if that were somehow keeping her going.

The doctor excused himself from the room momentarily and returned with an announcement.

"I think we all need to give Sherri some space for a while as we adjust a few things to make her more comfortable," he began, nodding at my dad and me. "We're going to adjust some medications, and I'd like to talk with her about a few things, if that's okay." He nodded in our direction. "Butch, you're welcome to stay, but I think it's best to just give us a second first."

"Butch . . . stay . . . ," my mom croaked, and he obliged. I left the room dazed, my body tingling, and rounded the corner, bumping right into my longtime friend RJ, brother of my friend Liz, who had died at age twenty-four a few short months ago. It was the grieving for her that had shifted my half-marathon training.

"Hi," he said with a big hug. "How are you?"

"Um, well . . . ," I began.

"Are you by chance Sherri's daughter?" came another voice. "I am looking for her room." I turned slowly on my heel to see a stranger with short blonde hair peering into the windows of different rooms, pausing to ask that question with hope in her eyes.

"I am," I responded, "but she's busy at the moment. Can I help you with something?" I asked as I felt my brow line furrow, trying to place her.

"Oh, hello!" Her tone instantly became warm and her eyes brightened. "I am a friend of your parents from church. We all went to Israel together. I just couldn't believe this news when I heard it, and I wanted to bring her this card and visit with her," she said, rifling through her purse and pulling out a cream envelope.

I smiled to myself, thinking of the multitudes of cards that had poured in over the past month, each one expressing a message of hope, recovery, well wishes for a speedy healing, and detailing a story or memory of their interactions with my mom. It was truly humbling to see how many people reached out to her, to us all, and to see how many people with whom she had connected over the years.

I had always admired my parents for their outgoing attitude toward others. My dad, loaded with questions, would fire them rapidly at folks to get to know them in record time; my mom would connect people to any resource she knew of based on interests mentioned. They were both fans of giving helpful, yet unsolicited, advice. They welcomed people into their home and lives with warm, kind spirits, and wanted to make others feel comfortable, loved. Often, holidays were spent with friends who didn't have a place to go, or lived too far from home, and they were welcomed into the Bashaw family tradition as if they had always been there.

My mom built community with ease, and found ways

to interact with everyone she could, which made for some eclectically wonderful holidays. My dad saw others' stories of their experiences as puzzle pieces of their lives, and relished in hearing all about them as the picture of who they were came together in his mind. This "all are welcome attitude" was something I was so proud of my parents for creating, though it was much less embarrassing as an adult than as an angsty teenager. Something about their warmth was infectious; this woman in front of me was further evidence.

"It's nice to meet you." I smiled back, mostly meaning it. It was exhausting to retell the story of "what happened" so many times to strangers, often feeling the need to comfort them after I was done. "She's not doing too well at the moment, but you are welcome to wait and see if she's awake in a bit and say hel—" My sentence was cut short by a loud alarm sounding behind me.

I turned quickly to see nurses running from both sides of the hall, one pushing a crash cart with him and stopping at my mom's door. The other had a machine I didn't recognize.

"We need every nonessential person out," came the elevated voice of the doctor I didn't know. "Now!" My dad and two CNAs came out of the room, looking as if they were extras on a TV medical drama. I watched in slow motion as the nurses quickly pushed the carts through the doors and shut them both. They never shut both doors. I kept staring, hoping it would compute, but momentarily, both curtains were drawn to conceal whatever was happening inside. I had seen enough of Grey's Anatomy to know that this had just gotten very serious.

I turned back to RJ and the mystery friend, my eyes wide and panicked. RJ nodded.

"Why don't we go to the lobby waiting area," RJ said to my mom's visitor as he put his arm around her and led her down the hall, away from the scene.

RJ was a longtime friend and had been by several times to check on my family and me. He was a strong comfort for me in Colorado, a grounding force, and he knew this hospital well due to Liz's multiple admissions. RJ and his family had been through so much. He was the kind of friend who "got it" and understood the pain most didn't. The kind of friend who understood what wide, panicked eyes meant without having to say a word.

My dad was standing outside the closed glass doors, starring at the drawn curtains. I went over to him, my body completely numb.

"Why did they make you leave, Dad? What happened?"

"She was choking on all that fluid," he replied, emotionless. "She couldn't catch her breath. She couldn't breathe. They had to operate." Operate. The word hung heavily in the air between us. We stood there in silence, staring.

When the doors finally opened, I caught a quick glimpse of my mom, unconscious and intubated, breathing on a ventilator before the outline of the doctor made its way slowly toward my dad and me.

"Sherri's left lung collapsed," his tone was low and serious, "and we had to do a bronchoscopy to extract the fluid buildup so she could breathe. Her blood pressure dropped again in this process, and we adjusted some medication to stabilize that too." He continued: "She is minute-to-minute right now, though; I need you to know that. We won't know how stable she is for another little while, but we've got her on the ventilator right now, breathing for her."

"What's a bronchoscopy?" came my delayed question, my brain struggling to process his words.

"It's a process where we insert a very large and long needle into her lung to pull fluid into a syringe to alleviate pressure," he answered, not missing a beat. "Between the pneumonia and her feet, she's not been able to get up as much as we need her to in order to drain the fluid, which means it's just all building up in her lungs with no place to go. She will likely need assistance breathing for the immediate future."

I blinked. I was replaying the nurses running into her room with both machines, like a scratched record. I couldn't get past that image, much less process this news. I could feel my brain stall out.

"I know this is sensitive, but I advise you to start thinking about funeral plans at this point," the doctor stated matter-of-factly. "In a few minutes, if she continues to stabilize, you can go in and say goodbye," he said, immediately looking downward. "I am so sorry."

I looked at my dad, tears streaming down my face. No, no, no. This was all wrong. My mom was fine just a month ago. A month. This was insane. As I began wrestling with reality, my optimism sprang into action.

"She's going to be fine, Dad," I said. "She will fight and be FINE." I said it for us both. He was silent, just staring at her through the door.

"Three ICU patients are terminal," I overheard a nurse say behind me into the phone. "Send your rep over, and I will let the families know," came her voice, like monotone b-roll footage playing in the background of my consciousness. It was sinking in that my mom was now one of these patients. I briefly noted my curiosity about what any of that meant, and then refocused on my mom through the door.

Five minutes later, she had stabilized enough for us to reenter the room. I was thinking about saying goodbye, but had come up blank. My brain felt hollow. We stood there, staring at all the tubes and machines holding my mom together. Mat ran into the room, breathless.

"I got here as soon as I could," Mat said, tears overflowing his eyes as he spoke. My dad somberly gave him the update. After a while, we took turns saying our goodbyes, though I felt disconnected and robotic as I recited mine. And one by one, we exited the room, completely drained of the familiar, of all feeling, and mostly of hope.

FOUR EYES

I jumped awake to Mat's voice. We were all anxiously camping out in the waiting room, and had taken turns falling asleep in the furniture that was harder than you'd expect based on its appearance, waiting for news. Waiting to feel less anxious. Waiting to feel anything but fear.

"Lish, the doctor," Mat said again. I sat up, instantly at attention.

"We think she will be alright with more time on the ventilator," he explained. "But because of that, we are going to need to do a tracheotomy so she can be conscious at times and have the ventilator as a support mostly at night and for a few hours during the day."

I felt my shoulders sink in response, and only then realized how close to my ears they had been. This doctor had spoken so gently to us all day.

"We'll do that now, and she'll be all set for tonight," he said, lingering. "Also, someone from the local organ donation organization stopped by earlier to talk with you all about last wishes when she was still in critical condition, but since she has turned a corner, we sent them on. It may not be a bad idea to talk about her final wishes regarding that as this continues to unfold, though it's not an easy topic," he said as he raised his eyebrows at each of us individually. "It's just a good conversation to have in general, but . . . ," he exhaled, ". . . she has bounced back much stronger than we thought she would." And with that, a small smile crept onto his face as he turned to leave the room.

I closed my eyes and exhaled. Life, death, breathing machines, another procedure, more tubes, and . . . organ donation? That last one was going to take far more energy to sort through than I had left for today, so I purposefully shoved it all to the side, earmarking it for possible later conversations. For now, I was grateful to sit in the good news. Maybe this had turned into a happy Mother's Day after all.

CHAPTER 15

May 14, 2012, 10:43 A.M.

MY BLEARY EYES opened to Sniff wagging her curlicue tail at me and sneezing with excitement. With a low growl, she requested that my attention please remain on her for the time being. I smiled. Gosh, how I missed her back at school. Thoughts of my life back in Pittsburgh seemed ages old and very distant, though I had been there just two days ago. What a weird time-warpy existence, I thought as I rubbed the soft silver and black hairs on Sniff's head against their grain and let my hand continue down her snout. She playfully yelped and stuck her wet nose under my hand in revenge.

"Okay, okay, I'm up, I get it!" I said to her. I couldn't stay annoyed at her, and she knew it. Her incessant tail wagging and flattened velvet ears pinned back in the playful position only made me love her more. She was staring at me with her kind, soft brown eyes, and wouldn't let up. After a late night at the hospital ensuring my mom's stability, we were finally able to come home and get some rest that lasted into the late morning hours. I didn't argue.

I listened for signs of my dad being awake. I didn't have to wait long; sounds of his booming snores filled the hallway as

I stepped into it. I sighed. It was the first chance I had to be alone since returning home. I grabbed my school backpack to appease my inner tasky homework captain, and felt marginally better as I switched on the coffee pod machine for my morning coffee. My dad's sister, my sweet Aunt Dar, had given each member of our family one for Christmas a few years back, and there was something very homey about them, no matter where I used one. I thought about the mental list of people I had made to call with updates, and began to take my inventory of emotional capacity to do so. Man, was I ever tired. Yet the relief of yesterday's near-death adventure ending well carried me forward.

I pulled back the glass slider, and Sniff ran outside and went to the bathroom immediately.

Hmm, I thought to myself. My dad must have not gotten up at all this morning yet. Good. He needs the rest.

"Sorry, Sniff!" I mumbled as she rushed back inside and over to the 1990s oak-colored pantry for her morning treat, as was custom.

My mom had started that tradition years ago, after losing our first keeshond, Muffy, to an unknown disease when she was nine years old. My mom had spent the last six weeks of Muffy's life on the floor with her, administering subcutaneous fluids to her every morning and coaxing her to eat with different forms of "people food." Muffy finally ate some chicken and rice, and my mom swore then that any dog of hers moving forward would only eat healthy "people food." I smiled thinking of my dad resenting this fact vocally as often as possible to anyone who would listen. "The dog eats better than I do!" was his standard half-joking phrase that wasn't really a joke. To him, it was one more deviation from Western medicine that my mom had taken in service of all that "out there" stuff. This was an argument as old as I was, probably even older.

When it came to philosophy of medicine, my parents

could not be more opposite. My dad, the first in his family to attend college, arrived at the University of Michigan with dreams of becoming a doctor. He took premed classes and studied the sciences as he continued to learn what being a doctor would mean for a family life. Growing up in an alcoholic family system in the city of Detroit, my dad promised himself that he would build a family of his own and relish in the connection that sobriety and quality time with one another could bring. Things he was not privy to in his own childhood. The kind of family life he wanted, he realized, would not be as possible for him with the long hours and demanding nature of what being a doctor entailed. Torn, he eventually chose to pursue family life, and he used his knowledge of the sciences to teach them rather than practice medicine.

He enjoyed concrete answers, proof, evidence, and facts. I often remember feeling the need to create fake PowerPoint presentations in my head for my dad when I wanted to do something with my friends in high school that I knew would be a "no." If I presented all of the information in a way that made logical sense, though, and spelled out the reward for him that would happen if I was allowed to join my friends, maybe he'd let me go. Sometimes, it worked.

My mom, on the other hand, was a bit of a flower child molded by a harshly rigid religious system of moralistic blacks and whites. She took solace in thinking abstractly, creating things, connecting with and befriending many different people, and coloring outside the lines any chance she got. She became interested in homeopathic remedies and more Eastern medicine thought and practice in college, and expanded on these beliefs further into her thirties. She was the first to run to her natural remedies books when anyone mentioned an ailment, ready to intervene with a dietary supplement or an essential oil. She also took up thought field therapy for a time, which involved tapping certain acupuncture points in a certain order to alleviate emotionally and physically painful experiences. You can imagine how much my dad enjoyed that one.

A large part of my mom's holistic journey showed up in her relationship with Sniff. And was Sniff ever lucky! She reaped all the benefits of my mom's experiments with homeopathy, which resulted in homemade all-natural peanut butter treats, oatmeal with digestive enzymes, brown sugar and butter for breakfast, and some variation of chicken, rice, cottage cheese, and carrots or beans with the appropriate dietary supplements for dinner each night. Sniff was truly living her best life, and I think underneath my dad's jokes, he knew it too.

I reached into the treat bag for an anxiously awaiting Sniff and pulled out a bone shape this time. Cute, I thought. I haven't seen this one yet. Sniff, justifying her nickname, gingerly sniffed the entire treat before grabbing it and trotting off to the living room to enjoy it in her spot near the tall metal decorative birds.

My dad still wasn't awake, and I didn't want to wake him. Sleep had always been a problem for him, and he rarely slept the whole night through. He often claimed his best hours of sleep were between 6:00 and 9:00 a.m., which was not possible during his working years. In retirement, however, his sleep had become more erratic, and he began staying up later and later, indulging his true night owl (a gift he also passed to me), especially since my mom was in the hospital. He was an avid reader, and would often be up reading his latest choice. Sometimes they were Alex Cross mysteries, sometimes they were books about baseball, and sometimes it was the latest Men's Group book about spirituality or the roots of historical Christianity.

My dad grew up Catholic and used to attend services in Latin as a kid. He hated not understanding what was being said, and he was thirsty for knowledge. Especially why things were the way they were. He attended Catholic school growing up, and many of his questions about the Church, the world, and God were answered in what he called a "demanding setting," where he learned to stifle any questions or doubts he had. He told Mat and me many tales of how, as the youngest of four, he walked into scrutiny left by his two older brothers who did not love the rules and created a difficult reputation for the Bashaw name. My dad was scared into compliance, and tamed his searching and curiosity. Consequently, in his late twenties he began to dive into faith in a language he could understand, with an attempt to finally ask his questions and further understand. The work was never done.

Both he and my mom continued to explore certain faith practices and rituals the older they got, and especially once they had Mat and me. My dad was part of a Men's Group Bible and book study with three or four other men for most of my life. The original Men's Group consisted of several fathers of Mat's and my friends growing up, which led to the befriending of several families that developed a beautiful community over the years. Even after moving to Colorado, the Michigan crew visited when they could, and continued to meet with my dad through the wonders of video chat. He also befriended a group of men in Colorado after a few years that joined together to read and discuss similarly themed books.

My dad created solid friends in these circles, and used reading as a means to connect with others and talk about some of the mysteries of life. He was always after the "why," and reading gave him more knowledge to include in his equations of life: "What is the meaning of life? Why are we here? What does it mean to act like God would act?" My dad's deep thoughts were almost crippling at times, yet he always continued to seek answers any way he could. Given the current circumstance with my mom, no wonder he was tired.

FOUR EYES

His snoring continued, loud swirling inhales and long punctuated bursts of exhale. My coffee was done, and I poured the boring non-flavored creamer my parents had in their fridge into it until it was a medium brown.

This will do just fine, I thought as I returned to the couch and my pile of homework. Snore-two-three-four-five; exhale-two-three–long pause–four. Though the rhythm of my dad's snoring was uneven, it was strangely calming after a while.

"Maybe that's how Mom did it all these years," I uttered under my breath. Sniff looked at me and sneezed as if in agreement.

CHAPTER 16

May 14, 2012, 3:37 P.M.

THE IN-ROOM HOSPITAL phone rang. It was my mom's next-youngest sister, Patti. She had been calling my mom's cell phone to no avail. My mom was so weakened by the events of yesterday and the sustained response to no food that she was awake for only a few minutes at a time. I sighed heavily as I relayed the information to my aunt, completely understanding her disappointment and sadness. I was equally that.

Patti was a neonatal nurse practitioner in Michigan, and was a helpful medical ear and translator for us nonmedical lay folk learning a new dialect. She was arriving this evening after getting some time off between her shifts. She was married to my Uncle Tom, a witty guy and previous high school band director, who also needed her care and expertise, as he was living with some severe medical complications himself. I wondered how much of a "getaway" this would seem to her, surrounded by medical situations. My mom's youngest sister, Janet, and her husband, Jerry, would be coming in tomorrow for additional moral support. Everyone was camping out at our house, and it would be great to see them all. I confirmed details with Aunt Patti for her arrival later this evening and told her I would see her soon.

My mom's cell phone had died, and I slipped it into my pocket to take home and charge, expanding my ever-changing role of support system/daughter/part-time caregiver. I glanced over at my mom and winced for her. I hoped she wasn't in pain. The tracheotomy was in, and she had a large knob of plastic sticking out from her neck. It was connected to some crinkled accordion-like plastic tubing leading to the ventilator, which reminded me of one of Mat's and my favorite childhood toys that you swung around your head rapidly to make different tonal sounds. We called them bugles. The bugle-like tube in my mom's neck was gently being lifted up and down with each breath the machine was creating for her. I wondered how she felt in there. If she was present at all. Was I present watching her?

A doctor's shadow slowly loomed over my five-foot-one-inch frame. I turned around with tears in my eyes, trying to dab them away as best I could.

"Hey, Allison," he said, his salt-and-pepper stubble the first piece of him to come into focus. I didn't bother to correct him on my name. At least he got the "A" right. "She's been sleeping for a while now, and everything is going well. We are going to put a peg tube directly into her stomach this afternoon to feed her; she's gone too long without sustenance and is incredibly weak."

I blinked back more tears as I nodded in reply. He pressed some buttons and walked out. I had met this doctor once before when he was filling in for Dr. Stevens. I couldn't remember his name. I guess the feeling was mutual. Behind me was the tray on wheels for people to eat on when they are bedridden. It was covered with new mail for my mom, and I could feel the warmth emanating from the letters from six feet away.

"Let's open some mail, Mom, shall we?" I asked the robot-like frame posing as her. I proceeded to read aloud and update her on today's well wishes and prayers pouring in from all over the country. There were cards from old teaching partners, friends, coworkers, neighbors, our beloved family chiropractor, family members from Michigan and Florida, relatives I had never heard of, and, in today's stack, a former student.

As I read his card aloud to my mom, I was beyond moved at his thoughtfulness. He had heard she was facing some health challenges and wanted to repay her the encouragement he reported receiving from her as a fourth grader. Mrs. Bashaw, as he knew her, was his favorite teacher, and had inspired him to become an elementary school teacher himself. He included a picture of himself with his current young class, who had all drawn her pictures that were included inside the large manila envelope he sent. Each card was preciously decorated in crayon, colored outside of any lines present, and adorably misspelled.

Wow, I thought to myself, she is really something special to so many people. I began to set the cards and drawings up around the room to surprise her when she woke up.

"We're going to have to start a box to collect all of these memories and kindnesses you're getting, Mom," I said to the air.

In that moment, I began to realize just how wide-reaching one person's wake could be. Something new stirred inside of me. I was proud of who my mom was, and proud of her ability to connect with so many. I was proud of the way those who loved her had responded and extended her love at this scary time. What kind of person leaves that type of wake? Whatever kind of person that was, I wanted to be one too. I felt lifted, lighter, and attuned to something bigger, something ethereal happening all around me. It was a blurry mixture of love and mystery and true friendship and support all combined into one. It was a feeling I will never forget. One that has continued to shape me.

FOUR EYES

My dad sauntered into the room with a wide, audible yawn and incredible bedhead in the combover section of his dark brown hair from the lobby, where he had gone to rest on a chair that was not quite long enough for anyone to actually recline in.

"You almost ready to get Aunt Patti, kid?" he asked, rubbing his eyes.

"Yep," I answered. And with that, we were off.

CHAPTER 17
May 15, 2012, 10:02 A.M.

I WALKED OUT of my bedroom to find my aunts and uncle enjoying the bright morning on the back deck of our house with the amazing view of the mountains. It was comforting to have them here. So much of my childhood had been spent celebrating events with one another, and though this wasn't a celebration, there was something very calming about their presence.

The deck was a definite selling point for my parents as they were house-hunting on their quick "find-a-house-buy-the-house" spring break trip during their last year of teaching. Especially once the hot tub was installed and nighttime became mesmerizing.

My Aunt Janet and Uncle Jerry had arrived early this morning, which was midmorning to them on Eastern Standard Time. The three sisters were very different—and yet not—at the same time. It was fun to watch them interact with one another, as it had rarely happened since we moved. At times I would mistake my Aunt Patti for my mom, and at times my Aunt Janet for my Aunt Patti. They were all unique in their own ways, and yet I could clock their family-isms a mile away. Perhaps because I was one of them.

FOUR EYES

All three of them shared a stubbornness that, according to my dad, was genetic. The sisters called it passion. It was a well-worn-in fact that going up against one of them often resulted in the spouse's response of "Yes, dear." All of their husbands had learned this by now. Some the hard way. As stubborn as they all were, though, they were also equally as tender, especially toward animals. They grew up in western Michigan with their parents, me and Mat's grandparents, with whom we had a very loving relationship growing up. My mom's experience was a bit different, although she loved her parents very much.

My grandma was a very petite, slender, pretty woman with striking blonde hair and fair skin who was always dressed to the nines. My grandpa was over six feet tall with tanned skin, dark hair, and a slender build from his training in the Navy. He was also a very sharp dresser who loved Tommy Hilfiger. They called me "Sheshe" and "Trouble" growing up, respectively. I tried my hardest to live up to my grandpa's nickname.

In my mom's memories of her parents, my grandpa was as absent as my grandma was present. My grandpa was working hard to support the family, and my grandma took care of the girls the best she knew how—with singing, music, faith, and scraping to get by. Keeping up appearances was a prevalent theme. My grandma found herself pregnant with my mom at a young age, unwed, and in total need to hide this fact from the world. She existed in a very different era, one that was especially cruel and punishing to those in my grandma's situation. Her wedding to my grandpa followed this news, yet all details around it remained elusive and unattainable. This spirit contributed to a family pattern of sweeping secrets under the proverbial rug.

When my mom was a senior in high school, her classmates were all wearing their moms' class rings, and she wanted to join her friends in the trend. She asked my grandma if she could wear her ring and received a solid "no" for months on end. My mom became bitter at this answer and snuck into my grandma's room one day when she wasn't around to find the ring. She found it, indeed, as well as the answer to why she was not supposed to wear it. The year of my grandma's graduation from high school was unapologetically clear. My mom did the math to her birthday from there and discovered, at eighteen years old herself, that she had been conceived out of wedlock, a very shameful truth for the time. Though she mostly knew her parents loved each other, this revelation led her to question if she was a part of the reason they got married. Perhaps a 'should.' Or something to feel resentful about. Or toward?

When my mom confronted my grandma with all of her questions, my grandma's embarrassment and anger were overwhelming, and it was obvious how ashamed she felt. What my mom didn't yet understand was that the truth was not exclusive to either scenario, but more complex as my grandma was a product of her own rearing in a system that trapped her from moving past hailing others' perceptions above all else.

My mom struggled not to internalize her unanswered questions as a reflection of her, but a seed of shame nestled itself into her heart. It grew and grew, straining my mom's relationship with both her parents. It took her years to realize that she struggled with the deep shame of her own existence as she navigated through her college years and into her marriage to my dad. It was decades before she could see that her parents were doing the best they could with what they had and knew, despite the damage that was done. They had huge shame seeds of their own, with very valid origin stories, and though she eventually recognized this pattern, her shame seed had already evolved.

When my mom got pregnant with me in 1981, she developed gestational diabetes that never went away. This became her secret to carry, and a space to hold the shame at what this meant about her weight, her worth, and her willpower. Neither Mat nor I knew she was diabetic until we were in high school ourselves. The power of this secret ate away at her slowly, as her shame seed sprouted thick roots and blossomed in her self-esteem. Weight was always a struggle for my mom—another gift she passed my way. Yet along with the struggle of weight fluctuation, the unseen heaviness of what that meant about one's character and soul became the more damaging struggle. This, however, was something we did not talk about.

My mom and Patti were two years apart in age, but three in school. Janet was two years younger than Patti, and five years apart from my mom in school. The age differences were just enough that my mom never went to high school with her sisters, and she experienced a lot of her shame alone. The class ring reveal led my mom to feel slightly different from them, though she didn't let that get in the way of being there for her sisters as they grew up. Though they each developed in their unique ways, they all shared many things, including clothes and, often, hairstyles.

The girls' hairstyles told the story of the times, and all of them vacillated through various versions of long hair, shorter pixie cuts, and perms. So many perms. My mom ended up with a short, wavy brown/blondish hairstyle for most of her adulthood and my Aunt Patti with mostly medium-length straight hair with an occasional perm thrown in. My Aunt Janet stayed true to the medium-length perm for as long as I can remember.

The perm lineage was also passed my way. After a full day of what I remember as actual torture sitting in a chair in my kitchen growing up, my grandma would remove the soaking-wet cotton strip around my head that was holding the home permanent solution and all the rollers in, wash my still-rollered hair in the sink (the most torturous part), and then slowly free me back to being a kid by unrolling each roller and paper wrapper one by one, clinking them into the sink. I was always wiggly and cold, and my grandma was so patient, though I am pretty sure she was as annoyed as she was patient. My perms inducted me into the family forever, and you could always find me in a crowd due to the number of inches my curls soared atop my head.

My grandma sewed all the girls' clothes until well into high school, which wasn't as cool for them then as it might be now. My mom also learned to sew and became my lifelong pants hemmer, as pants were always too long for my short legs.

Tradition continued as my mom enrolled me in sewing class as a kid. I remember being so proud of my created wardrobe, the best of the early '90s gifting me a geometric black-and-white pattern with puffy hot pink flamingos that I made into shorts and a shirt. I was in my creative haven and took to sewing as often as I could. At the end of the class, there was even a fashion show that I was invited to walk in. I chose a sensible puppies nightgown, obviously, as the ten-going-on-forty-two-year-old that I was. I remember walking up and down that runway hugging my stuffed dog and best friend, Mutsy, for all she was worth. Though my mom's experience with sewing had been markedly different, her relaying the skill to me replaced some of the joy it had lacked for her.

As the oldest, my mom was a natural born trailblazer. After college, she left home to live with her aunt and uncle, my grandma's sister and husband, in Washington DC. They had three boys, who my mom helped care for while job searching. She eventually landed her first teaching job in Falls Church, Virginia where she met Carol.

Carol was her oldest friend, and she became the reason we road-tripped to Colorado. My mom was ever the explorer and credits this time in her life with the birth of her inner adventure seeker. Her drive to see the world and find her place in it led her on many exciting adventures, not the least of which ended in her meeting my dad in the Badlands of South Dakota when they both happened to be on road trips from Michigan.

"Hi, Aunt Janet," I said as she came inside for some more water. I hugged her and asked about their trip and gave her the update, which, by now, was fairly rote behavior. Some days, it seemed as though I could share without ever nearing a feeling, while others were so full of feelings that I could barely speak. Today was one of the former days. It felt like roulette each morning, never knowing how I was going to feel. These days were a bit surreal, though. I often questioned how I could function and relay the facts if I was feeling everything all of the time, so I was grateful that today, nothing felt real, even my own skin. I was floating.

CHAPTER 18

May 15, 2012, 12:30 P.M.

MY MOM WAS awake when we got to the hospital—my aunts, my uncle, Dad, and me. We led them down our familiar route, chiming "second floor" with the elevator as we took the familiar turns to the Cardiac ICU in stride.

"Sherri, it's so good to see you!" my aunts exclaimed as they hurriedly entered my mom's hospital room and began to engage with her. With the peg tube in, my mom was able to sustain sufficient food and nutrients to regain some strength and be able to spend less time on the ventilator and more time awake. She was there, silently nodding and more alert than I had seen her in days. She was still being treated for pneumonia and the lethargic beating of her heart and was still connected to a jungle of tubes. In addition, this time, she could no longer speak.

My aunts continued to talk to my mom and interpret her answers as they processed witnessing their older sister incapacitated. With the trach in, another version of communication had suddenly joined our family, and no one was really ready.

CHAPTER 19

May 16, 2012, 2:36 P.M.

"LISH, IS YOUR mom diabetic?" my Aunt Patti asked over the phone.

My head swirled with panic, a response that had been ingrained in me since Mat and I found out my mom was diabetic, and our family had erupted. I didn't know how to answer my aunt.

"Um . . . ," I started before flashing back to that hard memory.

It was the summer before my sophomore and Mat's senior year of high school. He had just returned from a camping trip to Colorado with a youth group, where he'd fainted and described having seizure-like muscle spasms and not being able to respond while hiking up a mountain. He was terrified and didn't come out of it until someone gave him some hard candy. When he got home, he accidentally walked in on my mom giving herself insulin and decided to confront her about what was going on. We had suspected this for years and it wasn't a big deal to us, but now that Mat had experienced a health incident involving blood sugar levels, it would be helpful to know any medical details that could affect us.

This was not, however, how my mom received the news. Her feelings cocktail of mortification, hurt, disappointment, and shame all came out in pure rage, and she didn't talk to Mat or me for hours now that we knew her secret. The shame seed was deeply grounded. It got so bad that I took off on my bike for a few hours until Mat came to find me to bring me home for a family meeting. A shame seed of my own began to take root, as I believed my mom's anger was mine to hold.

My dad facilitated the meeting; my mom was so impacted that she could not even talk or barely look at us. She assumed that we had known for years and was convinced that we had shared her most shameful detail with everyone we knew, especially her family, when she already felt scrutinized for her weight by her parents. We denied this, but she remained angry and didn't believe us. My dad redirected her into sharing how she wanted us to hold this information moving forward.

"This is no one else's business but mine, and you never get to share this with anyone, especially Grandma and Grandpa," she told us, steeled and prickly. "I am a very private person, and this doesn't get to come out."

I had never seen my mom cry so much. It took her a week before she started to talk and act like my mom again. As my dad wrapped up one of the most awkward conversations, I had ever been a part of, he added one last detail about himself that sent Mat and me into shock. He revealed that he was also diabetic and had developed it around the same time as my mom.

I remember Mat and I looking at each other in disbelief. "What?!" was the general go-to response for a while as we synthesized this information. My dad asked us to keep his information private as well, and I left that conversation feeling both sad that they felt so ashamed about their medical condition and angry that it had taken Mat almost dying on a mountain to reveal that important information to us, their children, who could also be impacted.

As I processed this event over the years, one thing was clear among all the confusion: I was not to tell anyone, ever.

"The nurse came in with insulin, Lish, and I just wondered. How long has she been getting insulin?" my aunt asked.

My mouth had gone dry, and I tried to swallow all the anxiety pulsating through my body.

"Yes," I started. "She has diabetes and has since she had me. My dad has it too," I spit out quickly, watching for impending lightning bolts to strike at any moment.

"Really?" my aunt asked, incredulously. "And we never knew?"

I explained the shame seed to her, and their request for privacy about this as we processed. I was only half present, though, as I was thinking about how my mom would react to her sister now knowing her deepest, darkest secret. I had done it. The one thing I was never supposed to say out loud to anyone. I felt the fear of my fourteen-year-old-self course through me as though no time had passed at all.

I called my dad to nervously tell him of the news, and my inner fourteen-year-old had a slight reprieve as he sighed and said, "Well, they were bound to find out at some point through this. Diabetes is a huge reason she's in this position to begin with. It's okay, and there's no reason to hide it anymore. I'm not hiding mine, either."

I let out a huge sigh of relief as I said, "Good, because I told Aunt Patti you had it too."

"There's nothing more to hide," my dad reassured me. "It just is."

"I didn't ask her not to tell Mom, so I'm afraid Mom is going to be really upset again," I continued.

"I'll talk with her and let her know. And if she's mad, she's mad."

My fourteen-year-old-self remembered what this

uncertainty was like and took over.

"That's terrifying, Dad," I said. "She's going to be really mad at me."

"Nah, she won't," he said. "You didn't do anything wrong. Now that she sees the damage diabetes has caused, she knows it was just a matter of time before they found out. It's okay."

I wrapped my arms around myself in a giant bear hug to calm down. Taking a few deep breaths, I chose to believe him.

CHAPTER 20

May 18, 2012, 5:32 P.M.

OVER THE WEEK that my aunts and uncle were in town, we all slowly began learning my mom's signals, needs, and wants through pointing, guessing, trial and error–ing, and a large ongoing game of charades. The whole process brought levity, connection, laughter, and some frustration to everyone, though by the end, we began to get it down. Our tiredness was worth it.

Luckily, with all the current happenings, my aunts and uncle learning of my mom's diabetes was nothing more than a slightly embarrassing blip for her on her current illness trajectory. I was beyond relieved. I would still clam up whenever a nurse made a comment about her diabetes when my aunts and uncle were in the room, bracing for the aftermath, but it never came. Privacy and modesty were a privilege at this point, one my mom had lost when her life was on the line. I was grateful that she was open to it, though it was still rarely spoken about.

My dad told me that she had taken the news well when he told her.

"Sher, your sisters and Jerry know about our diabetes," he told her one afternoon as she was awake and looking out the window.

She nodded in return and offered a shrug, as if to say, "Oh, well."

"It's not worth hiding anymore," he continued.

My mom apparently agreed with a slight nod of her head.

My family took to navigating this fact about my parents with ease and kindness, and it was only brought up when absolutely necessary. Once I heard this was their response, my inner fourteen-year-old was finally able to lower her shoulders after all these years. She was still jumpy, though.

We took turns sitting with my mom, all in shifts. It was a relief to get some sleep in the mornings, as my aunts and uncle were usually up and still functioning on EST. They took the morning shifts, and my dad and I took the late shifts. This was unlike any previous family gathering we had ever experienced. Mat would join after work when he could, and he brought Brooks as often as possible. My mom lit up every time she saw him, and he would usually bring "Gamma" a recent piece of his coloring artwork for her wall. They were both extremely pleased.

There was an underlying parallel process happening for me, as I was simultaneously present with my mom undergoing so many changes while also in grad school learning about the best ways to connect with people, all people. People of different backgrounds, abilities, ethnicities, races, faiths, gender identities, sexual orientations, beliefs, value systems, and cultural identities. Seeing people as versions of their own Truths and the experts on themselves left space for me to learn to check my biases at the door when interacting with anyone whose life experiences had molded them into very different expressions of my Truth.

Given this fuel, I began to view my mom as a new version of herself and tried to remove myself from everything I had known about her while she was relearning everything herself. This was difficult and exhilarating at the same time. I began looking through a clinical set of glasses as well as a family pair. In clinical mode, I found great space in which to be creative with my interactions with her, and space to practice some of the skills I continued to learn in school that built rapport and relationship with someone by meeting them where they were at. When I was in daughter mode, it was easier to get frustrated at things being so drastically different than they used to be. I tried to straddle the line in hopes of a balance, though that proved much more of a challenge than I thought.

"Mom, school has been interesting lately," I started one day, letting her know my latest learnings.

She nodded as I spoke, staring at the ceiling. A tear slipped out of her eye a few sentences later, and I asked what was wrong. She pointed to her back and tried to roll over onto her side. It was her bedsore. I got the nurse, and she was rotated and given some more pain meds before falling asleep.

My daughter lens was cracked, and to prevent my taking the hurt personally, my clinical lens took over. She wasn't able to meet me where I was anymore, at least not right now, and needed me to meet her where she was instead. The balancing act was nearly impossible, and it gradually shifted more and more into mostly clinical view. I learned to reserve my details for my dad, and even then, it was increasingly more difficult to talk about anything good in my life when their lives were so hard right now.

I grieved this part of the relationship with my mom that no longer afforded her the ability to listen to my details or be a supportive ear. And I knew I wasn't the only one. The chasm between "normal life" and her life was drastic, and it was growing increasingly more difficult for her to relate to others.

She began pointing more often to communicate, and I began to learn her language. Everything was about her pain. I felt so selfish, trying to still interact with my mom as if she were the same as she used to be. As if she weren't compromised. But she was, and daughter mode was getting less and less comfortable with showing up. My survivor's guilt was off the charts. I was reminded of this every time I tried to bring up my life or details and she met me with a request for water, more pain meds, tears, or falling asleep. I totally got it, and slowly put my daughter self away on a shelf in service of helping my mom stabilize. Daughter mode could come back down later. I hoped.

CHAPTER 21

May 21, 2012, 12:13 P.M.

"HI, SHERRI," CAME the soothing voice of the speech-language pathologist. "How are we today?" she questioned as my mom's eyes fluttered open.

My mom waved her hand at her and shrugged.

"My name is Sarah, and I am here to help you work up to talking with your trach in over the next few days," she said, pulling up a chair next to the bed. She was a petite woman in her thirties with long, curly blonde hair and a very caring tone. "How does that sound?" she asked my mom while looking at the ventilator settings.

My mom nodded in agreement.

"Well, I see Physical Therapy was here earlier," she said, noting the large plastic sewing needle threaded with yarn and halfway woven into a stuffed bear with large precut holes in it for children to learn how to sew. That made quite the statement, as my mom was an excellent seamstress.

I noted to myself how weird it was to see my mom needing to relearn basic motor skills. She hadn't had a stroke, yet she was very swollen from the pneumonia, all the medications she was on for various things, and her open-heart surgery. She wore a pair of fingertip-less compression gloves that her fingers stuck out of as if reaching for their own freedom. Motor skills, walking, talking, wow, I said to myself as I continued to pay attention to Sarah. Clinical eyes on.

"We're going to start by disconnecting the tube connected to the ventilator and capping your trach with this valve so you can breathe through your nose and mouth and not need the machine to do it for you," she said as she looked at my mom for her approval. My mom consented through frightened eyes.

Sarah began to unhook the tube and, before my mom could react, swiftly capped the hole, forcing my mom to breathe in through her nose and mouth. She transitioned with no problem.

CHAPTER 22

May 22, 2012, 7:32 P.M.

WE WATCHED MY mom excel daily in small ways, until she no longer needed the ventilator at all. Sarah returned day after day to work more with her on removing the cap from the valve for longer and longer periods to get her used to taking in air through her trach to be able to talk. This frightened my mom terribly, as her oxygen would usually tank in the middle of her lesson. The low oxygen reading for the week was down to 61 percent, and with that, my mom requested a hard stop with both of her hands for a few days.

My clinical brain went to work on finding ways to communicate that allowed her to still feel empowered, and I brought her a whiteboard to write on. She tried to hold the pen in her hand, but her hands were so swollen under the compression gloves that she couldn't grip the pen tight enough to write; it would fall right out of her hand. Back to the drawing board. I tried again, daughter mode now indefinitely paused.

On my way home from the hospital that night, I stopped to grab a roll of magnets from the craft store. I found an old cookie sheet and began to write on the white tape–covered sticky side of the magnet roll different cue words my mom could point to. When done, I cut them all apart and arranged them on the cookie sheet to bring to the hospital with me the next day. She could point to what she wanted from us, and I was excited to try this method of finding my mom's current voice in a nontraditional way. This brought me some peace of mind, yet I couldn't pinpoint why. Perhaps it was some kind of control, something tangible, something that made me feel like I wasn't powerless over the ever-unfolding monster of traumatic illness. Something continued to poke holes in my shabby belief system, which had already been pretty rocked over the past decade, and I began to cling to "searching to understand" as the answer rather than for the answer.

CHAPTER 23

May 22, 2012, 11:17 A.M.

MY JOURNEY OF faith had become a jumbled mess of confusion over the past ten years, and I had fewer concrete ideas about what I believed anymore. Along with the accompanying guilt that came with questions, doubts, and seeking without just believing, I began to realize how fear-based my faith had become. Especially now, watching my mom go through this hellish process. Her fate somehow seemed dependent on the loudest of my fears—that I had doubted too much and had messed it up for everyone. But did I really have that much control over this situation? Was God really using my mom to punish me? By punishing her? Was I that important? I truly didn't think so, but my fear that I could be was louder.

I knew there was something out there, and something somewhat true about the evangelical faith in which I was raised, but the harsh judgmental limits of rights and wrongs without any gray area only fueled the idea of conditionally loving others based on their actions or political affiliations or moralism. This was a concept I could no longer afford to adhere to, especially in my career path of counseling, which required others, not me or my beliefs, to be the experts on themselves.

This was quite the lesson to learn, as I had spent years being taught how to strengthen my apologetics and evangelistic muscles to debate with "nonbelievers" to convince them they were wrong. Something about that never felt right to me. It often felt sales-y or transactional, somehow skipping over the personal piece of authentic connection. I was learning that I despised inauthenticity. In those early debate-like talks with strangers, I would often end up talking with them about their lives and experiences, never getting to the conversion part of the conversation. Because of this, I spent years ashamed of my lack of faith, and it impacted my self-esteem in a dramatically negative way, where I became "never enough of God, and too much of myself."

If I was supposed to deny myself for God but couldn't bear to bring him up in conversation about someone's soul, then I was selfish—too in tune with my desires, wants, and hopes and not enough of God's. I needed to humble myself and keep quiet, submit to the will of God, and forget all the human parts of me in order to truly die to myself and fully be a channel for God to work through. I repeatedly failed at this.

Yet the connection I felt to God was what brought me through the endless bullying I received for being overweight as a kid. Being bullied by my peers, some I even considered friends, reminded me that I was different, and that different was not okay to most. Different, however, was okay with God. I was willing to do anything in order to be left alone, and God promised acceptance. I easily agreed to obey whatever he needed from me in exchange for the assist. At least that's how it felt.

I had spent the past few years specifically delving into the bigger faith questions I had, and pulling on the string that unraveled my whole sweater of beliefs. Another gift of my dad's. We would compare notes from time to time. As my mom got sicker and sicker, and possibly closer to death, my thoughts drifted back to a pivotal conversation I had had with a friend four years back about the afterlife.

"So, what does that mean?" I asked my friend. "You think my friend Devon is just buried in some dirt and that's it, then? He isn't in heaven or some alternative place? Or at least his soul isn't?" We were sitting in my 2001 forest green Jetta with heated seats, and I had just driven her home after attending a Bible study unlike anything I had ever experienced.

"I am not sure," she replied, "but maybe—?"

The statement hung in the air between us like staticky white noise I couldn't turn down. I had no context in which to process this thought, and mixed feelings of disbelief, fear, and relief all fought for center stage in my mind. I didn't know what to believe. The Bible study had not gotten to the afterlife yet, but I had a feeling that, given the trajectory of what I had experienced so far, it was somehow going to look different than what I had always envisioned. Fewer angels waiting for us on clouds with harps and bonbons or fiery demons waiting to take you to a burning lake of fire for eternal damnation and more . . . well, that was just it. More nothing. At least for now.

When this conversation happened, my friend Devon had died in his early twenties just over a year before, and I was struggling to make sense of it all. I was searching for the why, the meaning, and I was coming up short. What did it mean that he had become addicted to pain medication after being paralyzed from the waist down in a horrific car accident during a road trip with my roommate and friends? A road trip I had been invited on but could not go? How was that fair—to take something from someone as sacred as his relationship with basketball, to which he credited his vitality after a very difficult childhood? Things like this were not supposed to happen. To anyone, much less people I knew and loved. It was quite a rude awakening to the realities of life for my naïve, privileged, and malleable mind.

A friend I met working at the bookstore of the church I attended during college had invited me to a Bible study after several of our discussions led to questions like these. It was the first time in my life I remember being able to air some of these questions out loud. This study was based on the historical context of the Bible, the philosophy of truth, and de-literalizing the Bible and its stories while still holding it as the ultimate authority. I had never heard of this take on faith before, and a large part of me felt guilty for even entertaining any of its thought-provoking teachings.

The hope of this study was to meet folks where they were at, while gently tearing down old problematic beliefs that ended in moralism and behaviorism rather than a true relationship with God. Once that part was complete, the aim was to then reshape old versions of faith into a historically accurate and critically thought-out point of view based on context and facts. This would take the wind out of the sails of belief just for belief's sake. To me, it felt like having my insides hammered before being thrown out of a plane without a parachute.

I both admired this take on some of the lifelong truths I had thought about God and grieved for a system of belief that had carried me through my life up until this point. My faith was in a very fragile place, and I did not experience the "gentle reshaping" posited to me by the leaders. I was both broken and bleeding out while alive in a totally new and foreign way. Perhaps this was the actual intent. Either way, I had hoped for a parachute.

A month after Devon's accident, my friend RJ and his sister Liz were in a similar accident that paralyzed Liz from the waist down at sixteen years old. I was ready to entertain anything that would help me make sense of these tragedies. Devon and Liz were some of the strongest people of faith I knew, people who devoted their lives, souls, and existences to God. What did it mean that they were not "healed" by their faith? What did it mean that they were forever compromised? Why did bad things happen to good people?

By the time my friend and I were having the conversation about what happens after you die, my black-and-white, all-or-nothing faith had already taken a hard, potentially irreparable hit.

"I just don't know," I said to her. "Maybe we're just in dirt, but maybe our souls find heaven on Earth? Or maybe our souls wait until a later time to be taken? But what about people who are cremated? What happens to their souls? Do our souls exist between worlds for a time? Like purgatory? Do I believe in purgatory? I never did before, but I'm not convinced of anything anymore." My mind was spinning out of control. I didn't know what to make of any of this. I just wanted to know what happened to Devon.

Maybe we were all either just ash or just in dirt after death? And if so, what would this mean for my mom? It was a terrifying thought.

CHAPTER 24

May 22, 2012, 5:57 P.M.

MY MOM LOOKED peaceful as she slept. I wondered if she felt that way. The nurses had increased the frequency of turning her onto her different sides as her bedsore continued to redden and grow, breaking down the skin right at her coccyx. She didn't love the constant interruption to her sleep or rest, as her left hip caused her lots of pain to rest on that side. My mom had fibromyalgia and had struggled with hip and leg pain, mostly silently, for years. Between having her position shifted every two hours 24/7, all the finger pokes for blood sugar checks, and all the different departments coming by to check on her daily, she was completely exhausted.

The peg tube was only administering her thirty milliliters of food every hour. That was one ounce per hour; over twenty-four hours, that was three cups of food. All day. And night. She was weak, a very slow healer due to her diabetes and the small amount of food she was able to keep down, and in desperate need of protein.

My aunts and uncle had flown home the day before last, and after we said our goodbyes, we spent the afternoon at the hospital with Mat and Brooks.

FOUR EYES

"Hey, Mom," Mat said cheerfully as he entered with some bright, colorfully mixed fresh flowers for her room. "How are you today?" he asked as he pulled up a chair.

She raised her hand and tilted it back and forth as if to say "so-so."

Brooks jumped up onto his dad's lap. "Gamma!" he said, and my mom smiled back at him. I had almost forgotten what her smile was like at this point. Mat began telling the latest adorable story about Brooks, and he laughed along happily. It was a peaceful afternoon—the last one for a while, as my dad and I were back on the full-day hospital shifts and all their uncertainty.

On their way out, Mat pulled me aside.

"On the way here, Brooks asked where we were going, and I told him we were going to see Gamma," he started. "As soon as he saw the hospital, he yelled out 'Gamma's house!' I got a chuckle from that and wanted to share," he said, as we both smile-grimaced. It was not inaccurate. I wondered what Brooks would remember as he got older.

"Poxicle?" Brooks asked my dad on their way out, and I watched my dad's heart melt at his grandson's request. He walked them out, stopping at the fridge along the way.

CHAPTER 25

May 24, 2012, 8:42 A.M.

"HEY, GUYS," **DR. STEVENS** walked into the lobby to find my dad and me grabbing a short can of off-brand pop from the generous supply they kept stacked for visitors.

"It's not quite as good as the real thing," my dad would say each time he had one, referring to the old "Coke" slogan as if I had never heard it or his joke before. It landed somewhere between annoying and endearing.

My dad lived for cheesy dad humor. Especially science puns. He fit the high school chemistry teacher bill to a T. A large part of him took delight in his own positivity and ability to make life fun after growing up with my grandparents, who were largely negative and big fans of the bottle.

He used to revel in his yearly chemistry valentine that he handwrote inside the shape of a heart and printed on pink paper for all his classes. It started with "AU, you're gold" and ended with "I've got my ion you." He was ever so proud of it. I loved this cheese factor about my dad, and I took to following in his footsteps, minus the untied laces bit, which was still happening often.

We would often battle it out in epic pun wars, eliciting enormous eye rolls from those around us, but we didn't care. We could crack ourselves up.

"Hey, Dr. Stevens," I said, grateful for the momentary distraction, popping the top of my diet cola.

"We need to talk," he began.

My dad and I exchanged looks of uncertainty.

"We are concerned about Sherri and the care we can continue to give her here," he said. "As you know, MCR is a level-two trauma center, which makes us excellent at acute traumas and aftercare, with the intention of stepping patients down as quickly as possible into lower levels of care. With Sherri, however, it's been five weeks, and we are still not able to get her off the dobutamine to help her heartbeat strengthen and stabilize enough to beat as strongly on its own. Her heart took a big hit from the attack before all the complications, and we're afraid it's not getting any better. We've seen her through a lot the past five weeks, but we want to connect her to a team that specializes in long-term heart damage."

I'd never heard a doctor talk this candidly before. I was all ears.

"We have called the cardiac team at University Hospital in Denver, and we think it's best if she is transferred there for more specialized care. The ambulance will be here in about an hour unless you have any objections."

We trusted Dr. Stevens. He had been with us since the beginning and was an excellent doctor. My dad and I looked at each other, wondering just how worried we should be, and shook our heads silently. No objections here.

"How bad is it, Doc?" my dad asked, always one to read between the lines.

"Well, it's okay; we just want her to get better faster, and Dr. Wolf at University is one of the best for cardiac damage. University is also a teaching hospital; they have a large team working on all the cases, which allows for more technology and grants for the most up-to-date equipment there. We are concerned about her food intake; it's not very much, and we need her to be able to eat and sustain more than she is. We need to act." he responded.

"Okay, let's go then," my dad decided.

The energy of the former levity had been sucked out of the room completely. Everything changed. The little hairs on the back of my neck stood up, I was cold all over, and my ears started ringing. It was time to be worried again. Part of me was angry at the part of me that felt it was okay to leave the vigilance post to laugh, and another part of me wanted to give myself compassion in the midst of yet another scare. I didn't know who would win that fight.

I watched my dad turn serious, focused. He gulped the rest of his cola in one big swig and threw the can in the recycle bin on his way out the door and back to my mom's room.

"Lish, let's call Mat," he said, his words trailing behind him. "And pack up her room."

"Yep," I replied by rote, feeling my autopilot kick in. "On it."

Mat's phone rang twice before he answered.

"Hello," came his workday tone that sounded more like a statement than a greeting.

"Hey," I said. "It's me. Mom's getting transferred to University Hospital in Denver, which specializes in cardiac management. Dr. Stevens thinks it will help her. They leave in an hour," I relayed the facts to him, hollowly.

"What does that mean?" he asked.

"It means her heart isn't healing the way they want it to here, I guess? I don't fully understand it, but I don't think it's a great sign that she's not healing here," I said, feeling a bit out of my pay grade. "That's at least my understanding," I finished.

"Wow, okay. We'll meet you at University Hospital tonight after work then," he answered, equally hollow. "Shit," was his final summation.

"Yeah," I agreed. "Shit."

CHAPTER 26

May 25, 2012, 6:47 A.M.

EVERYTHING IN MY body was sore. I rolled over onto my back and slowly woke up. These ceiling tiles were stained with different shades of yellow. Yuck! I thought. The carpet that thinly veiled the concrete floor was not much of a pad; however, I was grateful for a space to sleep. I was in the lobby of University Hospital, and none of the benches or chairs were as comfortable as the floor. My dad had taken the chair-bed-mostly-uncomfortable thing in my mom's room for the night, as there was only one guest allowed in the ICU rooms overnight. The nurses kindly let me sleep in the lobby so that I could be here for team rounds this morning, which always happened between 7:00 and 8:00 am. They saved me an hour-and-a-half drive down I-25 in morning rush-hour traffic, and I was willing to be sore just for that. I gingerly stood up, began to fold the blanket they'd given me, and made my way to my mom's room.

Mat had driven down last night after work to check in before heading back home, needing to get up early the next day. Careers in construction started ruthlessly early. I was jealous that he got to leave, and also glad I was able to stay. I didn't know which was better or worse. Mat and I talked about this, and once I heard him share his concerns for not being able to be there in person more, it clicked. There was no clear answer or way to navigate a situation like this. I took in another level of privilege in an effort to keep my mind geared toward something positive, realizing that grad school was providing me so many opportunities to be with my family in ways that having a job would not.

My dad was still asleep in my mom's room, sawing logs per usual. I wondered if that was calming to my mom at all. She was also asleep and looking rather grim. She had lost a lot of weight over the past five weeks and was fairly pale. The small break I had from her overnight allowed me to see some of the changes in her more clearly. I could see what Dr. Stevens was talking about now.

I sat down, waiting for rounds, recalibrating myself to hospital time. My long brown hair was getting longer and longer, and I spun it around my fingers as I waited. Another game of "hurry up and wait," I thought. Just like airports. My mind drifted to the conversation about final wishes and organ donation I had shelved. Are we there now? My stomach flipped, and I hoped that meant we weren't.

I didn't know this hospital nearly as well, and the rooms were much smaller, almost half the size of the ones at MCR. It was a massive hospital, and the drab tan walls looked dingy in the fluorescent lighting. The weathered trim of the cabinets and furniture gave away its age. It was overwhelmingly impersonal. We found ourselves on the ninth floor, which wasn't even halfway up, and I missed the familiarity of MCR. I wondered if they had any free pop or poxicles or stale graham crackers for folks here.

The lights suddenly flicked on as a team of eight people slowly filed into the shoebox space and lined themselves one by one around my mom's bed. This woke my dad up, but my mom kept sleeping.

"Good morning, folks; I'm Dr. Wolf," the oldest of them all

began, barely glancing our way. "So, this is patient Sharon Bashaw," pronouncing our last name "Buh-shaw" instead of "Baa-shaw," a small detail that made me feel very cold inside. "She transferred from Medical Center of the Rockies last night after a quadruple bypass surgery over a month ago, and she is not able to get off dobutamine with an ejection fraction of 25 percent. She is weak from lack of food after nausea, pneumonia, and a tracheotomy. She has a peg tube in, and we'll need an order here from dietary to continue that. She is allergic to heparin, and it looks like she lost some toes from that." He paused to pull up the bed sheet and look at her feet, still in the wrappings.

He continued. "She is very weak and diminished," he said toward us, his face slowly following. He stood around five-foot-eleven, with a slender build and dark eyes. His nose was small, and his glasses covered most of his face. There was a no-nonsense air about him.

"Hello, I'm Butch," my dad began his familiar speech whenever we met a new doctor. "She goes by Sherri, not Sharon; she hates Sharon, and I am her husband." The doctor's eyes glanced my way.

"Hi, I'm Alisha, her daughter," I said, suddenly conscious of all the eyes on me, still in my pajamas after a night on the hard lobby floor. I was certain I was a sight, and nothing in me could bring myself to care.

The crew surrounding my mom was an eclectic group of residents or interns, I assumed. There were three women and five men, and one of the men looked more like a teenager than a young adult—a real-life Doogie Howser. I surveyed the ping-pong game they played with their eyes, back and forth from Dr. Wolf to whomever was speaking. I wondered what they were all thinking. More so, I wondered what my mom would have thought about all of this a month ago. Slowly, through this process, she had become more of an item and less of a person. She was always the topic of conversation in rooms these days, but rarely was she a part of the conversation. I felt protective of her in that moment, of her personhood. She was not a problem or a number or an experiment; she was my mom, with a whole lifetime of experiences and a personality and dreams and a strong voice. It struck me how differently she was being presented right now. Frail, fragile, diminished. The doctor was right. Diminished.

"Sherri has been struggling to come off of dobutamine for the last few weeks and can't seem to function without it," my dad began the story of how we ended up here.

As my dad filled the onlookers in on the details, I saw the doctor process this information through many different facial expressions, some I recognized, others I did not. As my dad wrapped up, Dr. Wolf's expression landed on a soft smile as he sighed.

"This has been a journey for you all, I can tell," he started. "And I'm sorry to say, but if she had been here a few weeks ago, we'd be in a very different place. She has needed the type of cardiac management she has not had. We will do the best we can with where she is right now, but she is very compromised. We are going to start with all the basic blood draws to get her levels, and we will make a plan from there."

With that, he turned to his team and began speaking in medical terminology, ordering this and that to "get to know her." I reflected on that phrase and thought how bizarre it was that a bunch of levels and numbers could ever suffice as "knowing" someone. Yet, when life is on the line, I wasn't sure how much room there was for favorite colors and the like. It just seemed cold, sterile. Like a job more than a purpose.

Starting with blood draws and levels seemed like a waste of time to me, and I was frustrated that this felt like a step backward. She was again not receiving food, and she looked terrible, not like herself at all. She needed to eat. Why were we starting with baseline bloodwork? Couldn't they get that information from MCR? We just gave them all the information they could need about her, and we've been with her, more present than she was even, to all the details. I didn't understand. Who knew how long the liquid food order from Dietary specific to her diabetic diet would take. They seemed to lack the urgent promise of relief we had felt so deeply at MCR about this transfer. I looked at my dad with wide eyes. His scared ones stared back. There was nothing we could do but continue to be her advocate, and this felt like starting all over at square one.

We took a few moments to gather ourselves as they continued talking about next steps. By this time, I started to feel that we were very important team players—maybe more important now, since my mom was so out of it and couldn't speak for herself. It was very strange to be thought of as a number to strangers who didn't have our backstory. How do you catch people up on who my mom was and entice them to treat her as if they loved her as much as we did? It was a very powerless feeling.

"Doctor, is there any chance we can get her some food ASAP, please?" my dad asked. "She just started making some improvement with food through this peg tube less than a week ago, and I am worried that with the continued lack of nutrition, she will regress further. We had to wait a long time to find something that could work for her with food, and I just don't want to see her backslide," my dad pled his case.

"We'll get Dietary down here to do their assessment, yes. In the meantime, she will need many heart tests after we determine what is happening," Dr. Wolf responded before turning back to his students and giving them the sign to exit the room.

They filed out of the room in the same way they had entered, in a single-file line, Dr. Wolf bringing up the rear.

"We'll be in touch soon, and back on Monday," he called

over his shoulder to my dad and me.

I sighed heavily. My dad looked at me and echoed my sigh. I had forgotten what day it was. Friday meant that the weekend was coming, and the weekend feel was very different from the weekdays in many cases. Not a lot could happen on weekends, and weekdays provided the structure we all knew we needed right now. I could feel my eyebrows furrow as this reality began to sink in.

"We have to start over with them, kid," my dad said. "And the nicer we are, the more they will like us and hopefully give Mom care that is above and beyond." I knew he was right. It was that much harder to treat a patient when those the patient came with were less than pleasant. We had seen that play out plenty at MCR. Not that we would ever be mean, but we did find that sharing as many details as possible very directly with the medical staff, in their language, bought some credibility. Yet too much sharing could bring annoyance and less credibility. It was an interesting space, and a very tender balance to find.

Here we go again, I thought. Weekends at hospitals were the worst.

CHAPTER 27

May 26, 2012, 8:30 A.M.

IT WAS SATURDAY morning, and I was still in my clothes from Thursday. Gross, I thought as I stood up. I could really use a shower. Things like showers became afterthoughts when you were on autopilot. Time and space seemed to pass in another plane when so many unknowns were present. My dad and I decided to split the shifts of overnighting with Mom. He had gone back home to Loveland late last night to get some sleep in a real bed and to grab Sniff from neighbor Lisa, who had been calling periodically for updates, offering her support.

"Anything I can do, I will," she said, repeatedly. "I just feel so badly for Sherri, and I want her to know she's not alone. And Butch needs breaks too," she kindly relayed.

Sniff wasn't allowed in the Denver hospital, and Lisa had graciously volunteered to take care of Sniff for as long as we were here.

I had slept on the chair-bed thing in my mom's room that was plastic and not quite flat, which made sleeping in my favorite position, on my stomach, impossible. I had asked for a toothbrush last night, and the night nurse gladly obliged. I was very grateful, and snuck past my mom, snoring softly, to the bathroom down the hall.

The lights flickered as I flipped the switch, bringing the yellowed light into sharp focus. I brushed my teeth and thought about how privileged I was to be able to walk down the hall, go to the bathroom, and brush my teeth. A privilege my mom had not had in months. She had had many catheters and bed pans for bathrooms when she was too weak or sick to get up. How perspective changes in moments like this. I grabbed a handful of water and swished the toothpaste around in my mouth, feeling like a brand-new person. I would take it until I could get home to shower. My dad was coming around midday, and when he arrived, I could take the car home and not come back until tomorrow evening. It sounded like the best vacation I had ever planned.

Back in my mom's room, I was shocked again at how much weight she had lost, and at the extensive curliness of her hair after all the medications and procedures. Her longtime hairdresser had come to give her a "haircut" back at MCR to get her bangs out of her eyes and back to her short curled-for-extra-volume cut. She was only able to cut the front, resulting in a mullet-esque shape, and though her bangs were still out of her eyes, her tight curls were now falling lower onto the tops of her gaunt cheekbones. There was still no order from Dietary for food.

A nurse walked in. "Good morning," she said. "How are you this morning?" She was tall and slender and had a very nurturing air about her.

I yawned and stretched before answering her.

"I know that feeling," the nurse chuckled. "Can I get you anything?" she asked as I was beginning to soften to the idea of new people being able to help my mom as well as the MCR staff.

"I'm okay, thank you. Unless you have a magic button that could make all of this better?" I said in response and wished for her inner superhero to bust out of her fitted burgundy scrubs and set everything to rights.

She smiled. "If only" was her kind reply, laced with a tinge of sad. "I'm happy to start with some breakfast, though, if you'd like," she said, handing me a menu.

"That sounds great, thanks," I said, feeling a tinge of guilt at another layer of privilege I had stumbled upon—eating. I chose the eggs and pancakes with some coffee, and ordered it to my mom's room, grateful I wouldn't have to go to the cafeteria just yet. Dealing with a lot of people sounded hard at the moment.

When the nurse, Leah, came back in the room, I asked her about the dietary order for my mom.

"Still no word," she responded, "but I put in another call this morning. As you know, they have to assess and then get a doctor to sign the order. The doctor this weekend is different than your mom's weekday doctor, so it may take a little bit longer for the orders to push through. But we are collecting all her test results and hopefully will have a better idea of what the plan is later today when the doctor reviews them."

I could feel the frustration build as I closed my eyes.

"You okay, hon?" Leah asked.

"It's so hard to watch her get weaker without food, and I know it's a whole process and she's new here and it's a weekend. It just seems like it should be so easy, and she is doing worse now without it, you know?" I replied, dejected.

Leah sighed a sigh full of compassion. "Yes, I understand. It is a really hard spot. Let me page the on-call doctor and see if he can write an emergency order. I know there were some concerns about her developing blood clots as well, so I am already anticipating his call."

"That would be great, Leah, thank you so much!" I replied, my relief palpable.

"Sure," she said. "I'll see what I can do."

My phone buzzed. It was my dad. I gave him the update on the latest dietary news. My mom was really out of it. He'd be up later this afternoon. I had some time.

There was a knock at the door. My breakfast arrived on the standard uniform gray plastic cart on wheels. The familiar black plate cover with the diagonal swirled design covered my pancakes and eggs. The scrambled eggs looked mass produced, and the pancakes were rather firm. The coffee was as dark as the night sky in the mountains when you can't see your hand in front of your face, and the two half-and-half containers they gave me barely changed that. However, it was the best thing I had eaten in the last few days. Satisfied, I put my tray by the door and began to watch TV.

My mom opened her eyes at the sound, and I apologized for the noise as I greeted her being awake.

"Good morning, Mom!" How are y—?" She was asleep again before I could finish the question.

CHAPTER 28

May 26, 2012, 4:01 P.M.

MY DAD ARRIVED at the hospital, and we exchanged keys in the parking lot. My mom had woken up off and on for the whole afternoon as I dozed. Nothing had changed except my level of hope. I was feeling pretty low about my mom's trajectory, and I was hoping some alone time and a shower would reverse that.

On the drive home, I tried to switch gears into school mode with the small amount of bandwidth I had left. My semester ended in a less than a week, and I had received a small extension on a curriculum I needed to create for adolescents processing grief for my Group Counseling class final. I hadn't started yet, and I was wondering how you begin to help others through a time of grief when you are in one yourself.

CHAPTER 29
May 27, 2012, 1:02 P.M.

THE HOUSE WAS quiet, but I couldn't relax. My head was scattered, and was I having trouble being in so many places at once. It had taken all I had in me to focus long enough to write one page of my group counseling curriculum yesterday. After fighting myself internally to press on, I conceded to my heavy eyelids and went to sleep around 8:30 p.m., not moving an inch until I woke up this morning at 10:30. My body was somewhat rested, but my mind would not stop whirring from the moment I opened my eyes. I called my dad for an update.

"Hey, kid," he answered on the third ring. "Did you get some sleep?" He sounded sad.

"I did, yeah; how about you?"

"Oh, yeah, the best. You know how comfy this chair-bed thing is here," he said sarcastically.

I laughed. "Indeed, I do. How's Mom? Did she get food yet?"

"No. I'm going nuts. You know how the weekends go, though. Everything is just so slow. She is not doing well, still so sick and frail. She is barely awake. I talked to the on-call doctor last night, and Mom went in for a quick procedure this morning to implant a heart monitor to test each quadrant of her heart's blood flow on a monitor we can watch, which will tell them where the problem is, and how to fix it. And of course, she couldn't eat before the procedure, so it's just more waiting. There's a new on-call doctor tonight, so I'm going to talk to them as soon as they arrive for an order. This is awful to watch, and they need to know how important this is; she is dying without food here!" He got more passionate toward the end, then took a breath and calmed down with a sigh. "They are also worried about clots in her leg and neck area after some tests and scans came back, so they are figuring out the plan for tomorrow after they know more from the monitor. They started her on another blood thinner, not heparin, but needed something to help the clots from forming."

There was a long pause as the air was sucked out of the room.

"How's your paper coming along?" he asked, shifting the conversation.

I could feel my nervous system shielding me with its autopilot armor. "Oh, fine." I said, throwing my loose plans to concentrate on my paper out the window. "I'll head down in a few, and see you soon," I heard myself say from a distant place. I didn't know where that was.

CHAPTER 30
May 27, 2012, 8:39 P.M.

THE ON-CALL DOCTOR was my age, in his early thirties at most, and swayed back and forth as he spoke. I walked in to see my mom sleeping and my dad sternly talking with him.

"This is no longer an option," I caught the tail end of the conversation. "She has been here for three days now and has not had any food after not having hardly any food up north for the previous three weeks. I don't understand the rationale to wait any longer. Please order her the food. Now."

The doctor responded in a shaky voice, explaining how everything is closed on the weekends and that her primary doctor would be back tomorrow. My dad protested, and the doctor agreed to place the emergency order despite it being Sunday evening and Dietary being closed.

I smiled. I had definitely been on the receiving end of my dad's stern voice many times in my life, and I was not jealous. His most famous line was quoted by Mat and me often, stern face impression and all. I imagined my dad speaking to this doctor in kind. "Your life is about to change. Significantly." When he said it, it was usually true.

Forty-five minutes later, a bag of liquid food arrived for my mom and her peg tube was connected. Like I said, when he said it, it was usually true.

CHAPTER 31

May 28, 2012, 7:15 A.M.

PAJAMAS IN TOW this time, I was marginally more comfortable on the chair-bed thing for the night. I stretched and rolled over slowly, my ears picking up on the familiar voices of Good Morning America, one of my mom's favorite morning shows. It was on before school every morning growing up. Well, that's a comforting dream, I thought. But as I blinked, the voices didn't go away. I sat up and looked at the screen; my mom was holding the remote, a faint smile on her face at the familiarity of her show. I took in the sight. It had been so long since I had seen her be anything other than "really sick," and to see her watching TV? I was elated.

"Oh, my gosh, Mom, hi!" I exclaimed, and she turned her bright and focused sparkling blue eyes my way. She was so present, and for just a moment I was transported back in time before any of this began. A wave of comfort passed over me as she smiled in my direction. My mom was back, and she was okay.

She motioned for the whiteboard, and I scrambled up to get it. I left the magnet word cookie sheet at home as she was seemingly declining, hoping for its eventual use. She was able to grip the blue EXPO marker enough to make out the words "first hope." It looked like Brooks's scribbles, and it was the most beautiful thing I had seen in days. A tear slid down my cheek, and she smiled at me, proud of herself for writing on the whiteboard. It was the first thing she had communicated clearly since her lung had collapsed.

"Yes, absolutely, first hope," I said, holding back more tears. "The first of many."

She smiled and pointed to the liquid tube-fed food with a thumbs-up. It was a true testament to the power of nutrition in healing, and something we had highly underestimated. I was instantly grateful for my dad's stern talk with the on-call doctor. I returned her thumbs-up with a nod and settled in to watch the rest of Good Morning America with my mom. It almost felt normal.

CHAPTER 32

May 30, 2012, 3:00 P.M.

I WAS HEADED back to Pittsburgh in another week and had begun to settle into this next "new normal" phase of my mom's recovery. She had slowly progressed over the past three days with food, and her current cocktail of medication had begun to fight the remaining pneumonia infection with brute force. I had brought the cookie pan magnets down to Denver, and she had begun pointing to what she wanted and needed and trying her shaky writing when she had the energy for the whiteboard. It was the first time I had felt real progress since my dad's birthday.

The relief of my mom's turn for the better freed the chains of my nervous system to allow me to focus on my paper, and I was one group lesson away from complete. I was back up home in Loveland, and Sniff and I were relaxing on the deck as I sat down to finish my paper. Halfway through, my phone rang.

"Hey, Dad!" I cheerily answered.

"Hey, kid."

Instantly, I knew something was wrong.

"What's wrong, Dad? What happened now?" I froze in place.

"Well, I hate to be the bearer of bad news, but I wanted to give you the update. I know you are working on your paper."

"It's okay, what happened?" I shifted the topic back.

"Mom has started bleeding internally in her GI tract, and they had to stop the tube feed last night. I didn't want to ruin your night, so I didn't call until today, and only because it has gotten worse. The doctor's won't feed her because she has had a lot of blood loss in her stool, and they stopped the blood thinner to slow the bleeding. She is going into surgery tonight to put in a blood clot catcher, since a blood thinner is not possible right now, and they are still worried about blood clots. They will also try to remove some of the fluid from her lungs while they are in there. I know this is terrible news," his emotionless voice reported. I could tell there was more. "Hon, the doctors told me we should start planning for her funeral."

The words hit my positive momentum straight in the face. My ears started ringing, and I was already texting the neighbors for help with Sniff.

"I'm on my way, Dad. Are you calling Mat?" I asked.

"Yep, he's next."

The tears began to pour out with no control as soon as I hung up and those words sank in. What if my mom died? I had never really considered this as an actual possibility. I had trusted that it would not happen, which now felt like a foolish belief.

Shannon was our next-door neighbor and over in a few minutes. She shared a birthday and a friendship with my mom, and she knew Sniff well. I thanked her, gave her a quick hug, and grabbed my overnight bag. I had never unpacked.

CHAPTER 33

May 31, 2012, 7:19 A.M.

IT WAS ROUNDS time, and my mom was sleeping soundly. Again. I had arrived last night with puffy eyes after crying the whole hour and a half to Denver to find my mom in the recovery room after the clot catcher surgery, stable. We were still urged to say our goodbyes, and Mat had arrived before me, as he came right from a jobsite in Denver. The mood was sullen, somber.

We all took turns saying our goodbyes to my mom for the second time. It was the worst déjà vu. This time, I told her that if she needed to go, she could, but deep inside, I really didn't mean it. I wanted her to keep fighting for as long as she could. I felt both selfish and grateful that she had been fighting.

The doctors had tried to remove some of the fluid from her lungs while she was in surgery for the clot catcher but had to stop once they saw the internal bleeding coming out of the suction tubing. She was in a very rough space and without food would continue to weaken, if she didn't die from the internal bleeding first. It was a no-win situation.

Conversation with my dad and brother last night drifted from the next steps in treatment to what songs she would want played at her funeral, and everything in between. My head was sore today from the whiplash. She was an organ donor and would advocate giving any of her working organs to others if she could help someone else live should she permanently decline.

Mat and I grew up knowing both our parents wished for this; we had sat through what would seem to an outsider an absurd amount of talks about the importance of the little hearts on their driver's licenses. However, talking about it in real time was less idealistic and peaceful than those talks had ever felt. Imagining giving parts of her away now incited a defensive rage inside of me that was surprising. She still had some fight left. How could we be talking about this right now? It felt so wrong. Like we had betrayed her in some way by even discussing it as an option. I had excused myself to go to the bathroom and then placed that topic back on its shelf in my mind while I made my bed once again in the hospital lobby for the short night of something that sort of resembled "sleep."

Dr. Wolf cleared this throat as he entered the room, his team trailing behind. Doogie Howser took the lead today, recapping the severity of her situation. My dad's shoelaces were extra untied today, and people kept telling him that his shoes were untied. He began tucking the laces into the sides of his shoes as Doogie spoke. His main point was that time would tell. They were going to monitor her internal blood loss and give her a pint of blood later today. Once there was no more blood loss, which no one could predict a timeline for, they would start the peg tube of food again. Until then, there was just the white noise of waiting for the unknown.

CHAPTER 34

June 3, 2012, 8:15 A.M.

"SHEEEEERRRRRRI," THE VOICE floated through the room, soft and velvety. "Good morning, Miss Sherri, it's time for your vitals." Gary was a new favorite nurse of my mom's, with big brown eyes and matching short brown hair. He led with kindness, and it radiated from every bone in his nearly six-foot frame. He looked as if he were in his mid-thirties but spoke as if he had the wisdom of ages. He was thinking of pursuing teaching at some point in his career and had spent a large portion of yesterday telling my mom about his ideas and experience when she was awake. She would write a word or phrase about her favorite teaching tricks and tips on the whiteboard in return. She couldn't offer much, but I could tell he had made her feel seen. What a gift.

I opened my eyes and closed them again. I wasn't ready for the world to start just yet. I grabbed the blanket tighter on the chair-bed thing I had slept on and stayed still. My mom groaned and lifted her right hand into the air, pointer finger extended and ready to receive the pulse-ox to measure her oxygen level.

Gary laughed. "Perfect," he said. "You are a true veteran

at this. Temperature time next here, but you can keep your eyes closed, that's okay." He stuck a thermometer into an individualized plastic sheath and placed it in her right ear. I heard the click that popped the cap off, and it landed in the trash with a small clunk. I could see this situation unfold, even with my eyes closed.

I smiled, knowing that my mom's eyes were also closed. "The apple doesn't fall far from the tree," I could hear my dad saying in my head in an overly dramatic and playful way, offering both confirmation and condolences that Mat and I were forever connected to them.

"I think you'll like this next part, Sherri," Gary started, and my mom made a high-pitched squeak in return.

There was a sloshy swish noise of a viscous liquid inside a plastic bag that reminded me of a reusable gel icepack that had lost its hold on the cold. "Is that . . . ?" I half said out loud as I rolled over and sat up, stretching and echoing Gary's "Good morning." Gary flashed me a smile that showed off how truly white his teeth were as he adjusted some tubing and hung the new bag of tube feed from my mom's IV pole before connecting it to her peg tube.

"Did the bleeding stop?" I asked, wide-eyed and suddenly very awake.

"There was no blood loss overnight, so the doc ordered some tube feed this morning, to be dispensed slowly; we'll go from there. It's good enough news to try some nutrition and get you healing, Sherri!" he reported enthusiastically.

Gary had been with us on the roller coaster of monitoring blood loss for the last two days, and I was glad he was the one to connect her food tube and bring her some hope. Tests had revealed that she had some bleeding ulcers in her stomach, and the doctors hoped that with time, they would begin to heal and allow food to pass through without rupturing. Time was no longer a luxury her body had. This had to work.

CHAPTER 35

June 4, 2012, 9:47 A.M.

THE OPPOSING PARTIES were in the boxing ring, ready for the fight. Guilt in one corner, swinging mightily at the air, warming up. Weighing in at 250 pounds, it was a solid wall of intimidating, stocky muscle. Its fans screamed at its opponent loudly, relentlessly. Individuation stood in the opposite corner, observing. Its wimpy and rail-thin 130-pound body shook out its lanky limbs and adjusted the sweatband around its head to prepare for battle. Its fans were not heard under the roar of those in support of Guilt. The tension inside me built and built, awaiting the first blow. The fight seemed stacked, for obvious reasons—one that should never be, and yet one that would forever shift my life, no matter the outcome. This was not a scrimmage match. It was the match.

It was time to decide how to proceed for myself and my relationship with school, in spite of what was happening with my mom. My school had been very kind to me and continued to be flexible however they could. Some of my professors truly modeled walking the counseling talk of taking care of self and others, which only reassured me more of my choice of this particular master's program, though it was across the country from my family, my known, and my comfort zone. All the doors had opened at the right times in order for me to land a graduate assistantship with a professor who had been a staple of this program for decades, Dr. Bob Witchel. I was helping out with the department website and newsletter in exchange for half off my out-of-state tuition bills. It was one of the many doors that had opened. I didn't want to close it.

Another opened door was my relationship with Dr. Witchel. He was a quirky man in his early sixties with a lifetime's worth of stories and wisdom that he imparted to his classes through his 1970s-style PowerPoint presentations. He deeply cared about his students, and as his graduate assistant, I got to know him well. He was kind, just countercultural enough to make a few waves, and was very supportive of me throughout the struggles with my mom, even deeming himself my "Pittsburgh dad." I was very grateful for him, and all the support he offered.

Alongside him, three other professors made my graduate school experience a very healing one to occur concurrently with my mom's illness. Drs. Bruno, Cato West, and Marshak were not just supports but true mentors in how they navigated with me through the unknown. They used each new up and down as a learning experience for when life would happen outside of work in the future and demonstrated through action the blending of caring for yourself while also entering the world of caregiving for others. This echoed the process I was learning personally, and that it was reinforced professionally only strengthened Individuation's voice.

I wanted to be present with my mom, and to be there for my dad as best I could. I had a strong connection to my parents, and I felt very torn about continuing to pursue my own life and development while they were struggling so much. Many times, I had considered dropping out of school to help care for them, or at least be closer to home, but the voice of Individuation began to speak in soft whispers more often, and . . . it made sense. Something was pulling me back toward school, and its whispers were asking me to find a way to do both what I needed to do alongside what I could do for others, rather than sacrificing myself completely. This was a newly emerging idea. I was used to being all in for others and had learned to honor others before myself my whole life. I had interpreted that to mean instead of honoring myself not in addition to honoring myself and had had a hard time differentiating the two. But my decision to go to grad school across the country, despite it not making the most sense to my family, was one of the first major decisions in my life that I had made for just me, based on my gut feeling alone and not others' opinions and thoughts. It was big.

I began to get to know Individuation as a gentle guide and a strong advocate. Guilt had always portrayed it as selfish, arrogant, and only interested in personal gain. However, my experience of going to grad school had proven the opposite. Instead of selfish, I felt like I found my tribe of people, like I was in alignment with my calling and purpose, like I was furthering my desire to help others with a backed skill set. I had started to call Guilt's bluff, ever so slightly, and I hadn't been wrong. Yet it remained a moral boxing match that took its inner toll, and one I began to question again when my mom got sick.

The night before, my dad had offered that he did not want me to give up my life and pursuit of something in which I had finally found such joy. Hearing this was incredibly helpful, and with the promise to myself and to my dad that I would come back as often as I could, I made the hard decision to back Individuation in the ring. The fight was on, and Guilt had just been surprised by a sneaky right hook.

I got on the plane back to Pittsburgh two hours later.

CHAPTER 36

June 6, 2012, 11:35 A.M.

"LISH, IT'S AMAZING. Mom is getting transferred to a long-term acute care hospital back up in Loveland, right across I-25 off 34 later this afternoon!"

All the words tumbled out of my dad's mouth so fast, I had to think twice about what he was saying.

"Woah, what?!" came my astonished reply.

"The food has been working, and there's no more bleeding. And because of the food, it has helped her heart too. She is off all IV heart meds, and the team of doctors said they are no longer concerned that she is in any danger. She can leave the ICU and get started recovering now, finnnnnaaaaaallllllllyyyyyyyy." He dragged out the last word in a singsong tone. I hadn't heard him this happy in months.

"Really!" I said, as more of a statement. "This is awesome news! Is she excited?"

"She is, yes. She is using the magnet word board you made, and is able to mostly communicate what she wants, but I am dying to know what she has been thinking about this whole time. I can't wait to actually talk with her again."

My parents had always been deeply connected on many levels, some unseen. Though verbal communication was not possible right now, I was certain they were still very connected nonverbally, and it was driving my dad crazy.

"Wow, that's great, Dad," I said, meaning it. "When will she go?"

"This afternoon; they are arranging transport. It will be into the acute care side first, and then to the rehab side, where she will start to regain her strength by rehabbing for three hours a day. I'll call to update you on the new beige walls once we get there," he joked.

"Please do," I laughed back. I thought about how long it had been since I had spoken with my mom and pondered how different this experience had been—just talking about her, but never with her. Even before her trach, she was so out of it so often that the pattern of relayed information through my dad now seemed normal. As I parked my car and walked into the high-rise building ahead of me for class, I wondered what it would be like to actually talk with her again.

CHAPTER 37
June 18, 2012, 4:15 P.M.

THE PAST TWO weeks had been a consistent uphill climb for my mom, for which I was so grateful. I was able to jump back into my summer classes and begin to really focus on both worlds in a way that I didn't know I had capacity for. I talked to my dad every night, still, and he gave me the latest update. My favorite so far was the story of my mom being able to sit in a wheelchair, wearing her floppy yellow sun hat outside in the sunshine for the first time since this whole mess had begun. That one made me cry as I imagined her small body sitting with her face turned up to the sun with a slight smile, taking it all in. We were all so grateful, especially my mom.

I began to pray more often, hating that it seemed to make me a conditional pray-er, while also glad for the chance to reboot my faith some. Faith in something greater than myself was still so very important to me, and it was getting easier to engage with again as a lifeline rather than an afterthought. The gravity of my mom's life-and-death situations gave me the opportunity to reassess what was important to me; I had refound some faith, for which I was very grateful. It felt good. Familiar. Homey.

FOUR EYES

I was still hesitant to share my association with the Christian faith with my new friends at school, as present-day Christianity had become more of a set of beliefs and behaviors that labeled, moralized, categorized, and politicized so many issues and people rather than leading with love in action to all, because all are loved, and all are worth it. It broke my heart that the church as a collective had hurt so many in the name of God, and I found myself within the tension of wanting to share my beliefs but not wanting to be judged for them. This reconnection was the first breath of fresh air I had inhaled in years regarding faith, and I became increasingly grateful for the good, despite it stemming from all the pain my mom had suffered. Was that the point of it all? What a price tag. I just didn't know. An old thought crept in: "God works in mysterious ways." Indeed.

CHAPTER 38

June 20, 2012, 9:42 A.M.

I WAS ABLE to create a six-day break in my school and work schedules to head back home, and also stand as a bridesmaid in my best friend Elle's wedding in Montana. My great friend and old college roommate Becky and I were going to road-trip there from Denver, and it felt great to look forward to something other than hospitals while home. It also felt good to focus on a new hospital that was focused on rehabilitation rather than problem-solving.

This time in the airport, I felt much lighter and moved more quickly through the terminal to Baggage Claim. The golden animals engraved in the floor were still eye catching, and the familiar bear I often passed seemed to wink at me this time thorough as if he were cheering me on.

The reports from my dad had been slow but progress based. My mom had been able to sit up in a chair on her own, but she was still struggling to keep food down. Her peg tube was still going. Nevertheless, she was getting stronger by the day. This afternoon, I was told, the trach was going to be removed; I couldn't wait to see my mom be able to talk again after so long.

Guilt and Individuation were at it again in my mind about

FOUR EYES

Elle's wedding, and I tried to let each side say its piece before recognizing that by going to Montana, and visiting my mom before and after the trip, I was able to do both what I needed to do and what I could do for others. Yet, Guilt was still pretty loud.

This echoed what I continued to learn in school, about finding ways to assertively state my needs and care for myself in the same way I was learning how to guide people to do so for themselves. Though it was often easier said than done, the situation with my parents was great practice.

My dad met me at Arrivals, and we were off to the new hospital up north. It seemed like I had just been here.

My dad pulled the Focus into the parking lot of Northern Colorado Long-Term Acute Hospital, and already it felt more user-friendly. It was only one story, surrounded by many trees and flowers, and it looked like there were a few walking paths surrounding both sides of the building. Called LTACH for short, it contained two wings: a medical side and a rehab side.

My mom was in the medical complex side, where they had been working on getting her off the ventilator permanently. Her trach had been removed earlier today. My dad reported that it had gone well; she was even able to stand up and march in place today. After exerting energy, she was tired, and he had left her sleeping to come get me. She hadn't spoken yet. Her throat was too sore.

I had packed my carry-on knowing this was the plan and prepared my party hats, a Bashaw family tradition when it came to celebrating. We walked inside the building and were instantly hit with the smell of commercialized food and old mustard. I wrinkled my nose.

"Oh, wow," I said as my dad laughed.

"You get used to it after a while."

"If you say so," I said, shaking my head in return.

My dad was in on the surprise, and we walked down

a corridor that looked remarkably similar to all the other hospitals we had been in recently. This one had salmon-colored signs outside every room, accenting the cream-colored sterile walls. The handrails on each of the walls were a light brown, muting it all.

My mom's door was cracked open. We put on our party hats, and I was ready for a different experience than the one I had come to expect in hospitals. I watched my dad out of the corner of my eye extra carefully—he was prone to snapping the elastic bands of party hats on your chin if you weren't paying attention. It seemed we were in a momentary truce as we walked into her room yelling, "Congratulations! You can talk! Way to go, Mom!"

She was propped up on the bed with some pillows and looked up at us, totally surprised. I was so happy to see her up, with no plastic tubing sticking out of her anywhere. It was truly incredible, and I recognized that she was regaining some sense of herself. Her hair was somewhat curled, a daily routine she rarely let slide, and I could see that she was even attempting to do some makeup again. This was totally unexpected.

"Hi, Mom," I said, rushing over to hug her.

"Hi, guys," she croaked back at us with a smile. Her throat was sore, and she swallowed slowly, but she was able to speak for the first time in nine weeks.

My dad was grinning from ear to ear. "Hi, my love; it is so good to hear your voice and see you up and at 'em," he said, approaching the other side of the bed for a big hug and a kiss on her cheek. "I'm so proud of you, honey. You are one tough fighter!"

My mom nodded and motioned for some water. As I stood up to get it, she realized, as did I, that she could now speak again and laughed.

"Whoops," she said, followed by "thanks" as I handed it to her.

FOUR EYES

For the next couple of hours, we chatted slowly and caught up. I had really hoped she would be okay, but somehow, seeing it was another experience altogether. Getting up to go to the bathroom, I left my parents talking, holding hands, and recapping my mom's journey thus far. A strange feeling came over me that I couldn't shake. I wanted to cry and laugh and dance and sleep all at once. It was so strong that I almost didn't recognize it as relief.

CHAPTER 39
June 24, 2012, 6:47 P.M.

THE JAGGED MOUNTAINS of Montana shrank in the distance as Becky and I drove back from Elle's wedding. The windows were down, and our hair blew askew in the welcomed wind. Laughter filled the car and the hot Montana air as we reminisced about our old college days as roommates and caught up on life's current happenings. It felt amazing to laugh. Becky was seven months pregnant, yet still up for the adventure of a road trip. She was that kind of friend. Pregnancy also came with frequent bathroom breaks, which my small bladder didn't mind at all. It was a refreshing change of pace. Urgent-less.

Elle married the love of her life, Tim. They both loved the wilderness and had decided on a beautifully remote location in Montana that was special to them both. The downside of the remote space was, of course, no cell reception. This was the first time I had been out of reach since my mom got sick, and my anxiety showed all weekend through my restlessness and bouncing knees whenever I was sitting. Becky noticed and did her best to distract me. Mostly, it worked. I kept hoping that everything was okay, and as soon as we crossed into cell phone–reception land, I turned my phone on.

The voicemail icon showed, and I checked my missed calls. There was one from Mat, and three from my dad the night before last. Uh-oh, I thought, as Guilt threw an uppercut right into Individuation's nose. I felt the sting shoot through my body as it stiffened.

"Hi, Lish, it's Dad. I know you don't have reception right now, but Mom had a really big scare the other night, and I wanted to let you know. She was doing fine Friday night, but when a nurse came back to check on her, she was unconscious; the nurse thought she had had a stroke. She was rushed to MCR's emergency room, and they found that her blood sugar was dangerously low: 22! She had been getting around-the-clock tube feeding to help stabilize her sugars, and but then her blood sugar dropped drastically. They thought for sure it was a stroke."

Oh, my gosh, I thought. And here I was on a road trip with my friend, not able to answer the calls and having a great time. I felt a combination of Guilt telling me how bad a daughter I had become and Individuation trying to level with me by sharing the relief I had for not being present for that one. Mat's message added that the nurse who found her had also washed her hair earlier and had forgotten to reconnect the feeding tube afterward, leaving her without food for several hours. Once MCR stabilized her, she was readmitted to LTACH later that night. They also looked at her bedsore. It was continuing to fester and cause a lot of pain, so they gave her some more pain medication for that as well. The word "fester" made me squirm. What had we missed there?

Becky could tell instantly that something was wrong, and as I updated her, I could feel the air being sucked out of my lungs. I was in panic mode again and needed to call them immediately. Guilt: 2, Individuation: 1.

CHAPTER 40

June 25, 2012, 10:45 A.M.

AUNT PATTI HAD returned to help out with my mom and help her transition into a healing mindset that could get her strong enough to transfer to the rehab side of the hospital. She was there when I got home from Montana, and I was so grateful that my mom had Patti with her. It was my parents' thirty-fifth wedding anniversary today, and my dad had ordered a sheet cake for the staff to share in celebration.

I got the update late last night once home and tried not to over-apologize for being out of cell range. The mood was less frantic than what had been conveyed on the phone, and I was very grateful that everyone had seemed to get through the scare fairly unscathed. I tried to follow suit.

This morning we were off to celebrate and loaded ourselves in the car to make the hospital trek. My mom was up and waiting for us when we got there, dressed even. This was a rare find these days, and one she had been working on with the CNAs so she could learn how to do this for herself again.

"Hi, guys! How was the wedding, Lish?" she asked, wasting no time.

"It was really good! It was remote and beautiful. Elle and

Tim say hi and send their best," I reported. "I heard you had quite the scare Friday night! I'm so sorry! How are you now?"

"Oh, fine," came her confident reply. "That was pretty scary, but I'm glad to be back here." She had such a good attitude.

"Well, I wanted to come and celebrate your thirty-fifth with you guys for a while before I have to go to the airport," I offered, matching her positivity. "Congratulations! You have made it through so much," I said to both my parents.

"Thirty-five big ones," my dad replied. "We sure have. The best years of my life," came his response as he moved toward the cake he had set on the table.

"Yes, thirty-five is big," my mom concurred. "I'm so glad to have spent them with you, hon," she said, looking up at my dad with her piercing blue eyes. As different as they were, they did really come as a package deal, and there was something I so respected about their ability to really be there for each other through it all.

"Let's eat," my mom said, and my dad got the nurses to join us in celebration.

Guilt had been quieted by this interaction, but it puffed up again as the clock inched closer to when I had to leave for the airport.

I told my mom how proud I was of her, said I would call to check in now that she could talk again, and hugged her tightly. I hugged my aunt goodbye and was very grateful for her presence there with my mom. I could feel my shoulders relax. Maybe this would all be over, now, finally. My mom just needed to figure out this stomach thing and she'd be all set. Non-medical-related thoughts began to reenter my mind, put back into motion by my thawing nervous system. I hugged my dad at the airport and took the familiar route in the doors and down the escalator to the security lines. At my gate, I felt my eyelids droop hard. I couldn't fight them any longer; I slept the whole way back to Pittsburgh.

CHAPTER 41

July 31, 2012, 2:14 P.M.

THE MONTH OF July had flown by between a full course load, working, keeping updated on my mom's status, and processing some of my emotions from the last several months that had been stuck inside. Grad school itself was hard to get through, but this was a different version of hard that stemmed from different reasons and hurt in different places. I had asked Dr. Witchel to recommend a local counselor so that I could start to unpack some of my feelings. It was somewhat easier to do now that I wasn't in the middle of the pain. He gave me a name, and I pursued therapy with a woman who had also experienced a sick parent while she was in graduate school. It was a much needed and very helpful connection.

As I spent time sorting out my recent experiences with my new therapist, my dad continued the updates. My mom was still struggling with nausea and vomiting, though she had been moved to the rehab side of LTACH near the beginning of the month. It seemed she was getting better, especially since she began eating food again with tube feed. The doctors didn't know what to do with her stomach upset other than to treat the nausea and monitor what happened.

She was able to walk slowly, but often my dad pushed her in a wheelchair; they ate meals together in the cafeteria, adorably twenty years younger than everyone else.

My dad was growing tired of the long days and was beginning to wrestle more with his own depression. He shared with me how hard this had been on him, and how he was losing steam. It sounded like he knew Guilt as well as I did.

My mom's bedsore continued to get worse, and they began to treat it with a wound vacuum, which pulled fluid from a tube inserted into it, aiding in the healing process as well as helping pull the sides of the wound together. Aside from that, she was doing fantastically. She was able to participate in three hours a day of rehab with physical, occupational, and speech therapy, where she was relearning how to swallow and say certain words. She had even gone back to University Hospital for a heart checkup, and the doctors were pleased with her sustained progress. They adjusted some med levels and attributed her upset stomach to a bug going around.

Without many reserves, it was taking longer for her stomach to feel any better at all. She was vomiting up everything she tried. My dad reported catching something too, something that kept him home for only the second day since this whole journey began. It took him a full day of sleeping to recover. We hoped the same for my mom and understood her exhaustion as she was trying to fight off an infection in addition to healing. I would catch her on her phone now and then, but she was usually very tired by the time her day was done.

We had a family conference mid-July, and I flew home to discuss the future plan. One by one, the team reported their latest challenges and successes with my mom and gave a recommendation. They had all listed several things to continue working on but had unanimously stated that they thought she could go home in a few more weeks, once the stomach bug was better. A week after that meeting, they even took my mom back to our house, where she cried as she walked through the door for the first time in four months. All the welcoming comforts of home greeted her when she walked in, as did the sidewalks and driveway colored with loving chalk messages from the neighborhood kids. It seemed as though she was ready to make this transition. We were all excited, and also a bit nervous. It had been so long.

I had a ten-day break between my summer term and fall semester, and it started two days after my mom would be going home. It was perfect timing, and I excitedly told my dad I'd be home to help him with caregiving at home and also to support my mom. There would also be in-home nurse and physical and occupational therapy visits to help make the transition smoother.

My dad and Mat went to work installing new handrails by the toilets and showers and looking for a walker, a wheelchair, a shower chair, and an elevated toilet seat. Some of the items were easier to find than others. Mat was building a ramp entrance for our front door as well. They were discussing how to remodel the bathroom to make it more accessible for my mom, but decided to wait a bit longer to see how she adjusted first. As it stood, the bathroom layout was very difficult to navigate with much more than a walker and a shower chair to get the essentials done.

RJ's family had kindly offered many accessible items that were once Liz's, and on my quick trip home in July, I met up with Liz and RJ's mom to collect a wheelchair, a shower chair, and a handheld showerhead with a long hose. We gratefully crossed those items off the list.

These items, however, were so loaded with emotion that I needed to pull over on my way home to cry for a while. I just didn't want any of this to be true, but it was. Liz was gone, and my mom was now going to use her old items. While a very kind gift, I would have given anything for Liz to still be here and for Liz and my mom to not need them at all. I started to become very angry at the situation. Grieving my friend while also grieving a transition for my mom was a tall order.

The date was set for her to return home on August 8, and my ticket was for August 10. My therapist and I had worked on how to take some breaks for myself in a family system that was not particularly good at that, and I was mentally ready to continue to shape the boundaries of my involvement as much as I could. I also knew my dad would need a break, and Guilt and Individuation were at it again in my mind, in a stalemate at how that may look.

Mat was around too, but rarely did we cross paths when I was home, because when I was home, it was usually his break. He was also experiencing the stress of raising his young son while working full-time and had a large share of adulting on his plate too. This dynamic was so new for all of us, and I really wanted to approach it with the intention of doing it well rather than getting completely sucked in, if that was even possible.

CHAPTER 42

August 11, 2012, 12:45 P.M.

MY PLANE LANDED late last night, and for the week I was in town, Becky lent me a spare car she and her husband had recently acquired. It was a huge blessing, and I didn't even care that it didn't have heat or air-conditioning. Becky met me at the airport and took me to her house, where we hung out for an hour before I hit the road. It was nice to spend some time catching up with her, about nothing medically related, despite Guilt yelling loudly at Individuation and momentarily stunning it.

I had arrived home to quite the party. Sniff was her adorable wiggly-bodied self as I entered the front door, and I finally felt like things were again at rights. How they should be. My mom was already sleeping, and our neighbor Lisa was talking to my dad in the living room. I hugged them and then dragged my bag through the door and down the hall into the guest bedroom, noticing a pair of socks on the floor I had forgotten from my last trip.

Sniff was as excited to see me as I was her. She was such a smart girl, and always knew when I needed a little extra support or love. She came over and sat on my suitcase, insisting that I pet her, which was warmly comforting. In the hallway there was a long green tube running from my parents' bedroom to the living room.

"What's this, Sniff?" I asked her, half expecting her to answer as I followed the tube to its source in my mom's bedroom. It was connected to a big gray machine that made a steady hum. My mom was wearing oxygen equipment, and a much-shorter, clear tube was also hooked up to the machine and wrapped around both of her ears and into her nostrils. This must be a nonportable oxygen contraption, I thought. Interesting.

It was great to see my mom asleep in her own bed. She looked peaceful, and I wondered how, after sixteen weeks, her own bed must feel, or if she even remembered it. I could only imagine.

"Come on, girl," I said quietly to Sniff, and she gladly accompanied me to the living room, where my dad and Lisa were drinking coffee sitting on the adjacent brown micro-suede couches my mom hated with a passion. They had gotten the couches a few years prior, but my mom had suffered a strong case of buyer's remorse; she couldn't wait to get new ones. There was a third cup of coffee sitting on the table, waiting for me.

"Aw, thanks, Dad," I said as I settled into the stiffest part of the three-seater couch that no one ever sat on.

"Hi, kid," he started. "There is creamer in the fridge if you want. And don't worry, it's decaf."

"Awesome," I said. "I'll grab it in a minute." I saw the end of the green tubing draped over a couch and asked, "So, mom's on oxygen now, huh?"

"Yeah, they sent her home with it because she wasn't feeling great at LTACH the last few days. They gave her some antibiotics for an elevated white blood cell count that they think has to do with her stomach bug or her bedsore not fully healing yet; the oxygen just helps her breathe easier," he reported.

Lisa nodded.

"It's been pretty hard for her since being home," she shared.

Lisa was a shorter, slender woman with shoulder-length blonde-brown hair. She was a speech-language pathologist and had become my mom's best friend over the decade plus of neighboring. I was so grateful for Lisa, and that my mom had a friend outside of her family to talk to.

"Yeah?" I asked. "How so?"

"Well, she was doing awesome when she got home Wednesday, but she has really been struggling with strength and feeling capable to do anything since then," Lisa said.

"I don't know," my dad said. "I feel like she is used to having things done for her in the hospital, and I want her to get back to being able to do some stuff, not all of it, on her own. I think she needs that boost of confidence, but she is just so tired all the time."

"Yeah, it's good to have her home, but it's got to be so hard for her to adjust," Lisa said. I nodded in agreement.

"Maybe it will just take some time," I suggested, feeling as though we were at another family conference rather than in my living room with loved ones.

"Here's hoping," he said as I crossed my fingers.

"Have any of the in-home folks come to assess yet?" I asked.

"Yes, they have been very helpful," he said, "as has Lisa, giving me breaks. Mom just needs a lot of help with everything, and it's been harder than I thought. I am really glad you are home, kid. I can use the help."

Lisa affirmed my presence: "She'll be so excited you're here, Alisha."

I sighed audibly. I could feel Individuation shrinking back as Guilt was getting taller and taller. This was going to be a lot harder than I thought too. I feared Guilt would win.

The morning was full of activity and bustling around. My

mom needed help getting up from the bed to the bathroom and back to bed. She leaned on the walker to get there, but she wasn't yet strong enough to use it for standing up and/ or sitting down, which describes the entirety of the task at hand when it came to going to the bathroom.

She needed help carrying her wound vacuum; the tube inserted into the wound right above her coccyx ended in an external machine in a black zippered case that needed to go wherever she went. It was a strange but neat concept, and we all hoped it would work.

My mom's bedsore had been dressed and packed in tightly, and the in-home nurse assessed it each time she came to check on my mom. It was very painful, and Mom had a hard time getting comfortable doing anything. She was still not great on her feet, so my dad and I took turns spending time in the bedroom with her, playing "gopher" for anything she needed. Mostly it was to warm up a rice pack in the microwave or to refill her purple water bottle with ice. I could see my dad's point of wanting her to feel empowered enough to get up and do some of these things on her own. But she was so weak, it was really hard to tell when to encourage her and when to do it for her.

She needed help taking her meds on a schedule. Since all of this, she had been put on twenty-two medications, which she now needed help tracking and taking at the right times. And there was no way that some of those meds weren't contraindicating. I wondered how "typical" it was to be sent home with so many new medications. Some of them were pain meds for her bedsore, which she was beginning to complain of regularly. This meant she was also, with some frequency, rather high.

This version of my mom was so different from the one that had walked herself into all of this months ago. In a couple of days she was to have the blood clot catcher removed. All the doctors were in agreement that she no longer needed it, noting that it had done its job well and had caught a couple of clots before they reached her heart or lungs.

Our home care plan was to wait until the clot catcher surgery day and then reassess what was working and what needed some tweaking. In the meantime, my dad and I became the nursing staff 24/7; it was next to impossible to do much of anything else when the day revolved around the patient's needs.

CHAPTER 43

August 13, 2012, 5:37 P.M.

THE ROLE REVERSAL I felt was immense. We were now my mom's full-time caregivers, and I tried to give my dad as much of a break as possible, given that this would become his new normal and I had the luxury of flying away in a week. We had no idea how much work it would be to have her home, and she was only somewhat coherent for us to assess how she was really doing. She was so tired and slept most of the day. We got her to eat little bits at a time and helped her out to the kitchen table for breakfast in her wheelchair, after trying to get her dressed. Walking took too much energy for her. This was often a big deal, and breakfast was the biggest outing of the day. We focused there; based on previous experience, we knew how important nutrition was to her healing. That big outing to the kitchen from the bedroom took hours, never mind trips to the bathroom, and I could only imagine how slowly her acclimating back to feeling self-sufficient at home would actually be.

Guilt was screaming in my face and continuing to lunge ahead at full speed, while Individuation slowly began to slide out of the ring from underneath the ropes in the corner, one bit at a time. I could see it happen in slow motion, and I knew I was in trouble. I was losing myself.

This morning was no exception. We were up early for the trip to MCR for the surgery to remove the clot catcher. My mom was nervous and started to cry; she didn't want to go back to the hospital. I didn't blame her. Amid all the physical struggles, I could only imagine how all this was impacting her mental health—how often she felt triggered and scared that something else would go wrong. She hadn't spoken about this yet, but her personality was understandably so different now than it once was. I grabbed her hand as I helped her get into the car and told her how brave I thought she was, and how hard it must be to go back to the hospital.

She was a champion for the visit and the surgery, after which she was allowed to come home following a couple of hours of observation. It was a quick and fairly painless surgery, but still one that required anesthesia, so she was completely out of it when she returned. We considered the rest of the day a wash, as she needed to rest in order to recover.

It felt like it had been thirty years since I'd arrived back home. I checked my calendar to make sure I wasn't off. It had only been three days.

We were really hopeful for tomorrow—maybe she'd finally begin down the illusive path toward recovery and some self-sufficiency. I couldn't help but think about how much that could mean to her, as she had been so very independent before any of this. I didn't blame her at all for being so tired. This was maybe the first time she had truly stopped in years. She had a lot of sleep to make up.

CHAPTER 44

August 14, 2012, 4:37 P.M.

"HI, MOM," MAT began. "I just stopped by after work to check in on you and see how you are doing!"

My mom was sitting on the edge of her bed, counting.

"One, two, three, upppppp"; she drew out the "up" as she tried with all her might to get herself to a standing position, hands gripped tightly on the walker. It didn't work, and she exhaled loudly on her way back down the few inches she had achieved.

"Hi, Mat," she said without looking back. She tried again.

"One, two, three, upppp," but this time she didn't leave the bed. She was frustrated.

"Come on, arms!" she begged them.

"Want some help, Mom?" Mat offered.

"Sure," came her fast reply.

"Okay, here we go; one, two, three, uppppp," and with their combined effort, she was mostly up. She gripped the walker with both hands and stopped to catch her breath. Breathing seemed to be more and more difficult for her, and I wondered if that was a normal part of regaining strength and ability or something was wrong. The oxygen helped, and Mat grabbed the long green tubing from the bed and

137

handed it to her. She leaned her elbows on the walker and placed the tubing in her nose and behind her ears as she took a couple of deep breaths. That helped tremendously, and she began the long ten-foot journey to the bathroom.

Sometime later when she was done, Mat rolled her out to the dining room in her wheelchair for dinner. It was the first time we had had dinner as a family since I had moved to Pittsburgh. It was nice.

My dad and I had prepared breakfast for dinner—a classic favorite—set the table and gotten everyone drinks. Mat rolled her up to what was typically her spot, but the wheelchair didn't quite fit in between the china hutch and the table, so I traded spots with her. We ate and caught up, and I summarized my latest experience at school in exchange for Mat's work updates, which included switching jobs to another construction company. It was thirty minutes or so later when my mom could no longer do it; she finished her last of four bites of oatmeal and fell asleep at the table, her head pitched forward. We chuckled and began the process of wheeling her back to bed. My dad took that job, and Mat and I cleaned up the kitchen.

"Gosh, it's just so weird seeing her so weak, isn't it?" I asked.

"Yeah, it's really different. I think Dad's in for more than he bargained for," he replied.

"Yeah, that's for sure," I answered.

We cleaned the kitchen quickly then headed back to check on the others. My mom was crying, not complaining of any pain, just crying. I headed over to her pills on the white ladder bookshelf scattered with her favorite CDs, books, and many different lotions, and started grabbing her nighttime meds so she could go to sleep. There were so many pills. I wondered if these were all permanent and noted this as a topic to ask my dad about later.

Mat refilled her purple water bottle and warmed up the

rice pack for her, and I gave her the pills. Something felt off, but it had been a big day after surgery, and she was exhausted. I convinced myself that she would be better the next day and told her as much as we said goodnight. Mat, my dad, and I talked a little bit more before Mat had to go; we decided to regroup in the morning.

CHAPTER 45

August 16, 2012, 5:37 P.M.

"I THINK WE Should go to MCR. It's time. Something's wrong," I told my dad. Things had only gotten worse since two days ago, and we were exhausted. He felt it too.

My mom woke up today in a lot of pain and had been crying all day. It had taken her hours to get up this morning, and when she made it to the bathroom with my dad's assistance, she didn't know where she was. He called me in to help; she now needed assistance with wiping, getting cleaned up, and changing her underwear, as she hadn't able to hold it before she got to the bathroom. This was a new level of engagement with my mom, one that didn't allow for any modesty. When I got back to the bathroom, there was urine all over the floor.

When we let her know she was at home, it took her a few minutes to register this as truth. She had just taken her pain medication and was really spacey as a result, so we thought it was that. We helped her back to bed, and she slept for a few hours before we woke her up for lunch.

"Mom, it's lunch time," I said, bringing in a burger she had requested this morning. I sat next to her on the king-size bed and started to cut up the burger with no bun for her. She was totally out of it. I would be too, on all those pain meds. Slowly, she woke up and began to talk with us.

"Where did you get that meat?" she asked.

"We got it from the freezer, hon," my dad said matter-of-factly.

"Oh, what about the lettuce?" she responded. My dad and I looked at each other.

"That was from the fridge, Mom, from the garden out back." It was my turn. Every year, my dad planted and tended a vegetable garden, and this year they added a birdbath to the raised bed in the backyard. My dad loved to take Brooks to show him the vegetables, and Brooks liked to "give the froggy a drink," referring to the stone frog in the birdbath. It was adorable, and the two of them had a special bond. Stories like this drove my mom toward recovery: a relationship with her grandson.

"Oh, okay." She took a small bite.

"What about the cheese?" My dad laughed. I smiled. She was high, and this was kind of funny.

"Well, we got that out of the garden too, Mom," I said, testing the strength of the medication.

"Yeah, hon; it grew on the cheese bush out back," my dad chimed in.

My mom stopped chewing and thought for a moment.

"Wait a second, do we have a cheese bush?" came her very earnest question, eyes wide.

My dad and I stifled a giggle.

My dad continued, "Yep, we just have to pick the slices and plop 'em onto the burgers to melt. It's real easy." He looked at her with a lifetime of love behind his eyes, begging her to joke back. Anything other than crying was incredible today.

"Oh." She studied his face, very carefully analyzing what he'd just said, then broke into a slight smile. "Really? Cheese doesn't grow on bushes, does it?"

With her smile, my dad broke, and we all burst into laughter, my mom the loudest.

"No, honey, cheese doesn't grow on bushes," my dad said, wiping his eyes from the tears of laughing so hard.

"You guys," my mom said. "You're trying to trick me!" She giggled. "Cheese bushes, ha!" She continued to laugh with us. It was the happiest we had seen her since I had arrived in town.

That was hours ago at this point. After taking only a few bites of her burger, she fell asleep again. She woke up an hour later, screaming.

"The little boy, the little boy, where is he?" came her terrified scream from the bedroom. My dad and I had been watching one of our favorite shows, The Mentalist, enjoying a small break when we heard this. We sprinted around the brown buyer's remorse couches and down the hallway to her room.

"Sher, you're sleeping, honey, wake up," my dad said as he sat next to her and touched her head. She was warm, but not feverish.

"We have to find him now! He's in danger!" she screamed, inconsolable.

"He's okay, hon," my dad said.

My mom gripped his arm and stared at him; her blue eyes as wide as I'd ever seen.

"You got him? Is he okay? Where is he?" she asked, looking around.

"I've got him, Mom," I said, moving back into the hallway. "I'm going to take him to the bathroom." I stopped just outside of her line of sight to hear the rest.

"Oh, good. He was in trouble, but the little girl was okay," she began to tell my dad, crying as she told the story that made no sense. She was growing more animatedly afraid as she recounted the danger the children faced in her dream reality. I knew her pain medication was powerful, but I didn't know it had such hallucinogenic side effects. My dad talked her down from the fear, and thirty minutes later she was asleep again, complaining of pain but not able to locate the source.

When she woke up screaming again an hour later, this time about the little black-and-white dog that wouldn't stop licking her face, I asked my dad if we could call the in-home nurse. He did that while I sat and talked with my mom about the dog. She would flinch and scrunch her face as if the dog were real, and it struck me then just how terrifying this must be for her. I decided the quickest way to alleviate her perceived anxiety was to play along. The next time she winced, I grabbed the air near her face, pulled it away, and sternly told the air dog, "No." This seemed to soothe her momentarily, and she asked if I would please take him away. This was a sure sign that it wasn't her; my mom was such an animal fan, she would have welcomed any dog licking her face. I noticed that her water bottle was empty, and I took it back to the kitchen for a refill as I was taking the air dog away. She relaxed some as I promised to take away the offender and also return with some new ice water.

On my way back toward the kitchen, I heard my dad hang up with the nurse. I motioned "one second" to him with my index finger and returned to my mom with fresh water. She was asleep again, with a furrowed brow, and was mumbling something in her hazy sleep. She looked miserable. This felt like more than her just being high. Something was wrong.

My dad met me at the end of the hallway.

"The nurse said she could be just really reactive to the pain meds or something could be off. She said we should follow our gut, and if we are worried, we should call an ambulance."

My mom started to scream again. I raised my eyebrows at my dad.

"I think you're right," my dad said. "I'll call the ambulance."

We were waiting. Always waiting, it seemed these days. My dad and I had talked in the car as we followed the ambulance to MCR about getting her admitted; we didn't know what else to do to help her at home. We were on the same page, and both of us were completely tapped of all energy.

The emergency room was fairly quiet tonight, which made the waiting that much more frustrating. The paramedics had given my mom some more pain medication to calm her down when they arrived, and she was crying uncontrollably, not making any sense. She now was passed out in the hospital bed, hooked up to more tubes and monitors, and something about that felt like relief. Hopefully, the doctor would be able to help. This room was tiny, with paper-thin curtains separating the room from the hallway. All the lighting was fluorescent, and it shined brightly down, casting a deep jaundiced hue over everything. There was barely room enough for two chairs on one side of the bed, and the other was full of medical equipment. It was cozy.

My patience was growing thin. "Where is the doctor?" I almost said aloud as he entered, apologizing for his tardy arrival.

This doctor was in his late fifties with a stout frame, dark hair, and an accompanying mustache that made him look even older. He asked us all the basics as well as "the history of the patient," and my dad started on the epic tale of my mom. I tuned back in around the time of her coming home and relayed my experiences with her that afternoon around the hallucinations and the extreme fear she was exhibiting. The nurse had taken all the vitals and the blood samples when we arrived, but the doctor had none of the results yet.

My mom moaned and moved around in pain, unable to get comfortable. The doctor asked her what was wrong, and she just repeated that she hurt. We told him she had been like this for the past couple of days but couldn't tell us where she hurt. He decided to give her a dose of fentanyl along with some Percocet and summed up our visit by diagnosing my mom with severe anxiety. He prescribed some antianxiety medication and said we were free to go. Make that twenty-three prescriptions.

My dad and I looked at him in disbelief. I was annoyed that he didn't know the story, or any of what she had been through. He didn't know that this was abnormal behavior for her, even off her pain medication, and he wasn't listening to us. My dad asked about her white blood cell count as a sign of infection, since she had still been fighting something when she left LTACH. The doctor said that her white blood cell count was a little high, but nothing to be worried about. He offered that blood cultures have to sit for three days before they know what's in them, and without any firm reason to keep her, he couldn't admit her.

I sighed again. It made sense, but it was still hard to hear. She was so out of it that this definitely felt like an underdiagnosis, but there was no way for him to know that. I felt completely powerless, depleted. Maybe it was just that. We were extremely tired. Maybe she'd continue to heal and feel better with more rest. We all needed rest. But not until we loaded her into the car to take her home from here. She was barely coherent even when she was awake, but thanks to the fentanyl and Percocet, she was finally sleeping soundly.

This ought to be fun, I thought to myself as I dug deep for all the reserves I had left.

CHAPTER 46
August 20, 2012, 7:30 P.M.

THE LAST FEW days were excruciating. My mom was still in immense pain and was not able to participate in any of the physical or occupational therapy or CNA activities they wanted to do with her. The most recent CNA had been able to get her a shower one day, but that took her whole three-hour shift; once she left, my mom went to bed for rest of the afternoon and the night. In order to control her still undefined pain, she needed a constant routine of pain medication. This seemed a bit extreme for someone in recovery, though it did seem to be helping. My dad and I still rotated checking on her, playing along with any hallucinations she had, and talking with her as often as she was coherent, which was a rarity, to truly assess how she felt she was doing. For as much time as I had spent with my mom lately, I felt like I hadn't seen her in weeks.

Today she hadn't been able to get up at all and had been asleep all day. I had spent most of the afternoon in the bedroom with her, watching Hallmark movies. My mom and I loved the cheesiness, and over the years, that had become our thing to do together. We had both seen most of them already, but we still enjoyed watching them together.

I spent this afternoon updating her on the happenings of the movie in between her naps, as it was all new to her each time.

I went for a walk in the neighborhood to process my surroundings and what was happening. Autopilot mode was back. I was completely numb and supposed to leave the next night for my fall semester at school. But how could I leave my dad like this? There was no way one person could care for her with all the help she needed. I'd thought this would be a dramatically different adjustment to home life. I still swore that something was off. I rounded the corner back to the house and walked in the door with more questions than I had before I started.

"Lish, come here, quick," my dad yelled before I could even take my shoes off.

"What's wrong?" I asked, trotting down the hallway with my shoes still on, breaking the long-standing rule of "no shoes on the white carpet."

"I need your help," my dad said. "Mom doesn't feel good, and she thinks she's going to—"

Before he could finish his sentence, my mom vomited all over her pillow, the bed, and herself. She started to cry.

"Oh, no," I said. "It's okay, Mom; here," I said, grabbing some Kleenex from the adjacent bathroom for her face. My dad took them and helped Mom wipe her face.

"Let's see if you can get into your wheelchair and to the bathroom to clean up," my dad said and began to line up the wheelchair in a good spot next to the bed for her to get right into.

"I'll get the sheets, and a new nightgown," I said, keeping the mood calm and cheery. I didn't want her to think this was an inconvenience or a big deal, a trick we learned from all of the nurses we'd encountered. I stripped the bed, not breathing through my nose, and washed the sheets out in the kitchen sink before throwing them in the washer. I walked back to the bedroom and got my mom a new nightgown and underwear. I handed them to my dad in the bathroom and began to remake the bed.

My mom was still complaining of a stomachache, so I grabbed some of her anti-nausea medicine and handed it to her with her water bottle. She took the meds, brushed her teeth, and was rolled back over to the bed to try settling in again. It took her several attempts, but she finally got from the wheelchair to the bed; she wanted to stay propped up in case she felt sick again. I grabbed a couple pillows and made a back rest before we slowly turned her body to rest on them. She requested more pillows, and my dad went to go grab one from the room I was sleeping in. She closed her eyes.

"I don't feel . . . ," she started and burped.

I ran into the bathroom and grabbed the universal pink basin the hospital had sent her home with that was now holding some bathroom items. I dumped them out on the bed and handed it to her just in time for her to vomit again. And again. And again. She wasn't stopping. And this time, it was blood.

"Dad!" I screamed. "Call the ambulance right now!"

CHAPTER 47

August 19, 2012, 8:49 P.M.

THE AMBULANCE ARRIVED within minutes. My mom was dizzy but had stopped vomiting, for now. She wasn't strong enough to hold the basin, so I helped her hold it and looked the other way. When the paramedics entered, they took the basin, confirmed that it was blood and handed it back to me as they bustled around taking her vitals and getting her loaded onto the stretcher.

I looked down at the tub of my mom's blood vomit and realized I couldn't feel my feet. I had no idea what to do with the tub, so I set it in the bathroom and tried to answer any questions that I could. I looked at the bed and at the clean sheets I had just put on. There was bloody vomit all over them. My task brain took charge. "Strip the bed again and add them to the wash," it said. I listened.

"Lish," my dad yelled, "we're going back to MCR!"

I shoved the sheets in the washer and started it with the other pair I had loaded earlier. I grabbed my purse and patted Sniff on the head. She had been riled up with all the commotion, and I promised her we'd be back soon.

We followed the ambulance on the familiar route, parking in the side lot you had to enter after 9:00 p.m. We met my mom in the emergency room, and a nurse followed the same routine that had been done the other night all over again. Pain medication on board, she was completely out. A small feeling of relief and slight validation came over me as I began to feel like maybe we weren't wrong after all.

A doctor came in just as the nurse was leaving. He looked concerned as he read over the notes of the prior visit.

"I'm so sorry to see you folks back so soon," he started. "We are going to admit her to the Cardiac ICU."

"Really?" my dad asked. "Do we know what's going on yet?"

"Well, we grew those blood cultures from the other night, and they had some pretty gnarly bugs in them. When you were here three nights ago, her white blood cell count was still in a more normal elevated range, so we had to send you home. This is just some bad luck on timing; I'm so sorry it happened like this. We would have called you tomorrow to let you know about the blood cultures, but you beat us to it." He had kind eyes and a very empathic vibe. I liked him a lot.

"What does she have?" I asked, curious about what on earth could possibly be next.

Well, the folks in the ICU will be better able to assess exactly, but the culture was positive and showed that she has several different bacteria in her blood, which can result in cognitive disturbances, hallucinations, incoherence, increased pain, and pretty much all the things you folks reported the other night. Again, I am sorry for the timing on that; we will get her right up to the ICU to start some testing." He yelled something to a tech passing by, and she came back ten minutes later to tell us that my mom would be transferred within the next fifteen minutes.

"We know the way," I said.

Back in familiar territory, we said hello to the night staff and waited until my mom was settled before going home to get some rest ourselves. I helped my dad make the bed for a second time that night and cleaned up the blood vomit basin that was still where I had left it on the counter. I got in the shower, turned my face to the showerhead, and closed my eyes. There was no way I could ever unsee what happened tonight.

CHAPTER 48

August 20, 2012, 6:35 P.M.

"WELL, DAD, I guess that answers our question," I said, referring to my decision to go back to school tonight or not. With my mom back in the hospital, I felt just as awful, but a different kind of awful than leaving my dad alone to care for her in her previous state. I was planning on returning.

He agreed with me. I was going to take Becky's car back down to her house tonight after seeing my mom, and Becky would bring me to the airport. I was both excited and terrified about leaving.

What if something bad happens while I'm away? I thought. I would never be able to forgive myself if she died while I was off doing my thing. Guilt started using the "S" word again: "selfish, selfish, selfish."

On the way to the hospital, I turned the radio to a channel that played a lot of faith-related music and began to listen. It was the first choice I felt I had made for me in a long time. I wondered how my newfound relationship with faith would handle this twist.

Outside of my mom's room at the hospital was a rolling cart full of gloves and gowns and a sign that said "Mandatory."

FOUR EYES

This can't be good, I thought as my dad and I suited up. We walked in and found my mom completely asleep, softly snoring. She was heavily sedated and had had a catheter for urine connected and a fecal management system, or FMS, connected to her for defecation. The intensity I felt from previous visits to this floor began to return as I felt my limbs start to tingle.

Not long after we got there, a doctor came in to give us the update. It was a generalist; someone we had not yet met. He was young and kind and walked with ease into the room after putting on his gown and gloves. He introduced himself before giving us the news.

Tests had come back with positive results in several areas. They found MRSA in her chest wound that had begun to spread into her blood as well. In her bedsore they found three more infections, including vancomycin-resistant enterococci, or VRE, which is just as nasty a bug as MRSA, if not worse, and tricky to treat because the main treatment for MRSA is with vancomycin. Two separate strands of Pseudomonas were also found in her bedsore. In a person without a compromised immune system, these would typically not be a big deal. For my mom, however, they had become life-threatening. MRSA, being highly contagious, required the gloves and gown protocol for everyone who was in contact with the infected patient.

As the list continued, the knot in my stomach became more and more pronounced.

Holy shit, I thought. No wonder she was in such horrible pain. My poor mom! Her wound vacuum had not been working all that well, and the infections needed immediate treatment. They started with vancomycin this morning to work on the MRSA first. A concoction of other antibiotics were addressing the other three infections. Her bedsore was incredibly painful, and due to its location, it was so hard for her to find a comfortable position to rest. When the at-home nurse came to visit yesterday, she reported that she had never seen a stage-four bedsore being treated at home before. She was going to call it in to her boss to see how we should proceed. All the pieces were clicking and coming together, and Guilt was railing at me for not catching on sooner. My mom was a lot sicker than we could have even imagined, and life was the complete opposite of what was supposed to be happening for her right now.

"We are looking at ordering her a special sand bed while we treat her," the doctor said.

"Sand bed?" I asked quizzically.

"Yes; it's a bed that has constant air and sand running through it to help cushion patients who cannot lie on solid beds. It's what we do for this type of thing, though I don't know that we've ever seen one this bad."

I felt like I had failed my class in Caregiving 101 and had let my mom down. I had drastically underestimated the danger a bedsore could be and was suddenly realizing that they were no joke, and certainly not just for old people.

"So what's the plan now, Doctor?" I asked, curious how to fix this. How to make this gnawing panic I felt inside go away.

"Well, she will need to be bedridden for at least the next eight weeks for treatment and pain management, maybe longer, and we will start killing these infections, one at a time. We will get Infectious Disease up here to see what they can recommend in terms of getting that bedsore to heal. She will be in the ICU for the foreseeable future, unfortunately," his words ending on a low note.

My dad didn't have to say a word. I could already feel what he was thinking. All the recent progress and strength she had worked so hard to gain in rehab was gone. Eight more weeks in a hospital bed was a sure promise of muscle atrophy and then agony to learn how to walk all over again. The gravity of this was enormous; this was the biggest setback we'd seen yet.

CHAPTER 49

August 25, 2012, 6:14 P.M.

I HAD RETURNED to Pittsburgh as planned; said my goodbyes to my mom, who was completely high on pain medication in the ICU; and stayed in contact with my dad daily. My autopilot was on full speed, and I was able to somehow compartmentalize my daily activities.

My semester was getting more hands-on, and would start to involve working with real, live clients soon. I worried all the time about how that would go if I needed to go home at the drop of a hat. My body felt constantly shaky, and I built my camp in the territory of uncertainty. It was hard to concentrate at school, and yet I felt the strong pull to continue. It was a common topic of conversation for my dad and me, and every time it came up, he reassured me that being in school was the right decision. I chose to believe him, and handled Guilt when he had his rageful outbursts.

Yesterday, my dad called with another update, and Guilt went crazy. He lunged at Individuation with all that was inside him, and Individuation took a hard fall, landing with an audible pop.

Dr. Stevens had decided to treat the MRSA by reopening my mom's chest wound and scraping her sternum and the surrounding tissue clean of the infection before treating it with specific antibiotics. He had induced a medical coma and needed to treat the MRSA more than once, so he would be leaving her chest wound open and exposed for three days to aid in decompression and to increase my mom's cardiac output while he scraped her sternum as needed. OUCH! He would be closing it the day after tomorrow, with the future plan to surgically use a flap of skin from her calf to cover and close the wound. She would have some protective covering when he wasn't working on her and would remain open, still in a medically induced coma. This was the stuff of movies, or the future, or the very distant past.

Suddenly I was very glad that I was not there to see her like this. I could imagine my mom in such a situation, but I would never have the actual image of what it was like seared into my brain for life. Tears ran down my face thinking about it, and how absent she had become in this process. She had turned into a problem to be fixed, a constant anxiety, an experiment, a small hope, and sometimes even fear itself. I really missed her.

I couldn't sleep after that, and when I did sleep, I had very vivid dreams, dreams that seemed so real that it was hard to distinguish reality from fantasy when I woke up. All I could think about was my mom in a coma, a tube back down her throat, lying in some bed wrapped in saran wrap, open and exposed to the world.

Do I need to go home? I asked myself repeatedly. It was like slow motion shock.

My classes had started, and in a few of them I was only allowed two absences per semester before failing the class. I knew my professors would work with me, but I didn't know where the line was for continuing on with my beloved cohort, taking a semester off, or quitting altogether. It was always on my mind, and Individuation was perpetually trying to get back up, with no success. The floor in the ring was really slippery.

CHAPTER 50

August 29, 2012, 8:24 P.M.

TIME STARTED TO pass as if the world were suspended in water. Words that made up my thoughts were trapped in bubbles all around me, and I could only watch them float pass from my own isolated bubble. I wanted to speak, to cry out, to scream, but when I opened my mouth, nothing came out. I floated for hours, sometimes days at a time, existing dimensions apart from the rest of the world. Its pace hadn't changed, but mine suddenly swirled and swiveled much more slowly, allowing me to notice details I had so often missed before. Life was teeming everywhere, and I began to see it. Really see it.

Raindrops burst forth with shapes of meaning, a single blade of grass fascinated me by its sheer existence, and I was hyperaware of everyone and everything around me. I remembered that the truest things that mattered were not things at all. Life existed in the intangibles, and in the relation of myself to the world.

My senses tingled with awareness and took in the vibrant colors, the calming ocean sounds, the smell of seawater and sunscreen, the feel of the water slowing any movements I attempted, and the taste of salt water. I was the most present I had ever been while being so very, very distant.

I looked out from my bubble into the crystal-clear water all around me and watched as I hit a large, dark rock jutting out from an embankment. Instead of bouncing off and continuing to float, my bubble enveloped the rock and jarred my position within, adjusting to carrying more weight. Soon, several rocks were in my bubble with me, and floating became more and more difficult as the rocks weighed my limbs down even more. I was still floating, but down, down, down . . .

CHAPTER 51

August 30, 2012, 10:12 A.M.

BACK IN PITTSBURGH, I tried my hardest to focus—and took solace in my interactions with friends, trying to remember how to be a friend who wasn't weighed down with the existential dread of searching for the meaning of life amidst death. It was harder than it seemed. I was broken open inside, a mess of hot angry reds and searing streaks of yellows that burned so brightly into oranges and hues of pink when they merged. I was always convinced that others were privy to this view, and I tried to temper the streaks into societal standards, as was protocol for befriending others, but it only made the streaks hotter, flashier, angrier. My friendships surged with those who saw my flames and welcomed me anyway.

This past week's events included my mom's white blood cell count elevating to thirty thousand, when the level of "strong concern" was fifteen thousand. The doctors believed her gallbladder was causing those numbers and removed it, but her white cell count remained high. They started her on tube feed again, only to have the food get stuck and not be moving from her stomach. The news grew from worse to awful. There didn't seem to be one thing in particular that was harming her the most, other than the infections, but a combination of several systems that were no longer playing nice. Her cardiovascular system was compromised, which then compromised her respiratory system. Her skeletal system was affected by the reopening of her chest, her circulatory system was full of infection, and her digestive system was no longer willing to turn on. It was a stalemate. No one system alone was causing enough damage to harm her irreparably, but when they all danced together, it was a dangerous and unpredictable tango.

CHAPTER 52

September 8, 2012, 3:34 P.M.

MY GRANDPA SENT my mom an iPad to try video chatting. He had high hopes. I did not. I knew my dad would be the one attempting to use it, and he was still angry about having to pay for the "technologically advanced" call waiting service in the 1990s. I was certain this would be, at the very least, entertaining.

My grandpa had kept up on my mom's status as best he could while also caring for my grandma. He and my dad would often check in on each other as fellow caregivers, and my grandpa would always end the conversation with a joke about caring for yourself as a caregiver because, "you know what they say . . . the caregiver always dies first." Though meant as a joke, the sentiment hung eerily in the air over us all. They were both grateful for the other and for the subtle "me too" their conversations provided. The iPad was a physical representation of this connection.

I was the lucky guinea pig, and I coached my dad to set it up over the phone. After a lot of swearing, we finally connected, and he propped me up on my mom's plastic tray table on wheels so I could see them both. Aside from my screen's colors being a bit yellowed, so far so good.

"Hey, Mom," I called through the screen. Nothing.

"Hey, Sher, are you awake?" my dad asked softly.

She was snoring, as usual but, registering his voice, shook her head and answered faintly, "No."

I laughed.

"Ha-ha, okay. How are you feeling?" he asked.

She moaned in response. "Owwwww," she mustered.

"Earlier, Mom was in 1967, Lish," he said, smiling to the screen and almost finding the camera. "We've been through the decades today," he continued. "She answered with a different one every time she was asked what year it was, and I've started to use her answers as a guide for how lucid she is," he said in a loud whisper that wasn't actually a whisper at all.

"Owwwwwww," my mom groaned again.

"Yeah, I know. What hurts most?" My dad grabbed her hand, empathizing with her pain.

"My all," she replied.

"Anything in particular?" he prodded for more information. "We've got to get you feeling better because your sister Janet comes in tonight!"

"My softball kitchen," was her confident reply.

"Yep, I thought so." My dad sighed. She was back in the land of pain medication.

"Why?" she continued.

"Well, because you're kind of yellow all over," he said nonchalantly. "I suppose I should go get the doctor."

"Tell him I'll have a chocolate one," she replied.

"Will do, my love," he chuckled as he forgot about me on the screen and went to alert the troops of my mom's entire body turning mustard yellow.

"I guess it's not just my screen, then," I said as I listened to my mom's soft snores. She was definitely yellow.

CHAPTER 53

September 16, 2012, 11:09 A.M.

"WHAT?!" I TRIED to signal the comprehension section of my brain, to no avail.

"Yeah," my dad laughed. "I don't even know what to say anymore. She's so yellow. The doctors had moved her to the step-down unit, one lower than the ICU, because she was doing fine with all her antibiotics, and then she turned yellow, so she's back in the ICU."

"Why is she yellow? Is she awake? Coherent? How is she?" All the questions tumbled out.

"She is not coherent, and she's on a lot of pain meds all the time, especially after they debrided her bedsore and put another wound vacuum in it."

"Oh, God, that sounds so awful. And so painful." I was wincing.

"Oh, yes. Janet has been a big help here, though, and given me lots of time to rest myself. I am so grateful for her trip. They have given Mom lots of Versed, which makes her not remember anything, but I know she remembers Janet being here," my dad said. That was consoling.

"Oh, good. Can we get some of that too?" I asked.

He laughed. "Right? I wish." He sighed. "She's yellow

because a cyst in her liver is pushing on her bile duct, which is causing her jaundice. The docs put a stent into the bile duct this morning, and later they will try to drain the cyst to reduce its size so it won't push on the bile duct anymore. She should be returning to her natural color anytime."

"Oh my gosh, Dad, this is getting insane. Opening her up again? Is she in pain? Does she know she had that done?"

"No, she doesn't know. She's on so many pain meds and is so high." He sighed. "And at this point, she is so used to being poked and prodded, even if she were aware of it, I don't think she would argue. I don't know, kid. You may want to think about coming home again soon. I hate to suggest that, but this doesn't look like it's going to improve anytime soon."

"I'll think about it, Dad," I said, already knowing that that was the last thing I wanted to do.

CHAPTER 54

September 17, 2012, 7:58 P.M.

FAITH CONTINUED ITS elusiveness. My dad had written an inscription in a Bible my parents had given me as a kid, stating, "Life is a journey, and so is faith. May they both be good rides." Yet the church youth group in which I was raised didn't frame faith quite as adventurously. It was more of a set of rules to trust and believe in without question. Questions led to doubts, which were a clear indication of a lack of faith. And a lack of faith meant that it was my fault, my doing, my ineptness that caused my current struggle. So anytime a question arose, I learned to keep it in, and to check within myself where the resistance to belief was coming from.

It was similar to the logic of my Baptist college. Powerfully built on decades of fear, and then enforced as if it were the ultimate Truth, they somewhat jokingly purported that "backrubs led people to sex, one of the biggest sins if done before marriage, and sex led people to . . . dancing!" The horror! Questioning dancing's moralistic alignment became a sin itself, and another way to interpret that person's level of faith, dedication to God, and, perhaps, inability to "just believe." The ownership of the lack of faith or understanding always seemed to fall back on the person with the questions.

My lack of faith also meant that I could fix it if I changed my attitude enough, believed enough, repented enough. If only I believed more, sacrificed more of myself for others, fasted more, spent more time in prayer, or had more faith, maybe my mom wouldn't be suffering. But years of attempting, unsuccessfully, to "fix it" led me to a deep level of depression, consistently low self-esteem, a desire to please everyone around me without boundaries in an effort to please God, and a lot of self-hatred. I was never good enough. Something felt very off about this, and I couldn't get away from the thought that the conditionality of acceptance had run my life for years. It seemed so contrived. Transactional.

What about the unconditional love of God? If I obeyed a certain level of conditional rules, then I would earn the unconditional love of God? It was continuing to unravel, and I was afraid I'd be out of sweater soon. I didn't want to be doubting. I didn't want to disobey. But I truly didn't understand how, if God were love, and if I were made in his image, I could hate myself so much for not measuring up. I simply wanted to understand, and the more things happened with my mom, the less I understood them.

And while I knew in my head that my mom's illness had nothing to do with my faith, the small, terrified, rule-following part of me couldn't help but wonder if somehow this was all connected. I knew that if I continued down this path of thinking, I would end up back in the darkness of my depression and self-hatred I had worked so hard on in my twenties. Listening to my dad's heart-wrenching updates night after night led me to questions faster than to any answers. I didn't know anything anymore. I was scared. Overwhelmed. Exhausted. And perhaps it took all of that for me to leap into the mystery with both feet.

CHAPTER 55

September 20, 2012, 4:09 P.M.

"I'M SO SORRY to ask again, but I think I need to go home next week," I started the familiar speech, this time with Professors Bruno and Cato West.

"Oh, no," they both said. "What happened now?" came their concern.

My cohort of eighteen had become so used to my updates now, as we did check-ins at the beginning of each class, that I often forgot that the professors were often the ones without the latest information. I quickly updated them, and asked about possibly Skyping in to classes. They kindly complied, and we worked out the details as I worked on staying calm and professional. Their gentle reminders that it was okay to let myself be human in this experience gave me permission to head to the bathroom and sob after being confronted with such kindness. I was so used to my struggles being "my fault," and to have others meet me with such compassion was starting to open up a new part of me, showing me a way to be kinder to myself, especially when things were out of my control. And those things were innumerable these days.

The latest news was that my mom's bedsore had

increased to the size of a fist, and her white blood cell count continued to rise. I made a fist and looked down at it. It was not small.

There were now three bacterial infections and one yeast infection in her bedsore, and no amount of debridement or wound vacuum suction seemed to be helping. The doctors said these infections were proving harder to kill than MRSA, and they needed to bring in some really powerful antibiotics that had some serious side effects. My dad had called to discuss our choices, as my mom was incoherent; he had already spoken to Mat.

"Well, it's not great news," he started. "But it's at least somewhat forward-moving. Because Mom's white blood cell count keeps rising, they are resorting to a drug they have not used on anyone in the five years they have been open due to its potential side effects."

"Okay, what are the side effects?" I braced myself as I wondered about another appendage growing, or a third eye emerging.

"Well, it's a crapshoot. She could possibly lose her hearing permanently or her kidney function; we won't know what it will be until we try. But if we leave her untreated like this, she will die. Neither option is good."

Wow, I thought, starting to process this news. I liked the extra appendage and third eye options better.

"Dad, do you know what Mom wants in all of this?" I asked. We all knew she wanted to live, but with as many things as had happened to her, I wondered if she had updated her decision.

"I spoke with her for a small lucid moment last night, and she said she wanted to 'keep fighting,' which is not at all what I would choose if I were her. She's the strongest person I know."

"It sounds like we don't have much of a choice then, do we?" I said, not fully understanding the ramifications of either of the side effects.

"Not really," he said. "I just wonder how lucid she is in there, and I really hope we are making the right choice."

My defensive inner optimist spoke up without hesitation. "If that's what she wants, then yes, it's the right choice."

"But what if it doesn't work, kid?" he replied.

I was silent. I didn't know that answer. But I did know I had to get home soon.

CHAPTER 56
September 26, 2012, 1:15 P.M.

WHEN AMY AND I met in fourth grade, we knew we'd be friends for life the second the other mentioned Amy Grant. When she and her husband, Bryan, came to get me at the airport, seeing them yielded a familiar and peaceful calm. It was just what I needed. Amy and I knew each other's parents very well, and each set claimed the opposite daughter as their own. Amy and I spent large portions of our awkward teenage years at each other's houses reading Seventeen magazines borrowed from the library and dressing up our dogs. Amy and Bryan had moved to Denver right before I moved to Pittsburgh for grad school, timing epically failing us all. My parents' place in Loveland had been their landing pad when they first arrived until they found a place of their own in Denver.

Well-meaning friends and acquaintances offered their help often, yet sometimes the interactions were spent consoling them through their feelings about the situation, leaving me more emotionally depleted. I couldn't blame them, really. No one knew what to say. I didn't know what to say. I appreciated the gestures and felt awful realizing that I was slowly becoming a person who no longer wanted to participate in that type of relationship. Another point for Individuation, this one painful, and Guilt was not happy. I was so grateful that Amy and Bryan were not those friends, and I relaxed into their company with ease.

"So, what's the latest?" Amy asked. "And we're stopping at Good Times, by the way, our treat." She smiled at me from the front seat; Good Times was a favorite.

"Ha-ha, okay, great," I answered before a long sigh left my being. "Well, they gave her another really strong antibiotic that comes with some gnarly side effects, including possible hearing loss and/or kidney failure. But it was either that or she would die from the infections making her septic. She told my dad that she still wanted to fight, so we're fighting. But . . . she was on the drug for five days; her infections started to improve, but her kidneys stopped working. They are testing them now to see if they work at all or if her kidneys are shot."

I heard myself talking as if I were on another planet. It was so distant, so rote, so . . . emotionless. What was happening to me?

"We have a family meeting today to talk about next steps. I guess she has some options for surgeries, but I'll find out more tonight. I don't know anymore, guys."

"Wow, Lish," was all they said. And all they had to. It was dripping with empathy, and I knew I wasn't alone.

CHAPTER 57
September 26, 2012, 4:57 P.M.

ONE OF MY mom's favorite nurses, Ryan, was working when I came around the familiar corner leading into the Cardiac ICU, and she hugged me a big hello. She led me to my mom's new room, back to a windowless one with more gadgets for people who were as sick as she was.

There were two doctors already in there, a cardiologist that wasn't Dr. Stevens and a generalist who had just graduated from the University of Michigan. My dad was currently talking with him about his alma mater, one of my dad's favorite topics. The young doctor didn't quite share the spirit. The family conference was starting in three minutes. Experts representing each body system currently being treated had arranged for a ten-minute care consultation to talk with one another about next steps.

The generalist was humoring my dad and, soon enough, my dad gave up. He looked really tired.

"Hi, kid," my dad side-hugged me, resigned, staring at my mom. "Welcome back."

"Hi, Pops," I said. "You ready for this?"

"Sure," he said, not looking like his usual self, brimming with a million questions.

"You doing okay, Dad?" I asked.

"I'm just so tired," he said. I believed him. He looked terrible. I was certain he'd barely slept since I'd seen him a month ago. His skin was paler, and his hair was a mess. I knew it was awful, but this was the first time it hit me just how hard this must be on him.

"I bet." I answered. There was nothing else to say.

The doctors filed in sporadically over the next few minutes and surrounded my mom, asleep in her fancy sand bed. A GI doctor, the infectious disease doctor, a lung doctor, and the newest addition and last to arrive, a kidney doctor, or nephrologist. Another new word. Without any ceremony, they began. The infectious disease doctor went first.

He was a short man of Vietnamese descent and spoke with a thick accent. He had been with my mom since she had been readmitted and had been consistently debriding the wound without any improvement.

"I think the only move left for the wound," he started, "is to do a muscle flap surgery—take some healthy skin from her leg and attach the new skin to the sides of the sore, hopefully generating more healthy cells that will then grow together and close the wound. Her white blood cell count is much better, but it will get worse if we don't act soon to close the wound." He finished calmly and looked to his right as if passing a virtual baton.

"Respiratory thinks she is slowly dealing with chronic obstructive pulmonary disease, COPD, which is making breathing harder for her and taxing her heart. She will need oxygen consistently from this point forward," came this doctor's recommendation. He held up a breathing device in his large left hand and shook it against the air. "And a lot of this," he said, referencing the bizarre-looking device that looked like a mini version of the carnival game where you hit the base as strong as you can to try to ring the bell at the top. "She has to blow in this every day, working to get this ball to the yellow line in order for her lungs to grow stronger," he explained as he pointed. "We are doing medication treatments to relax and open up her airway, but they can only do so much." He finished by replacing the device on my mom's tray table with a snap. He patted the doctor next to him on the back. "Take it away, Doc," he said casually.

Without missing a beat, he did. "Digestive team thinks her GI tract is shut down because of everything else. We are anticipating GI function to resume once the antibiotics are at a reasonable daily dose, the infection is totally cleared, and cardiac output increases. However, until all of that happens, Digestive is at a standstill." He was a tall, slender man with deep blue eyes and a compassionate smile. I wondered how many times a day doctors like him did things like this. And how invested they could afford to get in their patients while caring for their own mental health.

Cardiac was next; I recognized this doctor but couldn't remember his name. He was in his late sixties with a head of gray and had looked after my mom a few times during her various stays. I liked him. He was quiet, smart, wise, and kind.

"She needs to get well with the wound closure first so that we can get her upright and back to gaining strength for her heart to heal as best it can. Congestive heart failure is present, but treatable. I haven't heard anything yet that sounds like a sure threat of death if we take the right next steps and work off one another in the proper order. Her heart is resilient, and her ejection fraction has moved up to 35 percent. If she can get through these infections, her heart will get stronger. I am a strong proponent of doing the muscle flap surgery to get everything back online."

"I disagree, doctor," the U of M grad began. He was no more than thirty-two and gave off a wave of arrogance. "She is so compromised that her body is going to prepare itself to only fight one thing. She won't last through the surgery; even if she does, she won't have the energy to fight anything else off. She will die either way, but if you put her through surgery, it's just one more round of pain for her to experience before passing."

My insides were frozen again, and I couldn't move, just stare. He just said it. She will die. She's going to die. She will not live anymore. I can't believe he just said it like that. Was he right? My head pounded and swirled.

"Forgive me, Doctor," the cardiologist replied, "but I have been doing this a long time and have seen many scenarios play out in many ways. I can tell you that if you proceed, her heart will recover. There is still work to be done here. She is only sixty-one years old. There's no need to quit right now," came his sharp rebuttal.

"I strongly disagree," the young grad fired back. "She is suffering. Why prolong it? Don't do anything; let nature take its course. Let her go."

"He's got a point, actually. She has been through so much, and more interventions may just lead to more issues. I would let her go too," the GI doctor seconded out of nowhere.

The cardiologist sighed. "Ultimately, it is up to the family; her husband has the power of attorney in this case," he said. "Do you know what she wants?" He kindly looked up at us.

"Yes," my dad said. "She wants to live." My dad finished, looking right at the generalist. "I am the last person who wants to put her through more pain and suffering, but she wants to live. She has two kids and a grandson and a whole family. I don't think we should go to any extreme measures to save her if something goes wrong during surgery, though," he presented his caveat. "I don't know that she could take anything more to her chest."

I looked at him, full of rising anger. This was something

I had never considered, and everything in me wanted to fight him on it. She wants to live! my head screamed. Let's do whatever it takes to make that happen! Why are we standing around her bed debating her life like a ping-pong match as if she's in some drugged-up dimension where she can't hear us?! Let's do something! But what came out was "I think we can talk about that later. But overall, she wants to live, so what can we do now?"

There was one doctor left to speak. I nodded his way. He had remained silent this entire time. Her kidney failure was the latest finding, and I was eager to hear what he had to say about that.

"This is a complicated case, no doubt," he started. "She has got a lot going on, and I think if we could get her into dialysis today and tomorrow, we could get some of the toxins out of her blood, some of the accumulated fluid off her, and reassess where she's at for the potential of surgery. The more medication she has in her, the more she will need dialysis to filter it out. We'll need to add dialysis to her schedule at least every other day, but for starters, for the next two days. I say let's try this, then discuss surgery."

I liked this guy. His name was Dr. Simon, and he was a tall, older man with gray hair and a very slender body. He wore a white button-down shirt with a pink tie. He seemed smart and practical. I liked his approach.

"What about food?" my dad asked. "She hasn't been getting nutrition, and without it, none of this sounds like it will go well."

"I think we can try IV feeds of TPN, if we are going to proceed," the cardiologist offered. "That way we can bypass the GI tract for now and get it directly into her veins."

My dad and I nodded. My Aunt Patti had been asking for weeks for TPN, or total parenteral nutrition, which brought nutrition directly to my mom's blood rather than needing to go through her digestive system. She had seen it work wonders in babies in her work. Finally, it would happen.

The final round of discussion ended with two votes for letting her go and four votes to intervene, none of which were my mom's. How quickly voices can get lost in this crazy medical world, I thought. A plan slowly developed to work out a surgery to knock out all the things she would need: the muscle flaps of skin to close both the chest and bedsore wounds effectively; an ash catheter implanted underneath her collarbone that would be her dialysis port moving forward; and, after a lot of discussion, a colostomy to reroute any feces that might interfere with the healing of the bedsore, due to its location.

It was a tall order. And one she would enter under a "do not resuscitate" order. Deep down, I knew my dad was right about that. She couldn't sustain chest compressions if she were to crash. The doctors left, and my dad and I walked down the hall to talk further. His shoes remained untied.

CHAPTER 58

October 3, 2012, 11:57 A.M.

SURGERY HAD BEEN delayed until today. The original date was three days ago, but it got pushed back by the anesthesiologist as they were on their way to the operating room. His gut was telling him that she would not survive the anesthesia with her heart so weak, and that she needed more dialysis before he would feel comfortable anesthetizing her. He was full of apologies to us, but firmly stood his ground that she would not make it through the surgery if we proceeded now. I was grateful for his discretion.

My mom had her first round of dialysis that afternoon, after they placed a Quinton catheter into her neck to use as a port. This was the most temporary catheter available; it would be replaced by the ash catheter in surgery. It was quite the contraption protruding from her neck, and at first sight, I was surprised that I didn't think twice about it. It was becoming normal to see her with tubes and contraptions, and I was disturbed that this didn't bother me more. She looked swollen and puffy, like she was having an allergic reaction to something.

Dialysis was on the fourth floor, in its own hallway and wing, and the dialysis techs rolled her fancy sand bed right up to the machine in the dialysis room while she slept through it. The process filtered all the blood in her body and cleaned it seventy-two times, I learned. After three days in a row, they had removed six liters of fluid from her body. She looked it.

I remembered donating plasma in college, and the feeling of the blood reentering my body after the plasma had been filtered out was so cold. I imagined dialysis was similar to that and felt for my mom. I was at least paid for donating plasma. I was glad she was sleeping through most of these days. I reflected on how long it had been since daughter lens had been out and made a mental note to check in with her later.

To tax her heart less under anesthesia, the doctors decided to split up the surgeries. Today was colostomy and chest flap day. The anesthesiologist had agreed that her heart would make it through these two procedures. However, we were embarking on a totally new journey with the colostomy surgery, and a bag we would have to care for, or rather my dad would have to learn to maneuver. I was still fighting to find the boundaries for myself amid the caregiving role, but I wanted to draw the line there.

Seeing my mom this way was already a tremendous knock to my childish belief that my parents were invincible, and watching my dad suffer watching her suffer was another level of hard. This wasn't supposed to happen. They were my parents.

My dad was starting to walk slower and needed more breaks to catch his breath. I was beginning to get very worried about him and the toll this was taking on him. He struggled with depression his whole life and was prone to severe depressive episodes. These days he was always exhausted, could never catch up on his rest without sleeping pills that kept him drowsy for days, and was growing more and more pale. He was falling asleep on my mom's bed daily, head on his hands, and not eating on any kind of schedule. I started to beg him to please talk to one of the cardiac nurses we had come to know so well, just to check in. He refused.

CHAPTER 59

October 5, 2012, 5:34 P.M.

AUNT PATTI HAD flown back in to be with us for my mom's second big surgery day. It was scheduled for the 8th, and my mom would have the muscle flap surgery to close up her bedsore and the ash catheter placed under her collarbone. Aunt Patti was such a welcome relief.

My mom was somewhat awake and took comfort in my aunt's presence. It was getting harder for her to live in the ICU, however. Between the pain of the bedsore and the beeps and buzzing of the medical circus surrounding her bed, she was struggling to relax. Some nights were more painful than others, and the nurses reported that she woke up screaming a few times from bad dreams and didn't know where or who she was. This behavior had increased over the last week or so, and I decided to get crafty to help calm her environment down some. Daughter lens.

I bought a flat, white bedsheet, found some of my mom's favorite fabrics in her collection in the basement, and cut out some leaf-shaped patterns. I glued the leaves all over the sheet, and the vibrancy of her taste for color instantly came alive. I rounded up a bunch of pictures we had of family and friends and pinned them on the sheet with safety pins.

I was hopeful this would bring her some peace when those moments of fear gripped her. I took it to her room and, with permission, hung it on the wall she stared at when she was awake. We were all in need of a mood shifter, and this delivered a small slice of just that.

My dad continued to worsen, and each day I asked him to please talk to someone. He finally caved and scheduled an appointment with his general doctor for the following Monday. Thank God. The more my dad slept lately, the lonelier I got. Mat was at work, and most of my friends had moved from the northern Colorado area south to Denver. I would call Courtney and Kelly from grad school regularly, but most days I craved in-person connection, and yet had no energy for it. I could feel my sadness increasing and my depression sucking the color out of my world more and more each day.

When Aunt Patti arrived, I was elated to have another person who "got it." She understood my mom so well and had known my dad forever. She was someone with whom I didn't have to explain anything. Plus, she knew the medical world and could translate when things didn't make sense. Spending time at Aunt Patti's house when Mat and I were kids was simply the best. Mat would play ambulance with her and "fix" her up with blankets and towels as bandages, and she ever so gracefully let me "do her makeup," which was more like me drawing all over her face with lipstick.

My mom was recovering well from the colostomy and the chest flap surgery; finally, things were starting to look up for her. At least for this moment. Her digestion had begun to process some things very slowly, and she was feeling much better with dialysis. These were very slow steps, but celebrated nonetheless.

My individual practicum class was meeting in an hour, and I was going to Skype in for the first time from the hospital. I set up a corner of the room to hopefully have some privacy and got into my gown and gloves, ready. Class began, and almost instantly my mom's monitors went off, alerting the nurses. Two of them came in to check on my mom, and with more voices came more distraction.

I realized how crazy all this must have looked on camera and confirmed that thought with a glance downward to see myself on the screen covered in a thin blue paper gown and blue latex gloves sitting in front of a bunch of tubes connected to machines, with people humming around my mom like birds. I looked like Scientist Smurf. The room saw more traffic in the hour I was in class than it had all day, and I couldn't control any of it.

CHAPTER 60
October 6, 2012, 10:35 A.M.

MY DAD WAS up early and off to the hospital, which meant he hadn't slept well the night before, if at all. He had taken advantage of my Aunt Patti's visit by making his daily schedule hours shorter than usual and coming home to sleep.

"Mat, I think something's wrong with Dad," I said into my phone on the back deck. "He's really tired all the time, super depressed, not eating well, and breathing heavily. He's getting spacey and taking forever to walk anywhere, but he refuses to get checked out until Monday. Still with his laces untied too," I vented. "What do we do?"

"We've all tried talking with him, and he just keeps saying, 'I'm fine.'" Mat exhaled loudly.

"I know! I don't know what else to do."

"I'll call him again at lunch and see if I can convince him to talk to someone," he said.

"Thanks, that'd be great," I said. My dad usually listened when Mat was insistent about something. And the more people who could talk with him about what he needed, the better. "I'll call you later with any updates."

"Thanks," he said, and we hung up.

FOUR EYES

I was enjoying talking with my brother more during this whole fiasco, a nice change from the past few years, when his family life and my school life had taken us down different paths. It was nice to reconnect.

Aunt Patti and I went to the hospital a few hours after my dad did and walked into my mom's room after putting on our Smurf uniforms. My dad was asleep in a chair, snoring very loudly, the arms crossed over his chest matching his crossed feet resting on the edge of my mom's bed.

I looked at Aunt Patti. "I don't know what's going on with him," I said, "but I'm worried." She nodded.

My mom vaguely nodded at us through her dopey haze of pain medication, and I could only imagine how much pain she was in from the bedsore. I kept praying that she wouldn't remember any of this.

Marni, another of our favorite nurses, walked in, and we caught up as Aunt Patti tended to my mom and deciphered her various sound effects. I followed Marni out of the room when she left, and quietly told her of my worries about my dad. She agreed. I asked flippantly what to do if he had a heart attack, and we made wide eyes at each other just at the thought before laughing.

"Can you even imagine?" I asked.

"In all seriousness," she said, "don't let him convince you to drive him here. Call an ambulance so they can start treatment on the way. Just in case."

I thanked her, feeling slightly better.

"Of course," she said, patting my shoulder and uttering an empathic grunt. I trusted Marni and her opinion immensely.

I took a small walk around the circular ICU and went to the bathrooms just outside the metal fire double doors enclosing the unit. It felt like a bit of a break. I took the long way back around the circle then grabbed another blue paper gown, unfolded it, put my arms through the holes, and tied it around my back. The gloves were offered in different sizes, and I alternated between medium and large, depending on how long I felt like wrestling with them. It was an uncomfortable getup, and it made my trips in and out of my mom's room more intentional than usual.

Suiting up, I could hear voices and then some stifled laughter. I smiled, excited for some levity. But when I walked in, I realized I had misread what I'd heard.

My mom was crying and begging my dad to get her back to the hospital. "Butch, please! We have to get out of here! They will be back soon, and they'll keep me here. Take me back! I don't want to stay in Mexico!"

I looked at my Aunt Patti. She was coughing to stifle a laugh while hiding her simultaneous worry.

"Sweetheart, you are in the hospital. I promise. The doctors didn't kidnap you. You are in Colorado, not Mexico. You are okay." My dad was also stifling a laugh while trying to calm her down.

None of us knew how to react, whether it was best to jump into a hallucination with her or try to talk her out of it.

Aunt Patti took a turn. "Sher, it's okay; you're not in Mexico. It's me, Patti, your sister. I came to visit you in Colorado."

My mom's eyes relaxed a bit as she tried to process this information.

My dad looked at me and said, "She thinks the doctors kidnapped her and took her to Mexico."

"I gathered," I replied, equal parts concerned and curious. "I'd be scared too if I were kidnapped." My poor mom. Pain meds were truly something else. I wondered how long it took to officially become addicted to opioids. She had to be close, if she wasn't already completely hooked. I was so glad she wasn't in her right mind to remember much, if any, of this. Her previous doctors had told us that the amount of pain medication she was on would most likely leave holes in her memory. It sounded like a blessing—and a curse.

She stopped cry-talking with my aunt, and within minutes was asleep again.

My dad went to sit back in his chair and assumed the sleep position. I couldn't contain my worry anymore.

"Dad, are you okay?" I tried.

"Yep," came his curt answer.

"You look so tired. I am worried about you. What if you talked with Marni today? We're in the Cardiac ICU, my goodness, and if anyone can help, they can," I pled my case.

"I'm fine" was his slow response. His eyes were closed.

I was upset and felt some of his icy exterior walls go up as I continued.

"Dad," my voice cracked. Then it all poured out: "Please, please, please, can you just talk with Marni? I don't want another parent to have a heart attack, especially if we could do something now to help you feel better."

He sighed but never opened his eyes. I stood my ground. My stubborn was showing.

Finally, he said, "Lish, I have a doctor's appointment on Monday, okay? I'll be fine until then. It's my life, just let it be."

I could no longer contain my anger or hurt at his dismissal of my concerns. "Fine," I shouted. "Do what you want; it's your life." With that, I turned sharply on my heel and tried to storm out, but first I had to remove the gown and gloves and wash my hands according to protocol in order to not spread MRSA to anyone outside the room. I made a dramatic show of ripping off my gown, but it got stuck on my sleeves. I grabbed at the gloves, hurriedly trying to release them from my hands, but my hands were sweaty and stuck to the latex. My hopes for a grand exit that made my dad rethink his behavior were dashed. It was probably a minute before I had everything off and finally managed to storm out of the room. I looked back through the curtain to see him fast asleep. Highly effective.

I walked to the lobby and then wandered outside for a while until I calmed down. I was so anxious and didn't know where to put all these feelings I had that things were not supposed to be this way. On my eventual way back up, I sat in one of the chairs overlooking the parking lot with a great view of the foothills and watched the clouds float by. I could feel my heart settle some as I began to entertain the idea that my dad might make the choice of not caring for himself as he needed to, and I had to be okay with that. It was an awful feeling, but one that settled in as a deep truth.

Back in my mom's room, my dad came out with the keys as I was suiting back up, slightly embarrassed remembering my melodramatic exit.

"I'm going home to let Sniff out; you and Patti can stay for the late-afternoon shift," he said, staring into a daze, totally unlike himself.

Resisting everything inside that wanted to continue trying to convince him to talk to someone, I simply replied, "Okay."

The afternoon passed uneventfully, and for that I was grateful. My mom slept soundly through the whole afternoon. Aunt Patti and I drove home around dinnertime and settled on watching some Hallmark movies to focus on happier, lighter things. Hallmark ran in the family.

I parked the car in the garage, and as I was going up the two steps into the house, my anger at my dad returned. I wondered how we would interact. Inside, I heard the TV from the bedroom blaring ESPN, giving away my dad's whereabouts. I relaxed a little.

Aunt Patti went to change as I created a veggie, cheese, and hummus plate for us to eat with our movie and settled into the buyer's remorse couches. She returned shortly, and we started one of the interchangeably themed Hallmark movies where the owner of a muffin shop falls in love with a commercial bakery owner after almost being bought out by them. It was exactly what I needed.

FOUR EYES

My dad walked out from the bedroom with his Detroit Tigers pajama pants on and no shirt. He was a lifelong Tigers fan. He'd grown up across the street from Tiger Stadium and had been frequenting the stadium since he was a kid. He credited his infatuation with all thing's baseball to this. He played baseball himself, coached high-school ball, coached some of my brother's teams growing up, and, until recently, had been umpiring for the City of Loveland's softball league.

He walked past us to the kitchen, saying, "A movie, huh? Good choice."

Looking pale and uncomfortable, he grabbed a Coke and some peanuts before heading back to the bedroom.

"Yup, I said," and, before I could stop it, "Are you okay?"

"Yeah, I'm just tired. I'm going to take some of my sleeping pills tonight to really sleep."

"Okay," I said as I watched him meander back to the bedroom. I was still angry—and still worried.

The movie got to the part where the owner of the muffin shop discovered that the commercial bakery was owned by her love interest. The drama ensued both on screen and off as my dad walked out of the bedroom, gasping for air with his arms crossed over his bare chest, pale.

"Dad, are you okay?" I jumped up. "Come sit, breathe," I said as Aunt Patti started asking him questions. He sat; he couldn't answer many of her questions, but he did give me my long-awaited answer.

"No, I'm not okay," he said, grabbing his chest with his left crossed arm.

Instantly, I ran for the phone. "I'm calling 9-1-1," I said, Marni's words playing loudly in my mind: "Don't drive him here yourself, call an ambulance."

The dispatcher answered, "9-1-1, what's the emergency?"

"I think my dad is having a heart attack," I said the words out loud in disbelief.

"Okay, I am dispatching an ambulance now and am going to stay on the phone with you to get some information about your dad."

"Okay," I agreed, not taking my eyes off my dad. He was focusing on his breathing, which was very labored.

"Is your dad conscious?" she asked.

"Yes, I'm right here next to him," I said.

He was turning gray.

"Okay, tell me about what's happening right now for him," she coached.

"He's pale, turning gray, not breathing well, holding his chest, sweating, not able to focus," I said as he stood up.

"He's getting up. Dad, what's going on? Where are you going?" I asked, my voice panicky, waiting for him to pass out and fall over like in the movies.

"Puke," was all he mustered as he made his way to the hallway bathroom and threw up profusely in the toilet.

"He's throwing up. A lot." I said into the phone.

"He's throwing up?" she asked.

"Yes," I said, annoyed. Terrified. My dad was having a heart attack. He could die at any moment. There wasn't time to repeat myself.

"Is he on any medications?" she asked.

"Yes, several," I answered.

"Can you get them together in a bag for the paramedics?" she asked.

"Yes, I will," I said, walking into my parents' bedroom and gathering the couple that were on his nightstand. "Dad, where are the rest of your meds?" I called from the bedroom, walking to the bathroom.

Done throwing up, he was standing again.

"Dad, can you sit down, please?" I begged as he walked back into his room and pointed to his meds on the shelf in his walk-in closet.

"Got them," I said to both him and the woman on the

phone as I swiped them all into my sweatshirt with a one-arm sweep. My dad was gone when I turned around. I grabbed him a shirt from the closet.

"Great, the ambulance is almost there," she said. "Would you like me to stay on the line?"

They were at the door. "They're here," I said. "And thank you." I hung up the phone and ran to meet everyone at the door. My dad had wandered back into the living room, and the paramedics were suddenly inside with a gurney, trying to convince my dad to get on it.

He was confused, and not certain of his surroundings. This was not happening.

"Dad, sit down here and let these guys help," I said, patting the gurney. Aunt Patti helped him sit on the edge, his legs dangling off the side. Instantly, the paramedics hooked him up to a portable EKG machine with circular sticky pads and printed out his heart rhythms. They gave him a nitroglycerine tablet to dissolve under his tongue as he lay back in pain. They confirmed that he was having a heart attack and asked for any medications he was on. I handed them the plastic grocery bag I had put them in as they placed an oxygen mask over his face. I handed him the shirt I had grabbed; he put his arms through and stopped to rest. The paramedics started to strap him into the gurney like that, and he didn't care. I could feel my nervous system tornadoing around inside me as they loaded my dad into the ambulance. Aunt Patti and I grabbed our purses and phones and jumped in the car to follow them. Aunt Patti drove.

"You did really great on the phone, Lish. Are you okay?" my aunt comforted me.

"Thanks. I think so," I said, looking down at my hands. They had started to shake. Here it comes, I thought. Maybe I wasn't okay.

But before my body began shaking all over to process

what had just happened, the ambulance flipped its lights and siren on and took off faster.

My body instantly stopped shaking; back in activation mode. Nothing about any of this was good.

CHAPTER 61

October 7, 2012, 11:30 A.M.

"WELL, IT LOOKS like we are going to adopt that teenager after all," my dad said matter-of-factly. His eyes were closed, and though he knew he was talking to his wife, he had no idea from where, how long he had been here, or what was happening.

"What?!" I could hear my mom's dazed confusion through the phone.

"Yeah, it looks like we're going to be parents again," he continued.

"Butch, what are you talking about? I don't want any more kids," she replied as her pitch rose in panic.

I started laughing out loud, but he didn't hear me.

"We make great parents, hon; we're going to have a baby!"

My mom whimpered. "Are you okay? Where are you?" My mom's questions hung in the air, suspending reality.

I heard my mom begin to cry from the next room through the wall. Sniff picked up her head from the corner and looked at me. I shrugged at her and laughed again. My dad's eyes were still closed, and his limbs were attached with soft ties to the bed rails so as not to disturb the balloon pump that had been inserted into his heart after surgery.

"Dad, I think she gets it. Let's just say goodbye for now," I said as I reached for the phone with the curly cord that reminded me of our house phone growing up. "Just tell her you love her and will see her soon."

"Okay," he said. "I love you, my love. I'm excited for this kid!"

My mom's confusion had turned to upset, and I heard my Aunt Patti grab the phone from her and begin to hang up at the same time I hung up my dad's phone. My aunt soothed my mom's mind that she was not getting or having another kid, and she seemed to calm down.

I looked at my dad. He was snoring again. I couldn't help but laugh and think, I have to write this down to tell them about later.

Last night's lights-and-siren ambulance show were the result of my dad's cardiac rhythms getting worse as the ride progressed. Mat met Aunt Patti and me at the emergency room. We sat with my dad for a second. After being given another nitro tablet, he was taken to the catheter lab, where a stent was inserted into one of his blocked arteries. It had been the "widow maker," and the doctors told us that if he hadn't come in when he did, he would have been dead within an hour.

By the time he was out of surgery, it was almost 4:00 a.m. Around 3:00 a.m. we ran into Nurse Ryan, who had been called in to help with another ICU admission. We shared a dumbfounded moment when she realized the admission was my dad.

He was rolled out of surgery into the room adjacent to my mom's. They now shared a corner. He slept soundly through the night in his anesthesia and pain-medication haze. It was eerily similar to my mom's situation, especially with the balloon pump helping his heart pump more strongly. Marni wasn't going to believe this. I couldn't believe this.

My parents on drugs was a very strange sight. Neither

was coherent, neither was present, and both believed just about anything told to them. It was both jarring and sad as I was confronted with the truths that my parents were (a) human after all and (b) perhaps more fragile than I knew. However, the deep sadness also came with the deep joy that they were both still alive and providing golden nugget moments like the one that had just happened, preparing me for the new sibling I was apparently going to receive from my sixty- and sixty-one-year-old parents.

My aunt came into my dad's room. We shared a knowing smile, and I went next door to help further calm my mom down. My mom was nervous that my dad was not where she had last seen him. We assured her he was okay, nearby, and that he was just catching up on some sleep. She finally exhaled fully, grateful to know his whereabouts.

"Oh, good. He needs that," she said. "He has that big game coming up."

My aunt and I exchanged giggles. "Yep, he sure does." I said just as Sniff entered the room. She took to her corner, lay down, and exhaled a big sigh.

"You can say that again, girl," I said. "You can say that again."

CHAPTER 62

October 7, 2012, 11:31 P.M.

THIS WAS ABSURD. I had been trying to sleep for more than an hour, but my thoughts were not on the same page. They continued to dance around my mind, sparking new "what ifs?" by the second. Guilt and Individuation were no exception. Both my parents were now in the hospital, next-door neighbors, after having heart attacks. What were the chances of this ever happening? It did not compute.

My dad had become a friend in this process, a constant "other" to experience this uncertain time with, the only other who knew what those twelve-hour days were really like in the hospital, always wondering what was coming—if my mom would ever get better, or if we were increasing her suffering by allowing all the testing and poking and prodding and surgeries to continue. He had become my rock, and we could depend on each other to "get it" when it was difficult to explain things to the world outside this medical bubble in which we'd been existing.

He also continued to push me toward doing what was right for me with school, continually reminding me that I had to "live my life." What did this all mean now that he was hospitalized and sick too? Could I lose them both? What did this mean for my role now? How was I supposed to get through the days on my own? Tears ran silently down my cheeks. My body began to shake—this was the most out of control I had ever felt.

My mom's last-chance surgery was tomorrow. Would this ever end? I was grateful Aunt Patti was still here, and would be for the next two nights before her flight home. I couldn't imagine what it would feel like when she left.

Sniff came into my room, jumped on my bed, and stuck her wet nose in my hand. I began to pet her methodically, and we both exhaled loudly. My body started to relax, slowly. A stunned hush fell over the chaos in my mind, and Individuation and Guilt retreated to their respective corners of the ring. For the briefest of moments, it was silent. It was unexpectedly beautiful.

CHAPTER 63

October 8, 2012, 6:30 A.M.

WE ARRIVED EARLY to the hospital this morning for my mom's surgery, at Pre-Op's request. After months of discussion and "will she or won't she make it?" events, "the butt flap surgery," as my dad had termed it, was finally here. This was the doctor's last attempt to get the stage-four bedsore to heal, and if this didn't work to help the wound grow back together, she would most likely die from the infections. The seriousness was in the air.

She asked for my dad, and the nurses told her he was nearby but not able to come see her.

"Okay," she said. "How about Sniff?"

My mom had trained Sniff to be a therapy dog years before, and she had visited many people for a few years at a local nursing home. Therapy dogs were allowed in MCR, and I had spent hours digging up her certification and vet records to prove her legitimacy to the hospital staff. Ever since then, she had been allowed to visit the ICU with my dad, and now for my dad, as often as she wanted. Thank God. She was my only other constant in those long days, and such a good friend.

"She's in the corner." One of the nurses smiled at my mom.

"Oh, good," my mom replied as Pre-Op entered her room. "Here we go," she said, unsure.

Aunt Patti and I gave my mom a presurgery pep talk that calmed her fears for a few seconds—the one that we only half-believed ourselves—and she was off. I wasn't sure how much more I could stand. I was running out of fight.

CHAPTER 64

October 9, 2012, 12:01 P.M.

WE WERE AT the hospital late last night, waiting for the moment in TV shows where the doctor comes out of surgery to talk with the family. I was acutely aware that we were now that family. Mat met us after work to hear the results and stayed with us all night. It was nice and having him around more was a gift to my loneliness. My mom had pulled through like a champ, and now the doctors said, we wait. What else is new? I thought to myself. We are pros at this waiting thing now. We all dispersed after she was returned to her room, completely out of it and resting peacefully.

I had tossed and turned all last night, worried that I wouldn't wake up in time to take Aunt Patti to the airport. We were up and on time despite our exhaustion. Her departing words were kind.

"Call if you need anything. I'll call this evening when I get home to hear how the surgery went," she said as we hugged goodbye at the airport. She looked so much like my mom that I did a double take just before I drove the hour and a half back up to MCR.

Sniff and I walked through the front doors and to the elevator, per usual.

"Second floor," the elevator dinged. We exited and turned left to head down the all-too-familiar corridor of the Cardiac ICU. The beige aesthetic mirrored how my insides felt: dull and bland. I worried that vast fields of nothing would take any remaining joy hostage. This territory was so unfamiliar.

Sniff ran ahead to find a surprise that the nurses had made for her; a blanket bed just for her in the corner between my parents' rooms with a folded pillowcase, a mint on the pillow, and a sign hanging above it declaring this "Zoe's bed." It was adorable, and I felt a tinge of warmth and gratitude. Maybe my joy would pull through.

I stopped by my dad's room first. He was asleep, snoring loudly. Marni entered soon after. I hugged her.

"Your advice paid off, you know," I started.

"Oh, Alisha, I am so sorry" was her kind reply.

"Thanks," I said back. I didn't know what else to say.

"And for Sniff's bed out there too! The mint was a sweet touch," I said, aware of my pun but unable to present it with my typical cheese.

"Of course; Zoe's a big hit around here," she began then switched topics quickly. "Did you know your dad has sleep apnea?"

"Not officially, but I suspected," I sighed. Given his snoring, that made sense.

"Yes. We observed him not breathing seven times in one-minute last night and think this could be a partial reason for his heart attack. We're going to get him set up with a BiPap machine immediately."

"Oh, wow! That's great!" I answered as she left the room to answer another patient's alarm. I clung to a strand of internal hope that maybe this would help my dad sleep better and then have more energy to take care of himself.

With that, he seemed to read my thoughts and snore-snorted so loud that he woke himself up.

"Hi, Dad!" I greeted him happily. "How are you feeling?"

"Hi, babes; I'm doing good. How are you? How's the snow?"

The only snow was that of his pain medication, but I caught my dad up on some details and how my mom was doing as Sniff came over to lick his hand.

"Yuck, Sniff! I guess that means you need to go outside, huh?" he asked to mostly the air.

I laughed. "I'll take her outside in a second. I want to ask Marni about something first," I said as he lay his head back to doze off.

"Okay, remember your hat," he said.

"Will do; good reminder, Dad," I said, shaking my head. This was entertaining at least.

Marni was back at the desk, and I asked her if I needed to order a BiPap machine for my dad at home as well. I wasn't sure how long he'd be here, and wanted to have it ready for him at home if he needed it. As if on command, his snoring woke him up again.

"You want to go out, Sniff?" my dad asked her again, and she happily wagged her tail and flattened her velvety ears to approach him for some pets.

I heard this from the desk, excused myself, and watched my dad try to get out of bed. The ties that kept him flat in bed had been taken off, and the balloon pump for his heart had been successfully removed yesterday.

"Dad, I will take her out; don't worry about it. I am just finishing up with Marni."

"I can do it," he tried to argue, raising himself to a sitting position.

"I know you can, but you need to rest," I replied. "You're just used to doing it from being here so long."

"Nah. I'll take her out. Where's your mother? Can you get me some mustard?" he babbled in a slur.

I sighed as he lay back down and then closed his eyes.

"Sure, Dad; mustard is on the way."

He hated mustard.

CHAPTER 65

October 9, 2012, 5:37 P.M.

I SPENT THE afternoon traipsing back and forth from my mom's room to my dad's, talking to nurses, and dozing off. I was in my mom's room when I vaguely felt Sniff's wet nose lift my hand and yelp a small yap. I petted her quickly and fell back asleep.

Fifteen minutes later, I awoke to the familiar beeping of the ICU; one of my mom's medications had run out. I stretched and yawned and went to find my mom's nurse as she slept on. I again found Marni, who let me know how to silence the alarm and said she'd be in in a minute.

I wandered over to my dad's room and pulled back the curtain, only to find that he was gone.

Suddenly wide awake, I began looking around frantically. Where could he have gone? Was he okay?

I walked quickly down the ICU hallway; no Dad. Back around the other side; no Dad. Into the family lounge; no Dad. My pace quickened as I pushed through the plastic faux-wood doors that blocked off the ICU and checked across the hallway. You needed a badge to enter there, and he didn't have one. I hit the elevator button and jumped in. Oh, my gosh. Could he be headed to the parking lot to drive home, as had been his daily custom?

"Lobby," the elevator dinged, and the doors opened in their own sweet time.

I jumped out and headed for the front doors. I didn't get more than a few steps before I saw them. My dad had Sniff's twenty-foot retractable leash fully extended as she was bolting for the door, creating a trip wire for many as they entered the hospital.

"Dad!" I shouted. He didn't hear me.

I ran up to them, apologizing to the folks who had been trapped by this situation; they nodded politely and quickly walked away.

"Dad, what are you doing? You can't be down here!" I spat out.

"I'm just taking the dog out. She has to go."

"Dad, you can't leave the second floor. You're a patient now."

"I'm fine," he said as he stopped and looked at me.

"Are you, though?" I asked as I pointed, and we both started to laugh. He was standing in front of the hospital's main entrance wearing only his hospital gown, wide open in the back for all to see, his compression socks up to his knees.

"You may want to take care of that," I said, as I took the leash from him and placed him on a bench to wait until we got back inside.

Sniff did her business, and we were back in seconds. My dad was still smiling.

"What are you smiling about?" I asked.

"How stupid of me to come down here to let her out but forget to bring my shoes!" he exclaimed.

I busted out laughing at his train of thought. He still didn't have a clue about his gown or about how many people he must have flashed on his way down.

"Okay, let's go back up, Pops," I said, "and you may want to tie your gown again."

As if it were a nonissue, he did so haphazardly, and we got off the elevator at the familiar "second floor" announcement. He headed through the Cardiac ICU double doors and down the corridor to his room. Sniff was stubbornly smelling something, and by the time she finished, we were well behind my dad. We walked through the double doors and into the hallway to laughter and clapping as my dad strode down the hallway, gown again wide open in the back, fists pumping in the air.

"I'm not lost, I'm not lost," he chanted on his way back to his room, assuming the laughter and clapping were for his return.

I couldn't stop laughing. Once back in his room, he pulled out his shoes before getting into bed, and placed them by the door.

"Just in case that happens again," he nodded at me.

"Yep," I stifled a snort. "Good idea, Dad."

Within minutes, he was asleep.

CHAPTER 66

October 10, 2012, 10:05 A.M.

"THIS IS SO nice, Mom!" I said to a groggy representation of her. "Your boss brought you a get-well package."

"She is so nice," my mom said from her left side, meaning it. Since her surgery, she was rotated every hour to give the muscle flap the best possible chance of healing. The ash catheter was placed under her collarbone on the right side, so she preferred her left.

"She really is," I agreed. I pulled out a red knitted blanket and held it up to show her before draping it over her shoulders.

"This is soft," she said, filtering her response through layers of pain medication.

Also included were some cards from her coworkers, a colorful new water bottle, and a book bearing a sticky note deeming it "a great read to pass the time." I showed her each of the items, and she smiled. An idea suddenly crossed my mind.

"Mom, this book looks good," I said. "Would you like me to read it to you?" Reading books aloud was something she and my dad did with Mat and me as kids all the time. My love for words and word pictures came from the unceasing number of books we were read as kids, and I cherished the memories dearly. Honoring the chance to return the favor, I picked up the book. It was The Hotel on the Corner of Bitter and Sweet, and I thought the title captured my feelings quite nicely.

"Sure," she said; "that'd be nice." And we were off.

The next hour passed uneventfully. We were engrossed in the novel, taking us back into a love story during the time of Japanese internment camps in the United States. When I needed a bathroom break, I stopped reading. My mom had been opening and closing her eyes off and on, but even when they were closed, I could tell she was listening by the small noises she made at key parts. I had no idea what was sinking in and what wasn't, but it seemed good, and it felt like this was the most connected to my mom I had been in months.

"I need a bathroom break, Mom," I said as I slowly stood up.

"Yeah," she answered. "I guess it's time for us to get back to our camps too." I smiled. "Does yours have a lot of steps in front of it? Mine does, and it's hard to climb them."

I chuckled. "Yeah, stairs are tough, Mom. I gotta get back to mine too," I said, playing along. She was clearly living in the book, and it was just as the book claimed—bitter and sweet.

"Wait, am I making stuff up again?" she asked, a moment of lucidity crashing over her.

"Yeah, you are, Mom, but that's okay," I said softly.

"Okay, well, just let me know, and I will tell them you had to come late," she replied, back in her haze.

"Will do," I said, and left the room smiling.

On my way to the bathroom, I stopped in my dad's room. Sniff was lying in the corner on her side, asleep.

My dad was sleeping soundly, snoring loudly. His BiPap was supposed to arrive later today. I was eager to see how this would help him. He had a bedside commode in the room, and would often get up to use it in a stupor. It was easier than being escorted each time he needed to go, and he wasn't in need of a catheter or a bedpan. This simple fact erased any remaining semblance of privacy, but it was a soft blow to the modesty of our family at this point. We were all cracked open, transparent for all to see.

Mat called several times throughout the day, and I kept him posted with updates. He was going to come after work today to talk with our dad about finances and bills. We had no idea how long he'd be in here and needed to understand what had to happen in their absence. This was a whole new experience. Mat also had temporary power of attorney for my parents' medical decisions, and we talked about every move we needed to make.

This was all new, and as I watched my parents sleep, the barren wasteland of nothing crept into my insides again. I felt hollow. What was I supposed to feel? I went for another walk.

When I returned to my mom's room, my dad was sitting in a wheelchair next to her bed, holding her hand. They were both asleep and both in their hospital gowns. My dad hadn't bothered to Smurf up, so they were matching as well. I took a picture. That, I thought as it felt like a warm breeze passed through me. That is what I am supposed to feel. Throughout this saga, my parents had continued to hold onto their love, literally in sickness and in health.

The ethereal thing took me over again for a moment, as I realized that I was looking at true, unconditional love despite horrific circumstances. Something about it was extremely peaceful, and extremely unexplainable. My inner knowing was back, but this time, there was no judgment or commentary on what this could mean about my faith status. It was simply peaceful. I liked how it felt.

Mat arrived with a legal pad to take notes, a chip off the old block, as my dad was the king of yellow legal pads.

"Hi, how's it going?" I asked.

"Ugh, it's been better," he answered, referencing the huge decision he had recently made to pursue divorce. This was taking up much of Mat's energy outside of both his parents being neighbors in the ICU. I felt for him. It was a lot for us all.

"Anything I can do?" I asked.

"No," he responded. "I'm really glad you are here to see to the details. Thanks for doing that. I just can't get out of work anymore than I already am."

"I totally get it," I said. "That's what our schedules have made possible right now."

"Yeah. We get to make these decisions together, though," he replied.

"Absolutely," I affirmed. "We do this together."

"Deal," he said. "Okay, I'm going to head in to see what I can get out of Dad," he said, shaking the legal pad.

I laughed. "Okay," I said, noting the legal pad. "Like father, like son."

He took notes for more than an hour with what looked like a half-present Dad. When he came out, he confirmed that not a lot of what he'd said made much sense, but he had gathered enough to hopefully take the appropriate next steps to pay the mortgage and utility bills.

I felt like I had aged twenty years, as we were now legally representing our parents' wishes and also responsible for their finances. I had always been responsible with money for myself, thanks to my dad's incessant "teachable moments" about savings and budgeting that were annoying while growing up but so helpful now. However, refinancing, escrow, real estate law, and money market funds were mostly just concepts I pretended to understand and then googled later. There seemed to be no break in the midst of all of this. One thing after another just kept coming.

Mat and I decided that he would largely look after my parents' finances and legalities, and I would focus more on the day-to-day happenings of navigating their medical worlds. When Sniff and I got home after the long day at the hospital, I was beyond exhausted.

The house was quiet. Too quiet. There was no background noise of sports or a crime show to ease my nervous system into knowing that someone else was around and experiencing this with me. There was only the noise of my thoughts and fears chaotically running amuck in my mind, scattering my focus. I would give anything for them to stop.

I made dinner for Sniff and me. We both had chicken, rice, and cottage cheese as I tried to distract myself with TV. Within minutes, I became restless and decided to go to bed. As I walked down the hallway toward my room, I stopped to grab my pillow and phone charger and continued on to my parents' room. I crawled into their bed, and Sniff jumped up next to me. It was the only place I still felt somewhat in touch with them, and not alone. Even though Individuation told me that it was weird to sleep in their bed, I slept through the night for the first time in a few days.

CHAPTER 67

October 11, 2012, 12:21 P.M.

PASTOR JAMES FROM my parents' church and their Israel trip walked into the ICU as I was coming back down the hallway from getting a tiny can of pop for some caffeine. He was young, only a few years my senior, and had black hair and dark eyes. He was slender and kind and very authentic. He had become a staple of my parents' faith journeys, one that would be helpful for my mom to process what was happening as best she could right now, especially after we told her that my dad had had a heart attack and was healing next door.

"Hi," I exclaimed, surprised and thankful to see him.

"Hey, Alisha," he said, his voice transferring compassion that I felt immediately. "How are you?"

I sighed. "I'm hanging in there, you know. I keep thinking that maybe Ashton Kutcher is waiting behind one of these corners to jump out and tell me I am on Punk'd at any minute. But, man, he's stubborn; he's waiting a long time for the reveal," I said as I began laughing.

Pastor James was laughing too. "Yeah, this isn't a very kind Punk'd if that's the case," he said.

In that moment for some reason, we both began laughing.

Hard. I hadn't laughed this much in months. It felt so good to laugh, to smile, to connect with another person in this way. We walked down the hallway to an empty small office and sat down. We caught up for the first few minutes and then began to laugh again at the insane absurdity of this entire situation. Twenty minutes later, I wiped my eyes from laughing so hard, and Pastor James headed down to my parents' rooms to pray with them or over them or for them, or however it worked these days.

This was the first time I had felt more like myself, more like my age, more like a child than a parent, in a long while.

CHAPTER 68

October 14, 2012, 5:14 P.M.

MY DAD CAME home two days ago and was recovering very well, completely to my surprise. I had expected him to be hospitalized much longer. I kept waiting for the other shoe to drop, but he seemed to have slightly better luck than my mom in his recovery so far. He began attending cardiac rehab at MCR three times a week, visited my mom before and after that, and then came home to continue resting. It seemed much more balanced and sustainable for him. For me, however, it was a different story now that both parents needed care.

As he continued to recover quite quickly and steadily, my mom, as was her pattern, was inching along. I would get the morning updates from the nurses that she was still waking up not knowing who or where she was.

Last night, she fell asleep to Law and Order and woke up terrified that she had been assaulted and believed she had lived the story of the episode's main character. The nurses told me that research was being done on this phenomenon for folks in the ICU, as their sense of time and reality were jeopardized by the constant beeps and buzzes; they easily believed they existed in whatever storyline they were taking in, whether it be on TV, from a book, or even a dream state.

This completely explained my encounter with my mom yesterday. When Sniff and I arrived at her room, she was furious, hurt and upset.

"Hi, Mom, what's going on?" I asked, sitting down, dropping my purse on the floor after Smurf-suiting. Sniff jumped at the thud of my purse and then wagged her body at my mom.

"It's just so infuriating! I can't believe he would do that," she said. "I guess it's just going to be that way."

"What did he do, Mom?" I asked, curious who the "he" was.

"Are you going to take me home, now?" she said, lucidly.

I was confused. "Mom, we're in the hospital, and you can't go home yet. You're in recovery after some major surgeries."

"Oh, I know that, but can we leave this place?" she answered.

I still didn't get it. "What do you mean?" I asked, trying a new angle. "Where are we?"

"This is so embarrassing!" she said. "Let's go. I can't believe he divorced me and left me in Sam's Club," she said as her face twisted as though she were about to cry.

"Mom, who divorced you?" I said, getting more details to make sense of her present delusion.

"Dad!" she almost shouted. "Can we go now?"

Somewhere in her mind, based on the recent events of life where my dad was less present than at other times, that translated to my dad divorcing her and leaving her in Sam's Club. I couldn't wait to tell him this one. Simultaneously, it was heartbreaking. And smart. My mom knew something had changed, something was different, and that my dad was not around as much as he used to be. Her pain med haze was on the case.

"We can absolutely go, Mom. Let's. But, just so you know, Dad didn't divorce you; he's just at home," I said as I grabbed her hand and tugged just enough to give her the illusion we were walking out.

"Finally," she breathed a sigh of relief as we exited the Sam's Club of her mind.

"And he didn't?" she asked. "Oh. Well, good," she said, as if that settled it.

The mind was an amazing thing. It was always trying to understand, to make meaning, to find the explanation. Even through mountains of pain medication, my mom's mind was still searching for truth.

CHAPTER 69
October 23, 2012, 2:09 P.M.

THE LAST WEEK had been full. My mom continued to wake up scared and screaming, so we brought her CD player into her room to play one of her favorite songs, "Blessings" by Laura Story, to calm her down in moments of distress. It seemed to help some. Some of my mom's friends in Michigan even made a recording of a prayer circle for her that seemed to help as well. She loved it.

Along with music, I made my mom a written statement called "Who I Am" for her to read when she woke up screaming, to help her remember what was happening to her. It included everything from her name to her family relationships to her location and her recent history with waking up scared. I could only imagine what she was experiencing. We left it on her rolling tray table, which looked more and more like her bathroom counter at this point, for her to reference in the night. The nurses reported that it was helpful, but not long-lasting. Each time she woke up, she was scared all over again.

She was so constantly drugged that we began to ask the nurses about lowering some doses of pain meds to see if that would help. When Ryan returned for her set of shifts last week and found my mom terrified of "Thomas, the little man standing in the corner with beady eyes," she called the infectious disease doctor in to assess the healing of her bedsore and chest wound so that she could begin to decrease the fentanyl drip. Both the chest flap and my mom's "butt flap" were progressing nicely, and the doctor cleared her for "as-needed" pain medication only.

Witnessing my mom's hallucinations was disturbing. They were wild and fantastical, and lately had all been based in fear. I was eager to see how she'd be with fewer pain meds aboard. However, she'd be, I wanted her to be it soon—I had to get back to school in person in order to receive credit for this semester. I didn't know if this was even a possibility.

CHAPTER 70
November 6, 2012, 5:30 P.M.

BACK IN PITTSBURGH, the familiar drive to school was comforting, predictable. I was grateful that school made me focus on myself. I was struggling lately with finding how to do that amid two sick parents. My dad called on my way there.

"She is really starting to turn around, Lish," my dad exclaimed. "She is swallowing and eating real food when she can. She's had her staples removed from her chest and bedsore wound, and she's even been up on this contraption they call the 'tilt table.' Since she hasn't been vertical in months, her legs have significantly atrophied, and they have these special leg massagers on her almost 24/7 to keep the muscles stimulated. Anyhow, they strap her to this table where she has support for her feet and handles to hold onto, and then they tilt her up to a certain angle for the blood to be able to flow vertically through her and for her to get used to being upright again. Today she made it to fifty degrees for twenty minutes before it became too much for her. Putting any weight on her legs right now is very foreign to her, so I think this will be a thing for a while." I hadn't heard him this enthusiastic in a long time. It was nice.

He was doing very well himself and reported sore hips as his biggest complaint. He had decided to care for himself as best he could in order to continue to care for my mom. It really was incredible to watch. He was even tying his shoes these days, convinced that it had been a good luck charm only leading up to his heart attack.

"That's so great, Dad," I said. "Dare we say we may be somewhat out of the woods here?" I asked.

"I don't know, kid," he said. "She still has some bad stomach stuff going on, and though she's eating, it's still not moving, and that makes her not eat, so we have some more work there."

I understood but was so overjoyed with both of them remaining alive that it felt like a minor problem, comparatively.

Being back in Pittsburgh meant that I was desperately playing catch-up for all that I had missed while in Colorado. My dad's updates were progressively happier. My faith continued its slow and steady climb toward trust again. The ethereal something was taking root deep inside of me in a way that both comforted and scared me. I was aware that I was no longer in control of any of the outcomes of this mess, no matter how hard I hoped, and I was acutely aware of all that I had. I wanted to show it in any way that I could, and I began writing daily gratitude lists to really recognize how lucky I was.

"That makes sense," I said. "I am just so excited that she is coming around."

"Me too," he sang.

My smile grew over my face. He was a terrible singer.

CHAPTER 71

November 18, 2012, 6:32 P.M.

THE SEMESTER WAS coming to a breaking point for Thanksgiving, and I was grateful for another week off to head back to Colorado. The constant battle between Guilt and Individuation would not stop, especially closer to the holidays, when I listened to Guilt's words that I should be home more often. I wondered how much the excitement for the holiday season that I usually felt would be tempered by the new reality of experiencing holidays in the hospital. So many changes.

My dad's latest updates were overall pretty boring. I had never been more grateful for boring. My mom's stomach issues were still a thing, and she recently had a peg tube put back in to get food directly into her stomach. My dad reassured me that it was temporary. I crossed my fingers and told him my flight details for next week.

CHAPTER 72

November 24, 2012, 10:00 P.M.

MY PLANE LANDED in Denver around 6:00 p.m. I couldn't wait to see my dad and hear how he was doing on a car ride north that didn't end immediately at the hospital, usually to address the latest emergency with my mom. My dream was soon shattered.

"Hi, kid," he sounded tired. He had lost some weight after his heart attack due to rehab, and I swore he had more gray hairs than last month.

"Hi, Pops," I said, hugging him hard, trying to sound chipper. He felt smaller. "It's almost your favorite holiday; how are you feeling about that?" I asked, referencing Thanksgiving tomorrow.

"Oh, kid, I'm doing alright," he said. "Better now that you're here." I knew it was coming. I could feel it. Where a pun would usually go was now just silence.

"What's wrong, Dad? Are you okay? Is Mom? What's happening?" I asked, my anxiety ramping up. Knowing it was coming, my body steeled in anticipation.

"Well," he started before sighing, "Mom has been so nauseous lately and has been vomiting often. The doctors found a bump on her pancreas, and they are testing to see

221

if it's cancerous. If so, she may have pancreatic cancer."

"Wha—?" I began. I was expecting a need for a higher level of care or a new issue with an already existing problem. This was one I hadn't even entertained. "Cancer?" I asked, completely perplexed. It felt wrong. After all of this, this was now suddenly a possibility too? Just when I thought it was safe to come out again after adjusting to a new normal? My body railed against its steely protective layer, trying to get out, but it was trapped. "When will we know?" I managed.

"Tomorrow. We'll know tomorrow," he said.

The car ride north was silent.

CHAPTER 73

November 25, 2012, 11:01 A.M.

WE WERE GATHERED around my mom's hospital bed watching her vomit. It was Thanksgiving. This was her third vomit of the morning already. She was crying, not able to focus on anything but her nausea. She kept vomiting into the rose pink–colored plastic semicircle containers angled just below her chin that I think were intended for just that. Things were bad again, and the continual vomiting was unprecedented. Her biopsy results were coming back later this afternoon. In the meantime, we were huddled around her bed, wishing to God that this was not happening.

Mat reached over and handed Mom a Kleenex. She blew her nose and continued holding the small pink tub close to her chest.

"This is awful," she said, crying. "Happy Thanksgiving." It came out drenched in cynicism. How disappointing this must be for her. She had come so far.

"What would you like us to do, Sher?" my dad asked. "Get the nurse?"

"I need some more Zofran," she said, her terrible mood both obvious and understandable.

"Okay," my dad said, and went to find a nurse.

We decided to watch a movie to try and focus on anything other than the present and pulled some uncomfortable chairs from down the hall into my mom's room. This was the strangest Thanksgiving, and I was on pins and needles awaiting results. We all were.

The movie ended, but the pain from the uncomfortable chairs did not. My mom had fallen asleep halfway through. We were hoping for the results at any time. Sniff was at my feet, and she let out a big sigh as she rolled onto her side. She looks so comfortable, I thought. I was jealous.

Several more long minutes passed until, finally, Dr. Stevens walked in.

"Good news, team," he said, beaming. My mom stirred. "The biopsy was negative for cancerous cells, which entirely rules out pancreatic cancer. It's most likely a cyst in there, causing pancreatitis. We try to avoid operating on the pancreas as much as possible due to its fragility and the possibility of doing more harm than good, so we will start treating it with medication. She should be feeling much better within a day or two."

I could hear my exhale before I felt it. I was discombobulated again, as if my mind were on a time delay from my body. My mom started crying and, as if in celebration, promptly threw up.

"Sherri, I am so sorry. Let's get you some X-rays to see what the peg tube is up to," Dr. Stevens said. "Radiology should be up here soon. For now, we can celebrate that you don't have cancer!"

"Thanks," she uttered softly.

"That's the best thing to be thankful for on Thanksgiving," my dad said, grabbing my mom's hand.

Radiology was up within the next hour, and the X-ray revealed that the peg tube had come out of her stomach and needed to be replaced. That was most likely the cause of her vomiting. They took her for the procedure, and Mat, my dad, and I went to Mat's house for a Thanksgiving meal, despite the current rocky status of his marriage. His in-laws were over, and I wasn't in the mood to socialize, yet it was Thanksgiving. It's what we always did.

My dad was depressed, sad, and flat for the gathering, and it was uncomfortable to vacillate between trying to socialize and wanting to hibernate. After an awkward two hours, my dad and I went back to the hospital with a plate of Thanksgiving food for my mom in case she was hungry and able to keep anything down. We said our goodbyes and left most of the social anxiety behind.

Back at the hospital, my mom was back from her procedure and sleeping it off. We brought her plate of food in and waited for fifteen minutes or so to see if she would wake up.

"Hi; you're back," she said about five minutes later.

"Hi, beautiful," my dad said.

"How are you feeling?" I asked her.

"Nauseous," came her familiar response.

"Want to try to eat a little Thanksgiving food and see if it helps to have food in your stomach after throwing up all day?" my dad asked.

"Maybe," she said. "What did you have?"

My dad handed her the plate, taking off the foil before it got to her. She looked at the options and took a bite of pumpkin pie first, followed by a bite of mashed potatoes and a sliver of turkey.

"I'm hungry, and this is—"

She stopped midsentence to grab the rinsed-out pink container to throw up. This was number nine for the day. She began to cry, and I did too. Happy Thanksgiving indeed.

CHAPTER 74

November 27, 2012, 4:13 P.M.

I NEEDED A break. I decided to take part of the day off to rest, and I slept until after 2:00 p.m. Transitions to and from home were getting increasingly more difficult, and I was requiring longer adjustment times in each place. My mom had finally stopped throwing up yesterday, and her spirits were starting to lift. She was able to sit in a chair now twice a day, though she was not yet able to stand. This roller-coaster peak was thrilling.

I thought back to the tilt table, and how the smallest increase in degree was such a success. How far she'd come to make it to sitting upright. Fear was becoming a more common experience, though, and some of her zest for life was dwindling. I was hopeful that this peg tube issue was the last setback she would have for a while so that she could regain some confidence. I could only imagine her reticence to anything new at this point after the amount of "new things" she'd had to endure. My dad's reticence too. Their limits were starting to show, and his own heart attack and recovery were often overshadowed by the extremes of my mom's instability.

I was dragging my feet leaving the house, and Guilt and

Individuation were at each other's throats over continuing to rest or going to the hospital. Guilt, as usual, was bullying Individuation loudly, and pressuring it into backing down. But suddenly, a quick burst of strength sizzled through Individuation and landed on Guilt's nose, momentarily knocking him out.

I felt my shoulders relax, put my pajamas back on, and lay on the floor next to Sniff in front of the TV. We watched the latest recorded episode of The Mentalist, which my dad had watched without me already, and I didn't hear from Guilt for the rest of the night. I officially took the day off.

CHAPTER 75

November 30, 2012, 3:46 P.M.

DIALYSIS HAD BECOME a permanent piece of life for my mom, and she hated it. We weren't big fans either, as it seemed to further complicate the already complex. The past few days had landed her a transfer back to LTACH's medical side. It was another facet of change to consider and adapt to in her treatment.

While at LTACH, she was able to have her first shower since August and cried because it felt so good. After all her surgeries, her hair had remained very curly, and she was enjoying doing it now that it was less upkeep. The Dykema family perm legacy was alive and well, this time no rollers or smelly perm solution was needed.

She had also been able to sit and stand up with a fancy lift like a giant hammock that she was strapped into to help her up and down as she regained her strength. One night into her stay at LTACH, she began vomiting again, the first time since Thanksgiving. This time, with an accompanying fever of 103 degrees.

LTACH needed to send her back to MCR for some testing they did not have the capability to conduct, and the giant yo-yo of "she's okay, no she's not" continued to throw us all for loops that weren't as impressive as actual yo-yo tricks.

MCR did two CAT scans that found no obvious issues and stabilized her with antibiotics overnight. Her white blood cell count was up again, and my dad and I begged the doctors to please check for infection anywhere they could. Yet until it showed up in a specific location, there wasn't much they could do but pump her full of antibiotics, which further harmed her digestive tract. It felt like constantly choosing between no-win situations, and each instance took a small chip out of who we once were and left gaping holes in our certainty.

My mom's spirit was struggling, and she began to sink deeper into depression. With both parents depressed, it was very hard for my own history and struggle with depression to stay at bay. Yet I knew that if I let it in now, the ship of chronic illness we were on would be left without anyone at its helm, and I wasn't ready to let that happen just yet. I was reaching my breaking point and was silently grateful for my return trip to Pittsburgh in two days to get away. Guilt was pounding at Individuation's insides with repeated blows, and Individuation was no longer strong enough to stand. It took to the fetal position and braced for the onslaught of pain.

CHAPTER 76
December 1, 2012, 11:31 A.M.

"HAPPY BIRTHDAY, DEAR Maaaaaaaaattttttttt," we droned. "Happy birthday to you!"

We were in my mom's hospital room at LTACH, trying to make his birthday feel anything but the gray blahs we had all been feeling lately.

I had purposely booked my plane ticket back to Pittsburgh for tomorrow to try to celebrate Mat with any sense of normalcy available.

"Thanks, guys," he said as I gave him some peppy jazz hands for a dramatic finish. It didn't really work.

CHAPTER 77

December 12, 2012, 5:13 P.M.

MY SEMESTER WAS coming to an end, and I was definitely phoning it in. My head was swirling constantly, and I was struggling to focus. My roommates were supportive and kind, and I didn't even want to talk to them. I felt so alone, and so scared. My dad's phone call didn't help.

"Hi, Dad," I answered, braced for whatever scare was to come.

"Hey, babes," he was too. "Got some rough news, and I am so glad you are not here for this."

He delivered the latest horror, and my nervous system remained steeled for protection.

"Well, they found the source of infection and finally linked it to her vomiting. It is the ash catheter she needs for dialysis. They pulled it after doing back-to-back dialysis for two days so that she could go a few more days before needing to go to McKee (the other hospital in Loveland that wasn't a trauma center) for a specialized doctor to replace it. She had the replacement surgery last night and has been bleeding profusely from the neck wound ever since. They can't stop the blood. It won't clot, and Mom can't stop crying. She thinks this is it, that she is going to die. It's bad. I feel so awful for her, and she just keeps counting towels soaked in blood from her neck that she is lying next to until they change them out."

"Oh, my God, Dad. Why all the bleeding? What is happening?" I sat straight up in bed from my reclined position.

"We don't know." He sounded so down.

"Did they nick something? What is happening?"

"We don't know, but they just now were finally able to stop the bleeding, twenty hours later. She has had ten liters of blood transfusions in order to stay alive." He started crying. "Lish, I have been pleading with God, yelling, screaming, crying, begging, pounding my fists on the floor in agony, begging him to help her, to intervene. I don't know how much more she can take! She is becoming such a different person. She is scared and sad and traumatized and anxious all the time, and I don't blame her one bit. It is so awful to watch. I can't imagine actually being her."

I was crying just listening. "I'm so sorry, Dad; that is so awful, so, so terrible. I wish I were there, I wish I could help; ugh, I am so sorry," I didn't know what else to say.

"No," was his strong reply. "I am so glad you are not here; you don't need to see this," he said, snapping out of his sorrow to protect mine. "You don't need any more of this engraved in your memory."

"But you do?" I asked, truly not knowing how much is too much for one person to handle and recognizing the traumatic impacts of this for both my parents.

"It's not your job." He reinforced my role as "kid," and thanked me for listening. I was grateful for the differentiation, and also curious how long it would last.

"So what's the plan?" I asked, trying to unimagine what I now knew.

"Well, next steps are to do dialysis two days in a row again later today and tomorrow, and then get back to LTACH."

"Okay," I said, completely numb everywhere. "Keep me posted."

It took me hours after that phone call to even remember what classes I was in, much less what final homework I had to submit. I gave up and lost myself in Gilmore Girls for the rest of the night, imaging living in Stars Hollow instead of my world.

CHAPTER 78
December 13, 2012, 4:15 P.M.

I WISHED MY dad knew how to text. Receiving information that way was preferential to the phone calls, where I felt every emotion in his voice in addition to my own. This was both my superpower and my kryptonite, feeling what others felt, and made it hard to differentiate what was truly mine. Guilt and Individuation were helping me find the balance between others' feelings and my own despite their slow and arduous timeline. This was all hard work, and I was left feeling drained, wanting to sleep for days at a time.

I dreaded the buzz of my phone alerting me to my dad's calls, and today was no different. His update included good news of no continued bleeding until partway through dialysis, when it started again for another five hours. They had to pull the ash catheter to stop the bleeding. It worked, but now how would she get dialysis? Her life depended on it.

CHAPTER 79

December 19, 2012, 3:13 P.M.

I TURNED IN my final projects for all my courses, not remembering ever completing them. I was packing to go home tomorrow for the three-week holiday and was trying to befriend my internal resistance. It was just so much.

My mom had received a new temporary catheter, the one in her neck again (placed on the opposite side of the bleeding wound), so she could get dialysis. She was healing from the bleeding incident until the temporary catheter became clogged and no longer worked. The surgery to replace the temporary catheter with another ash catheter was this morning, and my dad called to let me know that this time, the surgery was a breeze. There was no bleeding whatsoever. This confirmed in my mind that something had been nicked during the last placement surgery, and my anger climbed out of my mind as it turned into steam.

With all that my mom had been through so far, why did this mistake need to cause her additional traumatic stress of believing she was going to die as she watched herself bleed out? This seemed like completely unnecessary suffering, and I was beginning to question where God was in all of this. I was so confused, heartbroken for my mom, and devastated for what this may mean for her mental health both short- and long-term.

She was able to have dialysis in the afternoon with no bleeding and would be transferred back to LTACH tonight. It seemed that this could be the eye of the storm, but I didn't assume anything. I was learning to slowly let go of literally everything. With less expectation came less disappointment.

CHAPTER 80

December 23, 2012, 6:15 P.M.

"O COME LET us adore Him, O come let us adore Him, O come let us adore, Hi-im, Christ the Lord," the voices and notes rang out.

The scene was beautiful, and the ethereal presence was sucking me into its enveloping embrace as I watched the events unfold. My mom was in her bed at LTACH, still struggling with nausea, but feeling much better. There was no more bleeding, and dialysis occurred with no issue. She was given antibiotics to treat her infection from all the catheters and was present and clear-headed for the first time I could remember since right after her heart attack all those months ago. It was hard to believe that it had been less than a year. It felt like twenty.

Carolers were making rounds in the hospitals to sing for folks who were sick around the holidays, and tonight they had come to visit my mom. There were around fifteen of them, including one who played a viola. They had scrunched into my mom's room, and we had made as much space for them as possible.

The scrunch of people matched the scrunch of Brooks's forehead as Mat held him in his arms and he tried to sing along to the words, always a beat behind. It was precious. I was next to my mom at the head of her bed, and as the next song, "Jingle Bells," began, I was taken by the beauty this moment allowed. My mom was sick and hospitalized and had just recovered from yet another near-death scare, but she was now able to celebrate joy through some carols. I hoped this would encourage healing on both her physical and emotional planes.

The viola was beautiful, and made "Jingle Bells" sound more elegant, almost regal. Halfway through the second verse, my mom, unable to concentrate on them anymore, started crying and requested the pink semicircle thing that was apparently standard in hospitals and proceeded to vomit in front of all the carolers.

My insides twisted as the carolers stopped mid-song and slowly filed out the door to give her privacy. She continued to throw up and cry. It was simultaneously beautiful and heartbreaking. The ethereal presence suddenly cleared my thoughts of all but one truth: How could I know the elation of pure beauty when I didn't know the sorrowful depths of sadness? How much sweeter was joy when the depths of the pain were also known? An image of the two-sided coin floated around in my brain as I saw our situation through this lens. A shift in perspective, a "both and" rather than an "either or." It was awe-inspiring in my mind.

My mom kept crying and vomiting, and I grabbed her a wet washcloth from the bathroom attached to her room. My dad looked crestfallen, and Mat and Brooks had stepped outside with the carolers.

"It's okay, Mom," I consoled her as I placed the washcloth on her forehead. And when the carolers started playing and singing again from the hallway, I truly believed that it was.

CHAPTER 81

December 24, 2012, 7:00 P.M.

LAST NIGHT'S CAROLING incident lingered in my mind all day. Something inside had permanently shifted, and I could feel a layer of peace enfolding some of my unanswered questions. I didn't know the answers, but right now, at least, that was okay. I somehow knew I was not meant to.

When we arrived at the hospital tonight, we brought a small Christmas tree and our family gifts for one another, as was our tradition on Christmas Eve. We walked in to find my mom alert, sitting in a chair, and dressed. Her eyes were bright, and she greeted us with that smile of hers that I had forgotten existed.

I stared in disbelief. Was I dreaming? I dug my nails into my hand to make sure I wasn't.

"Merry Christmas, guys," she said as we all entered, and I felt a tear roll down my face.

This was truly a Christmas miracle.

CHAPTER 82

January 21, 2013, 4:17 P.M.

MY MOM HAD made tremendous strides toward her recovery in the past few weeks, and it was just the face-lift we all needed. The Christmas miracle truly stuck, and the ethereal presence was right; this joy was that much sweeter because of our intimate knowledge of the hard.

My mom continued her fight, and man, was I in deep admiration. She powered through her rehab, though painful and slow, and was now able to eat three meals a day while sitting up. The nausea had finally settled. Her infections from the dialysis catheters were completely gone, there was no peg tube, and she was off all but one of her antibiotics. She had progressed in physical therapy as well and had begun to regain strength in her arms and legs, though walking was still very difficult. She was determined. And when my mom was determined, the world had better look out. I proudly displayed my stubbornness as a gift from her.

Last week she was transferred back to MCR to their brand-new rehab program, where she would receive three hours of physical, occupational, and speech therapy per day. Speech was working on cognitive functioning with her, as her memory had become very hazy in part.

FOUR EYES

The doctors recently told us that due to the length of her time in the ICU, she could suffer some effects of "ICU delirium," which often presented itself in long-term cognitive impairment that looked similar to a moderate traumatic brain injury or a mild case of Alzheimer's disease. Though this was not pleasant news, it was generally accepted news—it meant she was still with us and able to live, like she wanted. The doctors stated that up to two percent of her brain function could be permanently altered, and that time would tell. Two percent didn't sound like a lot, but apparently it was. We accepted this with the rest and continued to focus on her progress, wondering how that would show up in the future.

Today's accomplishment was relayed to me from Mat.

"She was able to walk ten steps today, and she went to the bathroom on her own!" he said, excitedly.

This was a big deal, and I was struck at how rudimentary her progress seemed, and yet how rich it was in defining her determination.

"Wow, I'm so happy for her," I said. I noticed that I was starting to protect my excitement just a bit, just in case things turned worse again.

"Yeah, they even think she may be able to come home soon," he said.

Images of the last experience poured through my head, and my body froze.

"I really hope it's nothing like last time," I said as I convinced myself to exhale.

"No shit," Mat said, validating how rough that had been.

"Well, I am so glad things are slowly changing. Crossing my fingers they stay that way," I said, feeling the weight of Guilt jumping up and down on my chest for not being there.

I called her later to congratulate her on her progress. There was no answer.

CHAPTER 83

February 3, 2013, 2:17 P.M.

AUNT DAR, THE oldest of my dad's siblings, had flown in for my mom's grand homecoming to help my dad adjust to caregiving life. Aunt Dar and I were about the same height, had the same sense of humor, and looked very similar. When she was around, I often felt like I could see my future; we were that similar. Now that I had more clients to balance, I was not able to get the time off from my semester to go home as much, and I wanted to graduate on time. I was so grateful to Aunt Dar.

I had celebrated making it this far in grad school with my classmates a few nights ago at karaoke and had dedicated Pat Benetar's "Hit Me with Your Best Shot" to 2012. My attitude was fixed on forward motion, and despite Guilt's best attempts, I had made it back to Pittsburgh for Individuation to rest and recover. It was time.

It was Super Bowl Sunday, and Mat, Brooks, Aunt Dar, and my dad had all gathered to welcome my mom home. It was her long-awaited arrival. It had been almost a full year of hospitals, and I was sad to miss the grand homecoming. It was a huge accomplishment for her, and I wanted her to feel as celebrated as she was. They called just after they got her inside and settled.

"Welcome home, Mom!" I said, making celebratory trumpet noises with my mouth. "How does it feel?"

"Hi, Lish! Thanks! It's great. And a little overwhelming too." She choked up.

"I can imagine," I said, backing off a few levels of happy. She was so sensitive to emotion these days, and almost anything could bring tears to her eyes. In a moment of hopeful normalcy, I had forgotten. I hated being reminded.

"We're all here for you," I said, feeling Guilt laugh in my face. "I'm so sorry I can't be there today. I am so proud of you!"

"Thanks, Lish. Butch, can you get my water bottle for me?" Her attention shifted quickly. I was passed to Mat for a few moments before he had to go help with something. Aunt Dar got on for a quick hello and shared her pride of me for staying in school and studying hard. That small bit of validation rained on Guilt's parade for a brief moment.

"Thanks, Aunt Dar," I said, thanking her for being present for my parents in this time of adjustment.

"Love you," she said in her traditional sign-off.

"Love you too," I said, hanging up. I sat with my internal unrest for a while as I slowly convinced Individuation to keep working toward wholeness.

CHAPTER 84

April 26, 2013, 5:15 P.M.

MY PHONE CALLS to and from home had reduced from daily to three times a week, and it was an amazing vacation for my mind. My mom had continued to progress wonderfully at home, and I was so excited for her to feel like a person again. We had all been changed by this, her especially, and with time came the relaxation of my nervous system and the chance to begin to live without fear again.

I was currently in a class about disability and was learning so much about acquired disability like my mom's. I really felt for her and struggled not to become her therapist while also staying her cheerleader. It was a very fine line.

She had one return trip to MCR in March for an infection from her most recent ash catheter. My dad recognized the early signs of weakness, confusion, and hallucination, and got her in right away. He was right on. It was a strange phenomenon for her to be released after only a week— we were used to much longer stays—but a very welcome one. Since then, she had been working her way toward independence, but it proved a challenge, and her personality had become much more subdued.

My dad drove her to dialysis every other day and picked

her up four hours later. It definitely put a crimp in the days for them both, for different reasons, yet he continued to do it, elated she was home. Their schedule was full of home-care visits, follow-ups with various doctors, and dialysis. My dad began to realize the implications of caregiving—the thankless, unending tasks of housekeeping and the instability of making plans, as my mom's state could alter any plan set at any time without warning.

They were experimenting with her energy levels, and slowly finding an activity limit for the day that wouldn't wipe her out completely for the next one as well. They were adjusting to the truth that my mom would never make a full recovery, and that this was the new normal. Neither of them loved it, but they continued together, figuring it out as it happened.

I was in a parallel process, just across the country. My mom would never make a full recovery. Some days that sunk in deeply. Other days, I denied it and pretended my life in Colorado was that of a fairy tale. Kelly, Courtney, and Courtney's family were my constants.

I called Courtney crying one night after contemplating that my mom could actually die, and asked her what I would do if that really happened? Prepared for the "She's not going to die, she'll be fine" answer that was the more typical response from people, she matter-of-factly stated, "I don't know. But we can cross that bridge if it comes." I was shocked so deeply by her honest authenticity that I stopped crying. She was so confident in her answer that she didn't know. Maybe I didn't have to know what I would do either? The truth of that expanded into my lungs, and I felt air enter deeper into my body than it had been able to for weeks.

When my dad called tonight, my nervous system was fairly regulated due to the past few months' check-ins. They had been safe, and rather benign, so I didn't see this one coming.

"Lish," he sighed loudly.

Immediately, the hair on the back of my neck and arms stood on end. What now? I could feel the steely exterior getting into position.

"We're back at MCR. Mom was using her walker to get up the two steps inside the garage, and I was getting her wheelchair out of the trunk. She only got one of the walker feet on the second step, and when she put weight on the unbalanced walker, she fell backward onto the concrete garage floor and broke her hip and shoulder. She's in awful pain and doesn't have nearly the pain tolerance she had before. We just got the X-rays back confirming the breaks, and she is going into surgery for her hip in an hour."

My heart fell out of my entire body, and my limbs suddenly weighed hundreds of collective pounds. I couldn't move. She had finally been healing! I was crushed into immediate depression.

"Oh, no. This is so bad," I said, feeling it with my words. I couldn't find my actual feelings yet. "How is she?"

"Awful." It was all he said.

Point taken.

CHAPTER 85

May 25, 2013, 1:30 P.M.

I HAD MADE it back for a long weekend to visit my mom, in the MCR rehab program again. Today was music therapy, and I was going to go to the group class with her. I was so excited. Music had moved me since I was a kid, and I had grown up playing percussion and the piano, singing, learning the guitar in college, and eventually landing in the musical theater realm. I loved the power music held, and I was so excited to see how music therapy could help my mom.

My mom had learned how to walk for the third time now in her adult life, but it was very hesitant and slow. We started down the hallway well before group began to ensure we'd make it in time.

"I don't remember music therapy last time, Mom, do you?"

"No, they didn't have it then," she replied, still focused on placing one foot in front of the other with her walker.

"Do you like it?" I asked. "It sounds cool."

"It's good," she said. Her answers had become shorter over time. Most of her energy was going toward healing her body over and over and over again. It didn't leave much for conversations of substance.

We reached the door and walked in to find a group of ten people sitting in a semicircle. They were in various stages of present, and we joined them on the end near the door. Soon, a spunky twenty-something came over and passed out song titles to everyone while making small talk.

"Hi, everyone; I'm Stacey. Welcome to music therapy. Today we are playing Elvis or Frank Sinatra. But first, let's warm up by tapping our feet and clapping our hands to the beat of this song," she said as she turned on "Hound Dog" by Elvis and led the group through it by example. That's a really clever version of physical therapy rehab, I thought.

"Great job!" she said as she passed around a basket of smaller instruments for everyone. "Please take one of these instruments to play along with the music as we play Elvis or Frank Sinatra next."

Everyone complied. My mom got a small tambourine.

"Good pick, Mom," I said. She smiled.

"So, I am going to play a song, and one of you has the song title in your hand. When your song is played, you have to walk all the way up here and place it on the board under either the Elvis or the Frank Sinatra column," she explained. "Any questions?" she asked a silent crowd. "Okay then, let's go!"

The first song was "You Make Me Feel So Young," and an adorable man in his eighties healing from a knee replacement stood and shuffled his way to the front. He placed his title in the Frank Sinatra column as Stacey cheered; he took a minute to rest before heading back to his seat. The rest of the group played their instruments haphazardly to the beat, except my mom. She was hitting the tambourine on her leg to the beat softly and enjoying the song. I looked down at her song title. It was "Blue Suede Shoes," and we waited another three songs before it was her turn.

She used her counting "one, two, three" method to stand up with her walker, and slowly made her way to the board, where she confidently placed the song title in the Elvis column. Once class ended, we made our way back to her room, where she proceeded to fall asleep for the rest of the evening, completely spent.

CHAPTER 86
June 11, 2013, 5:32 P.M.

MY INTERNSHIP SITE for school required a physical, and I had returned to the clinic for my TB test results.

"It's definitely positive," he said.

This had to be a joke. I laughed out loud as I listened to the tech explain it again. He got out the ruler, marked the dimensions of the slightly raised red circle on my arm on a piece of paper, and told me to have a seat.

Tuberculosis? Really? Was this the 1800s?

After a chest X-ray proved I didn't have active TB, a doctor confirmed that my latent case could flare up in the future if I was ever immunocompromised.

I was still having trouble not laughing. This was ridiculous. I couldn't wait to tell my parents and commiserate with our family's medical plight of late. The doctor handed me a note and told me to report to the health department for nine months of medication and monthly blood draws. I wondered what I would name my TB baby at the end of all this.

CHAPTER 87

June 25, 2013, 6:00 P.M.

"HAPPY ANNIVERSARY, MOM and Dad!" I said into the phone.

"Thanks," they responded happily.

"What are you guys going to do to celebrate?" I asked earnestly.

"Oh, you know," my dad said; "only the finest."

"Sure. So takeout and a movie again, huh?" I laughed.

"Yeah," my mom said, very distantly. I heard her fumble with the phone and then ask my dad to bring her something from the living room when he came back to the bedroom.

This was becoming increasingly more common—my mom camping out in bed all day and my dad bringing her things when she yelled for them. He was beyond annoyed with this arrangement, yet compliant as he began to deeply understand my mom's limitations. She had come home the week after I was there last and had been continuing to heal slowly, taking a lot of pain medication again.

Mat's divorce had finalized last month, alleviating some of his ongoing stress. He started to give me updates from "kid eyes" when my dad's were clouded from the spousal perspective. I cherished these conversations, and it was great to commiserate instead of being in on the planning process all the time.

My mom had to go to the bathroom, so she set the phone down as I chatted more with my dad. I caught him up on my latent TB diagnosis, and we had a good laugh at my colonial times disease. He wasn't the least bit surprised. It took a lot to surprise him these days.

CHAPTER 88

July 14, 2013, 11:00 A.M.

BACK AT SCHOOL, I was in a one-week grief counseling class taught by my boss and advisor, Dr. Bob Witchel. Today was day three. It was heavy, which was both good and bad. This morning he had asked for volunteers to be clients with fake stories before his eyes settled on me and asked if I would do it with my real one.

I had been keeping him updated along the way, so he knew what he was asking. I could feel my heart beat faster as I thought about sitting in the chair in the middle of the room for the whole class to observe. Begrudgingly, I agreed, and he began. Partway through, I could feel my tears welling up inside; I was trying to hold them back, embarrassed.

"I can see you're having some feelings here," he said, pointing out my tears. "Can you tell me about them?"

I was angry, but my tears won out and spilled over my eyelids before the anger could reign them in. After several awkward moments of public crying in silence, I said, "I am scared that my mom will die."

"Yes," he responded. "I can see how that would be scary. Tell me why you're scared."

This was too real and hit too close to home. I felt both

overwhelmed and grateful for this experience, as contrived as it was. "I am scared that I will miss her, that I will be changed forever, that the waves of grief will drown me, that I will never recover, that my depression will win, that I won't have her anymore. I mean," I chuckled between my tears, "what am I not scared of?"

He looked at me with compassionate eyes that liked to push the envelope. "So it feels like you will no longer have access to her if she dies," he reflected what I had said.

"Yes," I answered, feeling the impact of that statement.

"Well, that depends on how you look at it," he said. "Have you ever heard the saying 'Death ends a life, not a relationship'?"

I looked at him through my blurred vision. I hadn't. It was strangely comforting.

"I don't think so, but in the middle of a breakdown, I can't really think straight," I said, trying to make a joke, to lighten the room a bit. It didn't work. No one laughed.

"I think of them more as 'coming togethers' than 'breakdowns,'" he said back. "Letting yourself really feel your emotions puts you more in alignment with you than ever."

This one did me in, and I started crying uncontrollably. He continued to ask questions and proceed with the "example," but my mind was stuck on the "coming togethers." There was more behind the wall of grief I felt, but class was ending, and I needed some air. As soon as class ended, I thanked him and he gave me a hug. I barely made it to the private bathroom before I continued to "come together."

CHAPTER 89

December 11, 2013, 4:15 P.M.

THE REST OF 2013 felt like a roller-coaster ride in the dark. Being vigilant the whole time, you had to wait until the ride was over to assess how it actually was. My mom's roller coaster was seemingly unending, and it was all I could do to keep up.

Her hip and shoulder had healed slowly with time, but with one step forward came two steps back. She had been back to MCR for more infections from the ash catheters than I could track, one placing her back in the ICU with a fever of 105 degrees and the need for a "cold suit," which was essentially being bathed in ice to lower her body temperature. The nurses told us that at 106 degrees, organs started shutting down. They acted fast, but it was yet another close and scary call.

Eventually, a skin graft surgery to place a permanent catheter in her right thigh for dialysis became the alternative to the ash catheter infections. Because her veins and arteries were small, she was not a good candidate for a dialysis port in her arm, so a skin graft was the last hope.

True to her pattern of "last hope" surgeries, it worked, and her infections dwindled. She had been home since

November 5th and, again, climbing her way to recovery, this time landing just a few steps below her previous climbs.

Thanksgiving was a quick trip home this year before the actual holiday due to school requirements and rapidly approaching graduation. My mom slept most of the day. My dad, Mat, and I called one another and expressed our gratitude for her being home—it was the first holiday she had been home since this began.

I needed to stay in Pittsburgh to finish my clinical hours for graduation. I picked up an additional internship at a drug and alcohol treatment center where my friends Courtney and Kelly were also interning to complete my hours. So much in the addiction world paralleled my personal life in terms of my mom's new relationship with pain medication. I really couldn't have had a better education.

Courtney and Kelly continued to be key supports in my life, and I couldn't imagine doing any of it without them. Kelly came over the night before last to write our final papers together, and when we finished, I had a giant pit in the bottom of my stomach that my time with her would soon be over when she moved back home to northern Pennsylvania. It was more grief, and I didn't want anything to do with it. So instead, we celebrated with a dance party into the wee hours of the night. It felt amazing to be done.

Courtney and her family had become family to me, and I had spent so much time with them as we sloughed through class after class and assignment after assignment. I was so grateful that they would be in Pittsburgh for the foreseeable future.

My question was, would I?

CHAPTER 90

December 13, 2013, 12:01 P.M.

IT WAS GRADUATION day, and I was elated. My dad and Mat had surprised me by coming into town yesterday for the ceremony. I couldn't believe it. They had arranged "Mom care," as they called it, and though my dad was in contact with my mom often, he reported feeling temporarily free from the caregiving responsibility as he pumped his fists in the air. He had the energy of a little kid, and I was so happy to see him feeling so good. I took them all over Pittsburgh to show them my world, and noted that it felt weird without my mom.

The ceremony was meaningful and intimate. Afterward, I got to introduce my dad and Mat to all my professors, and when Dr. Witchel met my dad, he bear-hugged him, telling him he was so sorry for all he had been through. I felt extremely warm inside and cared for watching my worlds meld. I wanted that feeling to last forever.

Later that day, my dad, Mat, and I went shopping, and watching my dad laugh and joke around with Mat and me at some of the ridiculous things we found was invigorating. For a brief second, we saw a less-worn-out version of our dad shine. It made us question just how good being my mom's full-time caretaker was for him, and it brought the question of what I should do post-graduation right to the center of my thoughts.

I had been weighing out heavily what I wanted. Or rather, Guilt and Individuation were. I had just spent the last three years making Pittsburgh my own, getting to know the city, and becoming connected. I had great friends, some promising connections for jobs, and a great apartment. I knew that I had to make up my mind before settling into the next part of my licensure process, as hours received for licensure in one state would not transfer to another.

For now, the plan was to continue at my original internship site as a part-time employee while I figured out what was next. What I really wanted was to buy myself time, and to make an informed decision.

It was comfortable here. I was comfortable here, and yet, I remembered Nurse Ryan's words when I asked what she would do in my shoes. "I think you should do whatever you can live with and not regret," she had shared from a place full of wisdom. It had become a guiding light for me in this giant decision, and at the end of the day, I simply knew I would not be able to live with myself if my mom died and I was not around. My answer was clear. But I kept that to myself for now.

CHAPTER 91

January 20, 2014, 11:37 P.M.

THE WEEKS SINCE graduation had validated my decision to move home. After Christmas, my mom had two more hospital stays from infections; this time, she turned septic with one of them. I couldn't take chances anymore with the unknown, and Guilt and Individuation were held fast in a leglock that hadn't moved in weeks. I needed to move home.

I observed how my parents were doing on my Christmas visit, and noted how we had yet to spend an actual Christmas out of a hospital since this dance with chronic illness began nearly two years ago. They weren't well but were status quo. My mom was a lot of work, and my dad was growing tired. I suggested additional help with home care, but my dad insisted that he could do it on his own.

I proved him wrong when my mom's colostomy bag had an issue while I was home. She was preparing for a shower and had asked my dad to remove her bag so that she could clean the area where the bag attached. He obliged. She was in her wheelchair, and he was about to wheel her to the shower when her stoma erupted. Everywhere. She immediately started crying, and my dad started yelling for me as he pushed her down the hallway as fast as he could, leaving a trail down the white hallway carpet. He got her into the tiled bathroom, and she worked on transferring herself onto the shower chair as fast as she could, which was not fast at all, as her stoma kept flowing. It was everywhere, including her wheelchair. When we knew she could no longer hear us in the shower, we laughed hysterically at the situation as we scrubbed the carpet. It was the humor that helped us get through the gross. When we could zoom out, it was a rather hilarious, albeit disgusting, occurrence. I wished my mom felt similarly.

We assured her that it was okay, but she was distraught for the rest of the day, cursing her colostomy bag until she fell asleep. I had such compassion for her, for anyone that needed one. They were brutal. My dad made a note to call about getting colostomy reversal surgery the next morning.

CHAPTER 92

February 26, 2014, 3:45 P.M.

THE COLOSTOMY REVERSAL surgery was postponed from early February until today because my mom got a urinary tract infection and went septic again. She pulled through like a champ. Today the reversal was completed, and I was hoping this would be the boost she needed to move forward.

The second septic scare extra-confirmed my decision to move home, and I was leaving in two weeks. Moving home without any of the protections of my friends or familiars would set me up for a pummeling by Guilt that I was not okay with, so in Individuation's favor, I got a cat. She was black and white, six months old, and adorable.

We stared at each other for a few days before I named her Olive, a sign of extending an olive branch of peace with God amid all the changes I was processing. My faith was still a swirling mess, and I hated that I had to choose between not being around if my mom died while pursuing an amazing career path or being present for my mom's illness and needing to start my life all over again in another state. I was bitter at chronic illness, at myself, and at the circumstances. And I knew it was my next right move.

At least I now had Olive.

CHAPTER 93

May 15, 2014, 9:01 A.M.

"HELP, HELP, HELP, help!" the screams filled the empty house.

I was half awake. I looked around the room to get my bearings. I had been sleeping in the downstairs bedroom lately when the low hum of my mom's oxygen machine and the loud punctuated air bursts of my dad's BiPap machine got to be too loud. I was more removed from the chaos of chronic illness down here, and every now and then, I could even hear my own thoughts and desires along with Guilt's chant: "selfish, selfish, selfish."

"Help! Please, please, Alisha, help me!" my mom's voice came into focus.

I jumped up and ran upstairs as fast as I could and back to her bedroom. "Mom, what's wrong?" I asked frantically, panting.

She was crying. The boot her foot doctor had given her recently for her right heel, which was developing a pressure ulcer, was stuck in one of the blankets, and she was twisted into an uncomfortable position. I quickly took to freeing her booted foot.

"Ow, ow, ow," she cried.

"What do you need, Mom?" I asked, recognizing how

quickly she flew into a panic these days over things that would normally not even have phased her.

"Ice and water in my bottle," she cried, searching the bed for her water bottle.

"That's it?" I asked, a little frustrated. "You scared the shit out of me!"

"Well, I'm scared!" she said, the mom I once knew gone.

Guilt surprised Individuation with a right hook, silencing it.

I softened. "I'm sorry, Mom. What are you scared of?"

"I don't know," she cried. This was becoming a theme, and we were all struggling with the adjustment.

"It's okay," I said calmly, turning on a nature sounds CD she loved so much. "I'll go and get some ice water, okay? I'll be right back. Do you need any meds right now?" I asked, wondering if she had forgotten to take them this morning.

"No, just water and ice."

"Be right back," I said, and sighed once out of earshot. Living at home was much harder than I'd anticipated, and she was a difficult patient. My patience was learning new ways of existing, and from time to time, I forgot that she was not her old self. I missed the old spunky, creative her. I wondered if she would ever be back.

My dad was meeting with his Colorado "Men's Group" this morning, and I was grateful that he had some time for himself, though I was also annoyed at how I woke up this morning in his absence. I didn't know how to feel.

I filled my mom's water bottle with ice, how she liked it, and returned to her room. Sniff and Olive joined the party. Sniff had started to lose her eyesight as her cataracts slowly increased, and Olive was a big fan of lying near her, knowing she couldn't see very well. It was cute, and brought my mom joy.

Sniff had been there for my mom when no one else could be, and she affirmed my belief in animal-assisted therapy even more. My mom sniffled and started talking to the animals, which helped her calm down. There was no way these weren't trauma responses. I had tried to steer my mom toward getting some help for all she had been through, but she refused, claiming she was "fine." I kept on, but she just shut down more when I persisted. I had to take intentional steps back and realize that I was not my mom's decision maker. She was. And even if I disagreed with her decision, perhaps that was part of the mystery. I didn't understand it, and it frustrated me to no end, but was it really mine to understand in the first place?

CHAPTER 94

June 16, 2014, 6:31 A.M.

I HAD HEARD about a well-renowned eating disorder hospital based in Denver at a conference, and I was excited to accept their job offer as a "Patient Care Assistant." I would start next week. RJ was spending the rest of the summer with his girlfriend in Ohio and had offered me his place to live rent-free while I started to look for a place of my own. A friend from Pennsylvania was moving out in September, and we were going to live together. It was all slowly happening in Individuation's favor, and Guilt was not happy.

Guilt reminded me of my mom's newish state of helplessness, chronic discontentedness, and the long-term cognitive function damage caused by ICU delirium. None of this was her fault, and yet there were times when my resentments about her not caring for her diabetes like she should have for all those years were loaded reminders of how deeply her shame seed was rooted. None of it felt fair, and yet no one entity felt entirely to blame either. She was becoming a different person, and no one could blame her.

I shared the "not taking care of the diabetes the way I should have" resentments about my dad as well when he progressively complained of neuropathy in both his legs and feet and the beginnings of glaucoma in his eyes, also complications of his diabetes. Perhaps the disease itself was to blame. Perhaps it was a combo. I didn't know. All I knew was that I was angry that it was slowly taking my parents away.

Regardless, I was starting my job next week in service of starting my new life in Denver.

CHAPTER 95

September 5, 2014, 4:32 P.M.

WORKING IN A behavioral hospital was a very different experience from anything I had ever done. I worked twelve-hour shifts, three days a week, and had four days off in between. I was loving everything about it so far, except the whole hospital part. But it was navigable, and I loved my work. I soon met a group of terrific friends that began to build Individuation up as a worthy competitor to Guilt for the first time ever.

I went home weekly to visit and check in and relieve my dad from the constant care my mom needed. It was a high-paced, high-energy, highly unsustainable way of living, but I was doing it. And I was doing it well. But I knew it wouldn't last.

My faith and my body were exhausted. I was confused about everything and was on the hunt for a therapist of my own. I just knew I had to keep going, but I wasn't exactly sure how that looked. My job was a welcome escape into the lives of others struggling, and it allowed me to pause my own struggle. I liked it.

CHAPTER 96

December 24, 2014, 1:00 P.M.

MY MOM HAD called last night in hysterics to tell me that Sniff was dying. We cried on the phone together, and Olive and I decided to head up for the next few nights and Christmas. I scribbled my roommate Jen a note that I was headed up north, and to have a Merry Christmas back home in Pennsylvania.

I arrived to find Mat petting Sniff, who was lying on her side, her breathing labored. He told her what a good girl she was, and that he loved her. She would pant and pace and find a new spot every few minutes, but never quite get comfortable. My dad told us that this had been going on for almost a week now. She was uncomfortable and would cough without relief for up to an hour at a time. Her meds for that were no longer working.

We had had our fill of watching suffering, and I was utterly devastated. I spent most of the night moving from place to place with Sniff, petting her and letting her know that she was so very loved. We were going to talk today about what to do.

My mom was ugly crying, and my dad was heartbroken. Mat left late last night to be to work early this morning.

FOUR EYES

We made a collective decision to put Sniff down after she was coughing and panting all morning with no relief. We couldn't watch her in pain anymore.

My mom still had dialysis every other day, and today was one of them. She had to be there at 1:30 p.m., and my dad had made the appointment for Sniff at 1:45 p.m. My mom had spent the morning saying her goodbyes to Sniff, and she couldn't stop crying. My dad asked which job I wanted—bring my mom to dialysis or bring Sniff to the vet to be put down. I wanted to do right by Sniff, but I couldn't bring myself to watch that happen. I had been there for our first keeshond's euthanasia when I was sixteen and still had those images burned into my brain. I chose dialysis.

My dad got Sniff in the car to go buh-bye, and I asked for a few minutes with her alone in the car. I climbed into the backseat, where she was standing, not assuming her typical front seat spot, and hugged her tightly as I cried into her neck fur.

"I love you so much, Sniff," I said. "I'm so sorry you're in so much pain. You've been the best dog in the whole world," I told her, sobbing. I didn't want to let go.

"And Sniff," I added, gently pulling her snout over to make eye contact, though she couldn't see much of anything, "thank you so much for being there with me through Mom and Dad's whole hospital stretch. I truly don't think I could have done it without you. You are more than a dog, you are an angel. You got it, and you got me. I am forever grateful. Thank you. I will love you forever." She licked my hand as if to say she understood.

I petted her until my dad came out and gently urged me out of the car. He was crying too, and it was time for all of us to go. And just like that, the only other being who truly knew what I had experienced when my parents were both in the hospital was gone.

I drove my mom to dialysis in tears and sat and cried

with her for a while until she fell asleep. The dialysis techs were very understanding and kind and told me they would take good care of her when she woke up.

Christmases had really taken a turn.

CHAPTER 97

April 28, 2015, 3:17 P.M.

THE YEAR 2015 blew in with some long-awaited normalcy. Well, normalcy for us, at least. My mom continued dialysis, and I helped my dad find a city-run ride-share service that picked her up and dropped her off so he could have more time in his days. My dad's depression was back, and he really needed some semblance of a life back to combat it. He was currently fighting it with bags of potato chips, Butterfingers, and Diet Dr Peppers. He had at least switched from Cokes to something with less sugar, as his blood sugars had been skyrocketing lately. He needed help and didn't know how to ask for it. Guilt told me to read between the lines of his communication and assume I knew what was best; Individuation told me to let us each adult on our own terms. I wanted to find a middle ground.

I got a promotion at work that included covering for therapists when they had time off, and I was pumped. I had just finished a two-week stint covering for one of the therapists on my team, and my career path was more validated than ever.

When my dad called me at work, I knew something was wrong. He usually tried to wait until after work to call with updates.

"Hey, kid, sorry to bug you at work, but I just wanted to let you know that Mom has a staph infection in her foot from a pressure ulcer on her heel. It is spreading up her calf, and we are at MCR again." His voice was monotone. He wasn't present.

"Wow, Dad. How are you?" I asked, taking my phone out into the hallway.

"I'm fine," he said. "Just hope it's an easy fix." There was no emotion left to express.

CHAPTER 98
May 30, 2015, 8:31 A.M.

I WHEELED MY mom into the lobby of the surgical orthopedic department on the third floor of MCR. Mat was loaded with coffee that his new girlfriend had given him for us all, and my dad was checking my mom in at the desk.

My mom's foot infection had gotten worse and had been progressing up her leg for about a month. The doctors recommended amputating her right leg from the knee down. We were all very distressed by this news. My mom had given it a lot of thought, though she really didn't have much choice. Today was the day, and we all took turns saying goodbye to her leg. She was crying but thanked it for its service and bade it au revoir. We followed suit, wishing it well. The ceremony landed somewhere between funny and melodramatic, but it was exactly what was needed. When we were done, they wheeled her back to a room; we all followed. As soon as they got her ready for the operation, they asked us to wait in the lobby until she was out of surgery.

Some of her nerves rubbed off on us, and my stomach let me know it immediately with its gurgles and flutters. Texts started to pour in from friends and coworkers, well-wishing the day. I was grateful for the support, as the familiar unknown started creeping its way into my psyche. Again. We played card games, and Mat told us about his new girlfriend, Jen.

Three hours later, the doctors emerged to tell us that the surgery had gone very well and that we could come back and see her. We walked into pure joy.

My mom reported that she had no pain whatsoever, and she was bright and alert and her old self. On pain meds, but still her old self. It had been so long since we had seen her. She was happy, and even smiled at my dad's joke about now having "a leg up on the neighbors." My dad was back. My mom was back. And we were all laughing. I wanted to bottle this moment forever.

CHAPTER 99

July 24, 2015, 3:30 P.M.

ADJUSTING TO AN amputation was more than any of us bargained for. My mom's mood swings were big, and they left an even bigger wake. She was depressed and falling further and further into depression. Everyone understood. She was in pain, again, and needed significant pain medication to manage it. A few times, she got behind in the pain medication regimen and spent the next day or so in agonizing pain trying to catch up to it. The most interesting phenomenon was the feeling that her foot still itched, though it was a phantom itch, and when she scratched where her foot used to be, it felt better. She had mirror therapy occasionally for the phantom pain, which involved holding up a full-length mirror to her left leg so that she would see two legs when she looked down. Her brain would register this as her still having two legs and send signals as it usually did, relieving pain. I didn't totally understand it but was fascinated that it worked.

Her wound healed nicely, though it took a while due to diabetes slowing down the process. As soon as it was done healing, she had a fitting for her prosthetic leg. Today the doctor was going to show us how to use it, though she was not looking forward to learning another, well, anything.

"Sherri, here we are!" the doctor exclaimed, holding what was to be her new right leg in his hand. He handed it her way, and she took it slowly, examining it.

"Neat, huh?" he started. "So, here's how this guy works," he said, and slipped a sock over her now stump, followed by a rubber brace-like thing. "You slip the inside of the leg over the rubber brace and then turn the rubber down over the leg to hold it in place."

"Wow," my mom said. "This is weird. I haven't had two feet in a long time."

The doctor laughed and asked her to stand up on it. She asked to wait until physical therapy to do that. After some arguing, the doctor finally agreed. She wasn't ready, and was very scared.

"Okay, let's try the slide board instead then," the doctor said as he took out a rectangular piece of wood with a glossy finish. "This can help you transfer from your wheelchair to any other chair by just sliding on it instead of having to stand up at all. You just stick one side of it under you far enough to feel that you are on it at least partway, and set the other side onto the other chair or surface you want to move to. What do you think?"

"That's awesome," she said. "But I still want to practice in physical therapy."

The doctor laughed. "You drive a hard bargain."

One week later, she sent us a picture that her physical therapist had taken of her standing up on her prosthetic leg between a set of parallel bars to hang on to. She had tears streaming down her face. This was her fourth time learning how to walk as an adult. The ethereal presence presented me with an overwhelming feeling of letting go to fully experiencing the joy from the sorrow and the good. Whatever it was, it was sticking around. I didn't mind.

CHAPTER 100

December 18, 2015, 4:56 P.M.

MY JOB HAD been increasingly stressful back in October, as I was covering indefinitely for one therapist who had quit while still completing my case management duties as well. It was all I had space for in my brain. I got home after work and flopped onto the couch daily, and I wasn't going to see my parents as much as I wanted to. I had little social life outside of work, and still felt pulled in many directions. After a lot of thought, I quit my job at the eating disorder hospital and took a job at an outpatient medication-assisted treatment center for folks struggling with addiction. I hoped the decreasing level of care from inpatient to outpatient would be helpful for my soul. And my burnout rate.

My dad called, and I lazily answered from my couch. "Hey, Dad," I said, yawning.

"Hey, kid, what are you up to?" he asked pointedly.

"I'm just relaxing. This new job and its 6:00 a.m. start time are nuts!"

"Yeah, I bet," he sighed. "I never was one for early mornings."

"Yeah, me either," I said. "What's up?"

"Well, the stupidest thing," he began. "You know how we

got that bedside commode for mom to use her slide board to get on and off in our room?"

"Yeah," I said cautiously.

"Well, Mom was transferring onto it, and her slide board fell. She fell too—and broke her other hip," he stated, angrily.

"What? She fell two feet and broke a hip?" I asked, feeling awful for her.

"Yeah, I know," he said. "It's crazy, and she's so weak. We're at MCR now, and they have to do surgery. Same as the other hip."

"Oh, my gosh, Dad," I was quiet. "I don't even know what to say."

"I know," he said. "Me either."

"How is she?" I asked, knowing the answer already.

"Exactly as you'd suspect. In pain, disappointed, and a mess."

"Yep, that is exactly how I suspected. So, another Christmas in the hospital this year?"

"We really have a special knack for that, don't we?" he said. "Let's get Chinese this year."

"Sounds perfect, Dad, absolutely perfect."

CHAPTER 101

February 14, 2016, 10:30 A.M.

"DO YOU GUYS think you can come to the show this afternoon?" I asked hopefully.

"Yes, of course," my dad answered. "We wouldn't miss it!" I had my doubts about my mom but was excited that they would try.

I had gotten involved in a church theater musical at Individuation's urging and had loved meeting new people and fellow musical theater nerds. It was an original, ridiculous show, but the right kind of campy ridiculous I loved. My mom was going to bring her portable oxygen, and Mat and Brooks were going to drive them down together. I was hoping my mom would be okay throughout the show. Sitting for that long in the car was hard on her.

They made it just fine and were in the almost-front row for the show. Carol met them there, and surprised me, too. It was fun to have them in the audience and fun to be in a musical again. I hadn't done a show in years.

Near the end, my brother left suddenly, and I noticed my mom nodding off. It was hard to concentrate on stage, and I hoped she was okay. As soon as the show ended, I booked it outside to find them. They were loading my mom back into Mat's Ford F150.

"Hi, guys, what's wrong?" I asked.

My mom stuck her hand out and squeezed mine. "You were great, hon!" she said loopily. She was high. Very high.

"She was in pain and took two pain meds at intermission. She ran out of oxygen toward the end and had trouble staying awake; we were glad the show ended when it did so we could come replace it," my dad said.

"Sorry I missed the last part of the show," Mat said. "I had to come get the truck."

"It's okay," I said, hugging them all goodbye.

"Thanks so much for coming down," I said, wishing they could stay and see more of my world. But they couldn't. Chronic illness only had room for its own world.

CHAPTER 102

June 9, 2016, 8:32 A.M.

I HEARD MY phone ring . . . once . . . twice . . . three times in a row. That was never good. I rolled over sleepily and looked. It was Mat. And my mom. I called Mat back first.

"Hey, what's up?" I said, half-awake, when he answered.

"Good morning," he said. "Have you talked to mom yet?"

"What's wrong now?" I asked.

"Mom called and said that Dad got up in the middle of the night because his blood sugar was low. He went to get a pop out of the garage but fainted and fell down the stairs, hitting his head on the concrete and cracking his head open. She said he was gone for over an hour, and when he came back to bed, there was blood everywhere. She cleaned him up as best she could with her limited mobility and begged him to go to the ER, but he insisted on going to sleep. She said he's got a three-inch gash in his head. When he woke up this morning, he seemed out of it. He won't answer his phone or the house phone, and she doesn't currently know where he is."

I was shocked. "What?! What do you mean she doesn't know where he is?"

"I told you it was a good morning," he said with a nervous

281

laugh. "She thinks he's outside."

"Oh. How the hell did he wake up after that?" I said aloud. "He is so lucky!"

"I know," Mat said. "He is."

"So, are you going over there?" I asked.

"Well, that's the reason for the call. Jen and I are already in Denver for the day. Do you think you could head up there if you aren't busy?"

I was busy but told him I'd see what I could do. I hung up to answer my mom's incoming call before I could call her back.

"Hi, Mom. Are you okay?" I asked, switching the conversation over on my phone.

"No. Dad fell last night and lost a lot of blood. He is not willing to go into the doctor, but he really needs to go."

"Yeah, this sounds bad," I said, finally able to feel my limbs again after their initial numbing with bad news. "Where is he now?"

"He's outside, I think, but he won't answer his phone. Hold on a sec . . . " I could hear the house phone ringing in the background.

"Hello," my mom answered. "Oh, good, okay, thank you so much Shannon. Please tell him I love him," I heard her say.

When she came back to my call, she sounded much more at ease. "Dad went next door to Shannon's, and she is going to take him to the ER now."

"Oh, good," I said. "Do you need me to do anything?"

"No," she answered. "I'll let you know what happens."

"Okay, thanks, Mom," I said, beginning to thaw the rest of the way out and into my tears. "Hang in there and call me if you need to."

"Yeah, you too" was her worried reply before we hung up. This wasn't good.

Two hours later, my dad called to report that he was

fine. "Just a little cut and a four-foot streak of blood in the garage from where I fainted." I told him I thought we had different definitions of the word "fine." He said he had eight staples in his head, and that the doctor didn't think he had a concussion. "They don't really know why I woke up when my sugar dipped so low after I fell, but I did," he said. "I guess I got lucky."

"Well, I'd say that's an understatement, Dad." I said, exhaling. "I'm really glad you're okay."

CHAPTER 103
August 19, 2016, 4:32 P.M.

MY DAD AND I were having margaritas at Amanda's Fonda, a favorite restaurant in Colorado Springs we had frequented many times before on our travels. He had asked me to come with him to get his BiPap machine fixed, as it was no longer sold corporately. He found a repair shop in the Springs, and we made an overnight of it, getting some neighbors to care for my mom. It was a wonderful getaway.

My dad was mesmerized by space, and he passed that captivation onto me. We were fascinated by the expanse of creation, the intricacy of the way the world and its inhabitants interacted just so, by the awe of being connected to something bigger, and by the wonder of the stars. This solidified his faith in God, and we had spent hours talking about philosophy, creation, theology, and science, and the possibility of God and the Universe weaving him and herself through it all.

One of my favorite things to do with my dad was to stay up late talking about the latest books we were reading and the new things we were thinking and learning. This trip was no different. The past few years had not been easy, and since then we had both been reading more about faith, growth, grief, having faith in both the good times and the bad, and what meaning and beauty can come from suffering. After health complications forever altered our family, we both grew, stretched, broke in half, and came out changed somehow. Different. Cracked. But just enough to let the light in.

Digging into existential angst for answers led us deeper into compassion for others and authenticity. And what we learned piece by piece was that though we could never make the uncertain certain, we could become okay with the mystery continuing to unfold in our lives, in our stories, and in the wonder and awe perpetuating what was to come. I so admired my dad for his wrestling match with his faith, as it made him stronger and more real. Talking with him gave us both new eyesight to see the incredible things we did have and know, especially when it was hardest.

We stayed up late talking.

"I don't know, Lish," he said. "I think things will go one way, and then they take a completely opposite turn. Good and bad things. I just can't fully understand why the suffering has continued for so long. What is the point of watching it all? Is it to recognize my own powerlessness? Is it for Mom to recognize hers? I know she gets it, so if that's the case, I cry 'uncle!'," he said, half kidding. "I am very grateful that Mom and I have had such a lucky life so far. We have been able to travel a lot, do what we want in retirement, move to Colorado to pursue our dream, and be around our grandson more. Maybe this whole thing is a lesson in gratitude and holding onto it every day because you don't know how long you have."

"Yeah, I like that explanation, Dad. What I can't make sense of is how to find redemption in suffering. If God or the universe or the Godiverse is supposed to redeem everything, I can't see it in this one. I'm trying to further understand that true joy includes the good and the bad but suffering with no motion toward growth or meaning is falling flat for me. And Mom has had so much suffering. I just feel myself becoming more bitter and sad. I can't find the point, and I'm growing tired of looking. Mom doesn't seem to be learning things through this other than she can be hurt at any time and so should be scared of everything. I hope there's more, but I can't see it."

My dad sighed heavily. "She is struggling to understand what her takeaways could be too, and she is starting to question God more about 'Why her?' which can get tricky to avoid falling into a victim mentality. But I don't blame her. She has had such a rough road."

"I know," I said. "I just hate to see her living with so much fear all the time, and if I'm honest, I hate that I am too. It has affirmed for me the need for something bigger in my life, as that's the only thing big enough to help me through the incredible anxiety I feel these days. I see Mom wanting the same, but she can't find it. It is really discouraging to watch. It seems that every time she tries to trust recovery, something else happens, and she just gets more afraid. That can't be what the Godiverse wants, can it? To be scared of everything?"

"No, it can't be," he answered simply.

"Then what could God want from this?" I asked. The question hung in the air unanswered. Neither of us had any idea.

Before long, it was well past midnight, and we were so very tired. We vowed to sleep in in the morning.

And we did. After a (very) late breakfast, we visited the science and space museum, the closest thing we could find to a planetarium. My dad held reverence for the expanse of the unknown being part of the Godiverse's big picture somehow, though at times it was couched in mystery. He consistently reminded me that faith is a journey and to never give up. I needed this reminder.

FOUR EYES

Once done at the museum, we headed over to the BiPap repair place and picked up his machine, good as new. He drove me back up to Denver, hugged me goodbye, and headed home before dark, as his eyes were getting increasingly cloudy. He had recently had a blood vessel in his left eye cauterized to slow the cloud from taking over his vision, and it made it harder for him to see in the dark.

CHAPTER 104
September 22, 2016, 3:13 P.M.

THE NEW REALITY of my life was currently exhausting. It was a pace I could not sustain. Work was intense and just as busy as my previous job. I knew that I had to change something soon. My aunts had called last week to tell us of my grandpa's fall off a ladder in his kitchen, landing him in surgery and eventually a nursing home. He had a brain bleed and was now in hospice. Mat and I were designated to represent our family and go to Michigan for his final days and the funeral. It was a tall order, and I was devastated. My emotions had been in a pressure cooker, and they finally all shot out at once.

My sad, tired, and defeated feelings of witnessing what had happened to my parents over the last few years as well as listening to my clients' struggles could only sit for so long. And now my grandpa was dying? I was so empty. I had nothing left. Numbly, I took a week off from work.

Mat and I road-tripped out and were able to say our goodbyes to my grandpa, arriving two days before he passed. It was so sad to watch my once very strong grandpa lying in a bed, unconscious, weak, and helpless. Hospice nurses came every day and slowly increased his pain medication.

Eventually, his heart could not take it, and it stopped. It was a horrific glimpse into what felt very much like euthanasia for humans. I remained numb.

We spent a week there, helping my aunts any way we could, and they amazingly put together a funeral in the time we were there so that we could attend. We went to the condo where my grandparents lived, and it brought back a flood of memories of my childhood. I called my parents from a bathroom inside and cried with them on the phone.

"It is sad, Lish," my parents consoled me from afar. "You can cry as much as you want."

My mom was crying too. She had been able to say her last goodbyes to her dad when one of my aunts held the phone up to his ear. She was feeling very guilty that she could not attend in person, and her shame seed was blaming herself.

My grandma had been living in a memory care unit of an assisted living home for the past few years as her dementia worsened. She was able to come to my grandpa's funeral with a staff member from the home, and it was both great and sad to see her. My grandma recognized my aunts still, but not Mat or me. When she erupted in laughter during the funeral for no apparent reason, her attendant wheeled her out of the service, adding another layer of sadness to my tears. She briefly recognized my grandpa's picture on the front of the memorial program, but we were all unsure of how much she understood. There was plenty to cry about.

The rest of the funeral was beautiful and an amazing testimony to my grandpa's life and legacy. It wasn't until it ended that his words to my dad that "the caregiver always dies first" flooded my brain with an eerie chill. In this case, he was right. I wondered if my dad had thought about that yet. Mat and I left the funeral to make it back home for Brooks's sixth birthday the next day.

CHAPTER 105

October 8, 2016, 3:34 P.M.

"HEY, KID," **MY** dad said. "I hate to bug you, but I have this back pain that won't quit, and I need you to take me to the hospital."

At a fall festival with some friends, I instantly turned on my heel when I heard this and started back toward my car.

"Oh, no, what's going on?" I asked.

"Oh, I don't know; I just can't stand up. You know how much I hate asking for help, but Mat and Jen are in Mexico on vacation, and I think I need some help."

"Absolutely, Dad," I said. "I'll be on my way in a few."

"Thanks, kid," he said before he hung up.

I filled my friends in on the situation and left for Loveland. They kindly consoled me and sent me off with a third of the caramel apple slices we had just jointly bought.

When I arrived, my mom was asleep and my dad was almost to the front door, crawling down the hallway.

"Dad, what is happening?" I asked, throwing my purse down. "Can I help you?"

"Look, kid; I made it this far!" He was so proud.

"Can you walk at all?" I asked, assessing this reality.

"Not really; it just really hurts," he said.

"Do you want to use mom's wheelchair?" I asked.

"No, I can do it," he insisted.

I had no chance in the stubborn department.

We managed to get him in the car somehow, and he reclined the seat to lie down on the way. When we got there, I asked him to wait while I got a wheelchair. When I returned with one, he was already using my mom's walker and halfway up the walk.

"Dad, take it easy!" I said. "Here, sit."

He wouldn't and kept going.

The ER wasn't very busy, and we were able to get into a room right away. My dad lay on the bed, and we began talking about the upcoming election and the reality show star that had become a party nominee.

The nurse came in, followed by the doctor, and we went through the same routine we had done with my mom a thousand times before. The doctor ordered an MRI, and the nurse took us back to the machine. I had texted neighbor Lisa to see if she could be with my mom and updated her with the current situation. Twenty minutes later, my dad was out; we went back to our original room to wait on the results.

"Well," the doctor said, walking in while looking at the scans, "you have some herniated discs in your low back, and they are pretty nasty."

"Oh, good," my dad said, his cynicism pouring out. "What does this mean?"

"Well, I definitely want to refer you to a low-back specialist for a second opinion, but I know that with these injuries, it takes time, time, time. Fifty percent of back surgeries on discs that low don't work, so it's a really hard call to make on how to proceed."

"Well, I'm not a big fan of surgery, so what's my other option?" my dad asked.

"Rest and pain management with medication," the doctor

said. "For as long as it takes. Sometimes, up to ten months."

The news hit me like a brick, sharp and unexpected. What were we going to do with both of them struggling to move and care for themselves? With both of them high on pain meds? This is a nightmare, I thought.

"Oh, awesome," my dad said sarcastically. "I kind of have to care for someone full-time, so what do we do with that situation?"

"Well, that makes it harder, but if you don't get better, you can't care for anyone else," the doctor replied, as if it were just that easy. Maybe it was? I couldn't tell anymore. "I want you to get that second opinion before we make too many plans, but you may want to look into in-home care for a bit," the doctor said, looking at me. I nodded.

"Okay," my dad answered. "Can I get anything for the pain right now?"

"Absolutely," the doctor said and returned with some meds in addition to prescriptions for more.

I sighed heavily. How was this going to go? I made a mental note to call on in-home care in the morning, and we started the long process of getting my dad back in the car to go home.

CHAPTER 106

October 9, 2016, 11:00 A.M.

I HAD SPENT the night to make sure my dad was okay, and to care for my mom. My dad white-knuckled it through his pain on the way home and was somehow able to make it into bed. I had dropped him off, gotten him into bed, and gone to get his prescriptions. He began his journey with opioids as soon as I returned. I shook my head in disbelief. What were the chances they'd both be in this state simultaneously?

My mom wanted to care for herself as much as possible so she could help my dad, but she could hardly move. Mat would be back from Mexico late tonight, and I would run some of my ideas by him tomorrow. I had spent the morning researching in-home care companies and had left a message at a few different organizations.

One of the agencies called me back later in the afternoon, and, after talking with them extensively, I hired them. They would be here tomorrow morning to help with whatever my folks needed. I relaxed a little and created an instruction guide for the company so I knew they'd be getting the right information. The kind my mom used to make for Sniff's sitters. It felt weird to do it for people. Even weirder to do for my parents.

My dad's back pain was significant, and he slept for most of the day. My mom was up off and on, and I told her the plan. She was on board.

Nervously, I left them in Lisa's care late that night to be able to go back to work tomorrow, with a plan to call them in the morning to see how it all was working out. Mat and Jen would be by tomorrow. I hoped this plan would be okay, and dove into the uncertainty at full speed.

CHAPTER 107

October 11, 2016, 2:32 P.M.

THE PLAN WAS working, and the in-home agency was straight from the Godiverse. I was elated. They had helped my parents make meals, get up and down as they could, get dressed, and get the right medications. My dad was now rivaling my mom's twenty-two meds with twenty-one of his own since his back diagnosis. It was unreal.

I saw "home" pop up on my phone screen and debated hard about answering. I was at work, so behind, and I had a client in twenty minutes. So often, these phone calls pulled me out of my life and into an unfolding puzzle, and I wanted to try to preserve my headspace as best I could while at work. Something inside told me to answer, so I did.

It was my dad. He was as high as a kite and feeling no pain at all. I was happy for him in that way. He had a question for me.

"Hey, babes, do you have my credit card?" he asked after we exchanged pleasantries.

"No, I don't think so," I said. "You're missing your card?"

"Well, it's not in my wallet, and I can't find it, so yes, I guess it's officially missing," he replied. "Unless the helpers took it to get groceries last night," he wondered aloud slowly as if the dots were beginning to connect.

This version of my dad was silly. I smiled as I entertained the conversation.

"Oh, well, that's a thought. Maybe check with them when they come back tonight?" I said.

"Yeah, I'll do that. Just check with them!" he echoed excitedly.

"How are you feeling, Pops?" I asked. I had called the back specialist for a second opinion, and they told me the soonest availability he had was seven weeks from now. That was too long, and I was searching for another doctor who could give another opinion.

"I am feeling soooooooooo, soooooooooo, soooooooooooooooooo," he dragged it out forever, "much better! These pain meds are miracle workers!"

"I'm so glad to hear it, Dad." I laughed.

"Yeah, have no fear, Mighty Mouse is here!" he said, emphatically increasing in volume as the phrase continued.

I busted out laughing. This only seemed to egg him on. He burst into the Lone Ranger theme song and ended with a strong "Mighty Mouse to the rescue!"

By now we were both laughing hysterically, and I could hear my mom snoring away in the background. After another minute, I noticed the time. I had to go.

"Okay, Pops; I have to go back to work, but tell Mom I said hi. I'll call you again later, okay?"

"O-kay-do-kay," he spelled out each syllable. "I love youuuuuuuuu," he sang as his exit.

"I love you too, Dad," I said as the clock turned to the hour. It had been twenty minutes, and my client was here. "Bye," I said as I hung up.

That made my day.

CHAPTER 108

October 12, 2016, 7:34 A.M.

I CAME BACK into my room from the bathroom half-dressed to two missed calls—one from Mat and one from home. I called Mat first. No answer. As his phone was ringing, I felt my voicemail alert buzz. I clicked on it and listened next. It was a police officer.

"Hi, Alisha. This is Officer Davis from the Loveland Police Department. I'm sorry to leave this in a message, but I'm calling to let you to let you know that your dad has suffered a medical emergency; you need to call your brother back as soon as possible."

My entire body hit the floor and I started shaking. I dialed Mat again. No answer. I called home. No answer.

My roommate Jen heard me thud onto the floor and came to check if I was okay. I filled her in, slowly, as I found my words and stood back up to get dressed the rest of the way and to gather what I needed. I hated being an hour away.

Mat called back.

"Hi, what's happening?" I said.

"I don't know," he said. I'm on my way there now. I got a call from Officer Davis, but she wouldn't tell me anything. Just that it's an emergency and that Mom is okay but couldn't talk. Lisa is there, I guess, with Mom."

"Is he okay? She wouldn't tell you?" I said, adrenaline kicking in.

"No, but she said they are taking him to McKee. I'm almost there; I will call you when I talk to Mom."

"Okay, I'm on my way," I said. I pulled on a hoodie and flew out the door.

I started my car and took off. I was speeding, but every time I looked at the odometer, it had barely moved.

Halfway there, Mat called back.

"I'm with Mom and she's fine. They are working on Dad," he said. "Something happened with his heart. Just drive safely up here and be careful."

"Okay," I said and switched into task mode. I called work and told the office manager what was happening. She was a calming woman and talked me into a slower pace and some deep breaths.

I called Mat back for specific directions to McKee, as I had only been there a few times and wasn't thinking clearly.

"Do you know anything else? What happened? How is he?" Mat's silence gave it all away.

"He's gone, Lish," he said finally, through his own tears. "They tried everything, but they couldn't get him back."

"What?!" I shouted. "No! This can't be happening."

My eyes blurred with hot, stinging tears. I vaguely heard Mat's response. "Lish, breathe, and drive safely; that's the number-one concern right now. Focus on the road or pull over for a second if you need to. You're almost here." Mat coached me through.

I inhaled as deeply as I could and focused on the road as I wound my way into the lot of the hospital.

"I'm out front when you get here," he said, and we hung up.

I saw him as I parked, and he waved. I got out of the car, totally numb, and made my way toward Mat. He hugged me and I broke. I was ugly crying and snotting all over.

"I know, I know," he said. We walked inside together, and he was crying too. He led me back to the room my dad was in, lying on a table. A nurse came to meet me as I saw him through the glass doors, pale, with a ventilator tube sticking out of his mouth. I crumpled, and the nurse caught me before I hit the floor. She was stroking my head and telling me to let it out. After a long while, I stood up and inched closer to the room's entrance. My mom was inside, sobbing in her wheelchair. I looked back at the nurse and told her this wasn't supposed to happen, that he was my best friend. She hugged me again, and my tears soaked through everything. I was numb, in shock. I slowly made my way into the room.

"Lish," my mom cried as I went to hug her and broke down again. We all stood around his body, crying for a really long time, speechless. The doctors told us we could stay as long as we wanted. My dad had a cut on his forehead, and a little blood was coming out. He was in a hospital gown. Eventually, I wanted to know more.

"Mom, what happened?" I asked her. She relayed her story through a waterfall of tears.

"Dad got up to go to the bathroom and then just fell over backward. I tried to get to him, but my boot got stuck in the sheets. I kept fighting them until I rolled halfway out of bed and couldn't go anymore. I found my phone in the sheet pile and called Lisa to come over and then 9-1-1. It was probably ten minutes before I could get to my phone, and he wasn't responding. Lisa got there, and then the ambulance, and they said they were working on him." She sobbed.

"It's okay, Mom. I'm so sorry," I consoled her.. "So, so sorry. That had to be so scary."

Mat continued and said the doctors told him that it was most likely over before the paramedics even got there, that he went quickly.

This made me feel somewhat better—both that he had not suffered long and also that my mom didn't have to feel guilty for her response time. I hoped it relieved her. I could only imagine how traumatizing that was for her. Lisa peeked her head in and asked about dialysis, and only then did I realize that Brooks had been with Lisa this whole time. Mat had mentioned it on the phone as I was driving, but I had forgotten.

"I'm so sorry, guys," she offered rubbing all of our backs. "Hey, Brooks and I are coloring around the corner, and I just wanted to offer to take you to dialysis today, Sherri?" she said, wiping tears from her eyes.

My mom started crying again. "I don't want to go to dialysis today," she said. Everyone understood. After a lot of talking, she agreed that it was probably better for her to stay on schedule so that she wouldn't get any sicker.

When it was time to leave my dad, we all took turns saying our goodbyes to his body, and Mat got his wedding ring off his finger. I hugged his gray, coldish body, crying and thanking him for being him. I left my mom to have her time last.

A few minutes later, we overheard her cry-yelling. "Why, Butch; why did you go? You weren't supposed to go! Why?" Mat and I went back in and consoled her until she was ready, choking back tears of our own. Mat wheeled her out, and I snuck a final look and told my dad how much I loved him. We walked back to where Lisa and Brooks were— Brooks was coloring a picture.

Mat had to tell Brooks what had happened, and he did it with the eloquence needed to convey the concept of death to a six-year-old.

"Buddy," Mat began, "you know how Great-grandpa just went to heaven, where he isn't hurting anymore?"

We were all crying.

"Yea," he said, confused.

"Well, Grandpa went there today too," he said. "Grandpa's heart was hurt, and the doctors couldn't fix it."

I wondered how Brooks would make sense of this when, just last week, my dad had picked him up from school and they had gone to the gas station to get "a cold pop," which was their "thing."

Mat continued, "Grandpa loves you so much, buddy; he wishes he could stay with you here, but he had to go." Mat's strong voice cracked.

"Okay," Brooks said sadly, "but I don't want him to go."

"I know, buddy, I know," Mat said as he hugged his son. "Me either."

When Mat let go, Brooks tightly squeezed a teddy bear a police officer had given him this morning. Brooks named him Grandpa Bear.

My heart broke for Brooks and my dad's relationship. It was so cherished by both of them, and the thought of my dad never getting to interact with Brooks again was devastating. Brooks hugged my mom and showed her Grandpa Bear and started to show us the pictures he had colored. We were trying hard to pay attention.

Finally, Lisa took my mom to dialysis. Mat had to go back to work for a meeting with his boss, and I took Brooks to school. I hated that the world still turned when mine had skidded to such an abrupt halt. As I drove away from Brooks's school, a shiver went up my spine as I remembered my grandpa's famous joke. The caregiver had indeed died first. Again.

I felt something break inside me, and knew it was irreparable.

CHAPTER 109
October 15, 2016, 11:00 A.M.

I HAD ALL the feels and needed to sideline them to plan for my dad's funeral. There were so many things to do, and yet doing anything right now was nearly impossible. The coroner ruled my dad's death a "massive cardiac event" based on the direction he fell when it happened. I remembered having the organ donation conversation about my mom as a family, but we hadn't even considered discussing it for my dad. His wishes had been clear since I was a kid. We were to donate any organ and tissue that were still good to others who could use them, and then donate the rest of his body to science. It was that simple. Knowing it with my head was one thing. Grasping it with my heart was completely different. Though I knew it was the right move, I was feeling protective of his body and wanted to preserve him for as long as possible just in case this wasn't actually reality.

My mom was not coping well, and I stepped in to coordinate many things that were too hard for her, including the body donation. It was something I knew my dad would be so proud of, and that brought a small ray of hope to the overwhelming sadness that moved through me.

I had found an amazing therapist in Denver, and she

called to walk me through any feelings I could find so that I wouldn't pressure-cooker explode again. I was staying at my parents' house for the time being. Right in the middle of the storm. I took solace in my therapist's calming voice and her years of experience working with hospice. She understood without my needing to explain it. I needed her to get through whatever was ahead.

I found Science Care online and told the hospital that my dad wanted to donate his body to them. The next day, they called to ask my mom a bunch of questions about my dad's health history. I picked up the phone as well, to help if needed. About halfway through the call, my mom started checking out and answering questions incorrectly. I heard her put the phone in her lap when Lisa came over, and I went over to hang it up. She was not well.

The conversation was jarring. They asked many questions about my dad's sex life to make sure his blood was not infectious to anyone working on the research they were conducting, and I tried to hold it together for as long as I could. As soon as I hung up, I went out onto the deck, looked at the mountains, and screamed. Dr. Witchel's words came back to me as I sobbed. Was this really me "coming together"? I just felt myself scattering more and more.

Mat furthered his financial and legal knowledge of what needed to happen now, and my mom and I handled many of the funeral plans. Mat joined us for a family conference with a pastor at my parents' current church who would be conducting my dad's funeral. After the pastor left, Mat asked about my dad's ashes. I filled him in. After Science Care completed their research, they would return my dad's remains via the post office. The box would be clearly marked as human remains, and I was to pick them up in three weeks as if it were any other package.

CHAPTER 110
October 25, 2016, 3:00 P.M.

MANY PEOPLE HAD flown in for my dad's funeral, including my friend Mandy from college. I was so glad I had a friend to be with during it all. I definitely needed one. The day was finally here, and most of the tasks were complete. Pastor Dan, who was conducting the funeral, was so kind, and he facilitated the whole thing beautifully. My mom also paid Pastor James from their Israel trip to offer some words. Aunt Janet and Aunt Patti were back, and several members of the Men's Group came to speak on my dad's behalf. I also spoke and had stayed up late the night before finishing my speech. I was tired, and my mom wasn't feeling well, which wasn't a good sign. She and I had been crying on and off for weeks now, and it was hard to differentiate the source.

It was a gut-wrenchingly painful yet beautiful service. One of my dad's oldest friends from college arrived out of the blue and cheered my mom up by reminiscing. But not for long.

Carol took my mom straight to the hospital from the funeral, where she was diagnosed with a urinary tract infection that needed more treatment. This was brutal. Where was the Godiverse now?

CHAPTER 111
November 13, 2016, 6:54 P.M.

MY MOM HAD needed additional care over the past few weeks, and I took FMLA (family and medical leave) from my job to move in with her and help. It was a long stay, and I experienced the full extent of caregiving that my dad had lived every day for the past few years. It was very confining. I was consistently sad for my mom and for myself, and I knew I couldn't live with her forever if I was ever going to continue my life. Again, I wanted to find a way to do both. Balance felt elusive.

Mat had begun looking into skilled nursing homes to see what options existed for my mom. He found a promising one near his house and arranged for her to move in at the beginning of November.

She was grieving the loss of her dad, her husband, and now her house. I felt for her so deeply, and Guilt and Individuation continued to rival within me. I wanted to help, and yet I knew I couldn't live with her like my dad had been doing. It was too much, too constant, and she needed more help than I could give her. It literally killed my dad to try on his own. And even still, Guilt had a field day with my "selfishness."

As she settled into her new surroundings, she set the goal of getting well enough to live in an adjoining assisted living building so she could get a therapy dog. This carried her forward. I loved that she had a drive for this, but I questioned the actuality of her being well enough to make that move. I called daily, drove up north to visit her, and brought her things she needed. She usually had a list waiting for me.

Mat visited much more often, as the facility was very close to his house. She liked it there but was very lonely. This broke our hearts. We didn't know what else to do. The last few times I went to visit her, I noticed her gaining more water weight and puffing out more and more, even after her dialysis sessions. Mat and I were concerned and called the dialysis clinic. I missed my dad so much in instances like this. We all did.

We arranged for her to continue attending the dialysis center in Loveland instead of transferring her to one closer to her facility in an effort to keep her as stable as possible amid all the changes. She had been denied the possibility of a kidney transplant a while back; she couldn't pass the required strength tests, and she was mourning that blow as well. The dialysis team had called back early yesterday.

"Alisha, hi. Yes, we want to connect about your mom. We have some news we want to discuss."

We arranged a meeting for this morning. When Mat and I arrived, there were many more people there than we had anticipated. After we sat down, they began. They explained that my mom's dialysis was no longer working and that her liver was now starting to shut down, causing toxicity that would start to mess with her clarity and mindset. This was why she had been gaining the water weight. I asked the question hanging in the air above us all: Did this mean she would die?

Others' eyes met mine, filled with sympathy.

Yes.

It would be a supposed "peaceful" death, but nothing about this felt peaceful. My skin was hot, my eyes welled with tears, and my heart was beating at an abnormal rate. I was struggling to remain present. I was certain I was floating.

They suggested that they would tell her this news at her next dialysis appointment. We were shocked and devastated, and the hollow took over my insides again. Was this really happening? First my dad and now my mom, so close together? This was unreal, and I couldn't find the ethereal presence anywhere I looked.

Her next appointment was tomorrow, and Mat and I both spent the night wrestling with this new truth.

CHAPTER 112
November 15, 2016, 10:01 A.M.

MY PHONE BUZZED. Instinctively, I thought it was my dad before remembering that he was gone. That was happening a lot lately. It was the dialysis clinic.

"Hey, Alisha. I wanted to let you know that we just sent your mom to MCR because she was so confused when she got here. She was calling us all the wrong names and blowing into a sticky note, thinking it was a paper bag. I didn't want her to suffer through another dialysis that isn't working," she reported gently. "I'm so sorry." She was crying. "We love your mom so much here."

"Thanks," I said. "I know you guys do. Thanks for everything you've done to help us out."

"Of course, sweetie," she said and hung up.

I called Mat. Back to MCR we go.

CHAPTER 113

November 16, 2016, 6:15 P.M.

THE NEPHROLOGISTS HAD come to talk with my mom both yesterday and today and laid out her options moving forward. Option one was to be hooked up to a dialysis machine for eight hours a day for the rest of her life, which, with that treatment, could be a month or two. The other option was death. Of course, she chose life. And as the toxicity and water weight continued to build, she became less and less lucid. Mat and I had her medical power of attorney authorization and were now responsible for making all her medical decisions. This was a terrible ending to a terrible fight. I was becoming increasingly more bitter. Every ounce of me hated this. We were completely in the middle.

Mat had arranged a lawyer to come and talk with my mom about her finances when she passed so that everything wouldn't end up in probate after all my dad's careful planning. Lucidity was needed, and we were running out of time.

My mom signed the required papers after sharing that she was having trouble getting out of the car and that her focaccia bread was burning in the oven. But the grand finale took the cake. "Alisha, I want to thank you for everything

Mat has done for me," she said as she put the pen down.

"You're welcome, Mom," we both said, chuckling. It was a pained moment of welcome relief.

The hospice folks came to talk with us after that and arranged a bed for my mom in their inpatient unit at McKee starting tomorrow. It was awful, knowing that my mom wanted to live; and yet the thought of buying her another month or two hooked up to a dialysis machine for eight hours a day was torturous. The skin graft over her dialysis port was in her thigh, which meant she would be reclining in a chair for eight hours a day, colder and more miserable than the four-hour sessions already were. Mat and I couldn't see how she would make it through any of that on a daily basis.

The nephrologists came to talk with her again and told her that her death would be slow and peaceful, to which she responded, "But I'm not going to die, so we don't have to worry about that." Try as they might to convince her of her fate, she continued to believe she would get better, like she had done so many times before. I didn't blame her one bit. She had survived everything life had thrown her way up until this point. Why wouldn't she believe that she would overcome this as well?

Mat and I talked to Dr. Simon as he was leaving one of those conversations.

"What do you think, doctor?" I asked him, searching for the slightest ray of hope in his answer that she could beat any of this.

"This is a really sad ending, but it is one of the most peaceful ways to go," he repeated to Mat and me.

"What about dialysis every day? What would that do?" Mat asked, on the same quest for hope.

"It would be in our lab on the fourth floor, and she would be inpatient for the rest of her life. It may extend her life a month or two, but I think it would be really hard on her mentally." He looked at us and sighed. He had seen her from the beginning. "And honestly, guys, I think her quality of life is so low as it is, that would make it even worse. But I totally understand whatever decision you make. She clearly wants to live, and I don't know how much of this she truly understands at this point."

There was no ray of hope in any of that. My tears spilled onto my face and then the floor. This was beyond awful.

"Thanks, Dr. Simon," Mat said. "We are thinking a lot about her quality of life too. There's no way dialysis for eight hours a day would do much to improve that," he said blankly.

"I agree. Hang in there, guys," Dr. Simon replied as he began to walk to his next appointment. "And I'm so sorry. Sherri is a great lady."

We nodded in agreement and looked at each other. There was really no question about next steps at this point. And we didn't know if our mom had the capacity to understand what was happening. We tried to talk with her once more.

"Hey, Mom," I tried. "How are you feeling?"

"There's a space part in the corner," she said.

"I see it," I pretended.

Mat tried. "Mom, what do you think about trying McKee out? We want you to have a good quality of life, you know? Not be stuck to some machine all day."

"Yeah, I was thinking about renting a hose for the garden," came her reply.

I hated that we held her powers of attorney. This was getting more painful by the hour.

We decided to proceed with hospice.

CHAPTER 114
November 24, 2016, 4:00 P.M.

HOSPICE AT MCKEE was a unit of around ten beds or so through a set of white double doors. It was sad, and when you saw others there, you instantly felt their pain. My mom had been here now for eight days and had fallen into more and more of a deep sleep state. This afternoon, Brooks had come to visit, and my mom's only lucid statement in two days was "I love you, Brooks," to him before she fell back asleep. It was beautifully sad.

I was sleeping on the twin bed next to my mom's bed in her room and had been since she transitioned to McKee. I desperately didn't want her to die alone. I didn't want her to die at all, but I was trying to make peace with it as best I could.

CHAPTER 115

November 26, 2016, 10:09 A.M.

"ALISHA?" SHE CALLED softly. I vaguely heard her gentle tone enter my consciousness.

"Alisha, honey?"

I groaned in recognition and rolled onto my side as I smiled widely. I was elated, still half in my dream.

"Alisha, sweetheart, is your brother on his way?"

My bleary morning eyes squinted up from my bed at the figure as her purple-and-green scrubs came into focus.

"Um . . . ," I trailed off, looking around the room. Where is Sniff? I thought. She's always here. But today my faithful, furry friend of twelve years was not in my room. My dad must have taken her outside, I thought, as was their morning routine. My dad was probably up late again, reading one of his crime mysteries or philosophical posits, his kind, deep brown eyes housing the collected wisdom. He had begrudgingly come to accept that Sniff would wake him up each morning to go outside, regardless of his bedtime. He would stiffly bend over each morning, pet her thick gray-and-silver fur, and feign anger. She would wag her curly tail at him, knowing he did indeed really love her.

I gripped the sides of the bed and hoisted my weary

body into a seated position. My hands didn't recognize the scratchy bedding between my fingers, and suddenly I was aware of an ache in my lower back.

"Alisha, it's getting close, honey. I didn't want to wake you, but I think you should call your brother."

Suddenly, and without warning, the memories came back, each one slamming into my recall a bit faster than the last, like a ten-car pileup on black ice. I was currently in my mom's room at McKee. Sniff, my daily companion throughout the medical nightmare of the last years, wasn't here because she had died two years ago on Christmas Eve. My head kept pounding with the realization of more truths as I winced my way awake.

I looked around the room. It was mostly the same as they all were, minus the mind-numbing beeps of machines and mazes of tubes in the ICU that reminded me constantly that everything was not okay. Hospice was different. It was bland, ordinary, not memorable or forgettable, just there. The walls held the disappointment of decline for millions of loved ones between the many layers of beige paint.

My mom would have had a field day with this place. She was a born creative and would see how to make everything feel homey and comfortable in just a few moments. She would welcome anyone into the space with warm conversation, some peppermint oil diffusing, and genuine interest in who you were. I imagined her decorating the drab walls with a few of her dried-flower art pieces and outlining the floor with painted cement rhubarb leaves in black wrought-iron stands. She would have delicately transformed the room into her warm aesthetic, donning the fused glass jewelry she had made, inspired by the last craft show we attended.

God, those craft shows. How many times had we hauled those cement leaves into and out of those buildings, excited about a few sales? How many times had they been kicked or knocked over with a cane by accident and broken? I giggled softly to myself, remembering my dad's standing comment when that would happen: "Well, one less to carry!"

My backache traveled to my neck as I looked down to stretch. The scratchy bedding was unrecognizable because it wasn't mine. I wasn't home. My body was aching because this was the ninth night in a row that I hadn't slept in my own bed. At least in hospice, it was an actual bed.

"Alisha?" the nurse asked again, dread sinking in with each syllable.

I stared at the sterile cabinets next to the door. Another bland color to represent the unknown, I thought. The nurse cleared her throat.

"I'll call him," I said, and reached for my phone.

The nurse's sweet demeanor was noticeably impacted as she gave me the look I'd come to see so much of over the last five years. The look of empty sorrow, hopelessness, and deep sympathy protecting the fear that lay beneath. The look that communicated it all. Something big was about to happen, and the owner of the glance was damn glad it wasn't about to happen to her. Ugh; I had become so bitter.

Mat arrived with breakfast shortly after I called him. An hour later, my mom was gone.

CHAPTER 116
November 28, 2016, 5:31 P.M.

I GOT UP and walked to get the mail from my parents' mailbox. I still couldn't believe this was real. Both of them were gone within six weeks of each other. A part of me was so happy they were together again; a bigger part of me missed them so much and would give anything to have them still here. I turned the small key in mailbox #1 and opened it to a small stack of letters. The one on top was from the Rocky Mountain Lions Eye Bank. I opened it on my short walk back to their house.

"Dear beloved family members of Everett (Butch) Bashaw," it started. "We want to thank you for your tremendous donation of your loved one's corneas to aid those fighting corneal blindness and other diseases of the eye. Everett's corneas were recovered and successfully transplanted into two others, who are both living in southern Colorado. One is a man in his seventies, and one is a woman in her sixties. Only one cornea is donated per person, to ensure that if there is trouble with the transplant, only one cornea will need replacing. Please know how important your loved one's gift of sight is to those who have not been able to see. It is a priceless gift that came at quite a cost. Should you wish to reach out to the recipients, please see the protocol we have for that on the next sheet and understand that all communications will be filtered through the eye bank. We thank you again for your generous gift."

Wow, that's pretty cool, I thought. I had no idea what happened after donating parts of one's body. This was the first bit of meaning I had been able to register in a long time.

CHAPTER 117

December 6, 2016, 1:00 P.M.

I CRACKED OPEN a Diet Dr Pepper from my parents' fridge in honor of my dad and poured it into my glass of ice. When the foam approached the top of the glass, I shoved my face down, lips extended, to suck away the bubbles before they spilled over the glass and made a mess. My dad called this trick "quick lips," and I thought of that every time this happened. It was endearing, sweet.

It was my mom's funeral today, and again, six weeks after my dad's service, people had flown in from everywhere to attend. I was so grateful for my Aunt Patti and Aunt Janet, who helped us plan and execute the last-minute details. It was another infuriating experience of being expected to do so many things while also suffering. Systemically, this was wrong. Yet I had to partake in it in order to get through the funeral. I was going to sleep really well tonight.

My mom's friends from Michigan who couldn't make it sent recordings and letters, and Mat and Carol read them aloud. I spoke too and sang my mom's favorite song, "Blessings." I had to reach deep to both craft my eulogy and not burst into tears while singing. Aunt Patti stood behind me as backup just in case I broke down or, as Dr. Witchel put it, "came together," in front of everyone.

I was on autopilot, and my friend Elle guided me around my own experience for most of the day. I was so empty inside and didn't want to talk with anyone. Another foible in the system for the bereaved at a funeral.

After the service, Mat, Jen, and I cleaned up what we needed to, and then left.

That was it.

Now what?

CHAPTER 118
May 24, 2017, 11:00 A.M.

THE PAST SIX months had been full of so many feelings and heartaches. Everything in my world had changed. I quit my job at the beginning of the year after my FMLA ran out in order to take some time off to grieve, stop, and work on cleaning out my parents' house to get it ready to sell. It was a huge undertaking, and one I often didn't think I would survive. Mat and I continued our deal of me taking care of the day-to-day and him taking care of the finances and legalities, of which there were many now that they both were gone.

Without the help of many extremely dear people aiding me in the process, I wouldn't have been able to continue, as I got swallowed up by memories lurking everywhere in their house. In my house.

My life had become a blank slate, a confusing mess, and, most definitely, overwhelming. My sadness was growing stronger by the day, and I found myself lost in it, as though the black hole of pain I woke up with every day would take over my insides and provide me nothing but numbness for the rest of my life. I couldn't see past it, and I was struggling to catch up on processing the past years' events. So much had happened, and I was still trying to accept what was. I was scared, lonely, often triggered, and very depressed. I was a young-adult orphan who didn't know anyone else in my peer group with a shared experience, though I was grateful for the years I did have with my parents; not everyone is so lucky. It was a strange, seeming no-man's-land in between childhood and adult status, and I felt very alone. Nothing was clear, and I questioned everything about who I was now.

I felt like an alien in the world, a responsible one who could sometimes function, but an alien nonetheless. What was previously important no longer seemed relevant. The pursuit of career, relationship, success, and money that often came in the thirties was no longer of great interest. I didn't know what was of great interest though, aside from my quest to at some point find meaning in all that had happened. I knew something was different in me. Something had forever changed.

Conversations with my peers became more difficult as I realized how involved in the world of caregiving and chronic illness I had been for the past almost five years. I had missed out on a lot of life as a thirty-something. Sympathy eyes were everywhere when I did share my story, and because it was such a long story to tell, I felt Guilt's old voice of "too much" and "selfish" rear its head and often stop me from continuing when I saw the blank stares from others who had no idea what to say.

Self-pity and victimhood stood outside my door every morning. With time, I began to resist them more, but it wasn't until I truly understood how I felt changed by all of this that I began to heal. When I realized that a previous version of me had also died along with my parents, I could finally recognize my own grief at the loss of my identity in addition to how I felt about losing them. The version of me that found purpose and connection simply by being in relationship with them and interacting together was gone. I could still talk to them, sure—or maybe it was the air—but regardless, it was so different now. It was a hard blow to take, and I often cried with Individuation as we continued along the path of developing a new identity together.

In cleaning out some old papers one day, I came across my mom's letter from the Rocky Mountain Lions Eye Bank. Amid all the commotion, I had completely forgotten about it. Her corneas had been successfully transplanted into two older women in Germany.

Germany? I thought. Wow! That's really cool! And in the same way the letter about my dad's corneas struck the meaning-finding chord, so did my mom's. I couldn't help but feel somewhat uplifted that their eyes were living on, and literally helping others see. They would have loved this. I'm sure they did. Somewhere.

CHAPTER 119

August 12, 2017, 8:00 A.M.

I WAS LATE, and I desperately didn't want to be. I had responded to a Facebook ad for an event the eye bank was putting on about eye donation. I was fascinated to learn more and kicked myself for not getting up at my first alarm.

I made it to the front door at five after, and no one was there.

Dang it! I thought and tried to call the organizer of the event. There was no answer. I left a message. There were chairs lining the wall, and I sat in one of them, waiting for a plan to come to my brain. It was too early for this.

I decided to e-mail the organizer as well, and as I was crafting the e-mail, he ran through the door, looking around and apologizing for being late. I breathed a sigh of relief.

"No problem at all," I said. "I was preparing to say the same thing when I ran in!"

I liked him instantly. He was young, taller than I—but then, who wasn't—with dark hair and very kind eyes.

"I'm Colton," he said.

"Nice to meet you; I'm Alisha," I said back, shaking his extended hand.

"Well, I think you're it for today, so let's just head this

way," he said, leading me up a short flight of stairs.

"Oh, really? Were there supposed to be more?" I asked, very surprised.

"Originally, yes, but they all had to cancel, so you'll get the one-on-one tour," he joked, opening a door to an office. "So, how did you find out about this?" he asked.

I wasn't sure if he knew what he was in for as my summary tumbled out. "I'm really interested in this process and all that happens. The advertisement said it was about possibly communicating with the donor recipients too, right?" I asked.

Colton was very empathic and wanted to answer as many questions as I had. "Yes," he began as he explained the nature of today's session was part information and part learning how to communicate with either donor families or donor recipients.

I was thrilled. And completely enraptured by the immense amount of information I was sponging up about the eye donation process. I learned that the word "harvest" was no longer used when referring to "recovering" eyes, tissue, and organs, and I learned that the eye bank partnered with Donor Alliance, which did all the tissue and organ recovering. The memory of the rep who had come to visit the patients who were terminally ill in the ICU when my mom was initially sick clicked as I recognized this person had been from Donor Alliance. The folks at Donor Alliance are connected with UNOS, the united network of organ sharing, and the national transplant list. The expansive web of the organ donation network illuminated the beautifully complex process. What shocked me most was that despite the public's general support of organ donation in theory, just slightly above half of the US population are registered donors. I wondered about this discrepancy and wanted to know more.

Colton continued sharing more specifics about eye donation. The process is fairly complex and must be completed within twenty-four hours of death to keep the cell count in the corneas as high as possible to provide better sight to the recipients. I learned that the cornea is a small slice of the eye, and that the whole eye including the sclera is not always transplanted for corneal blindness. This answered my question as to why my dad, who had been going slowly blind, was still able to donate his corneas. Also why his being colorblind had not been a disqualifier either. Apparently, blindness on any scale did not always affect the cornea, or rule one out for corneal donation. This fascinated me.

I learned that matching a donor to a recipient is more about the content and quality of the cell count in the cornea than anything else. At one point, Colton gave me a pair of glasses to look through that represented how someone with corneal blindness sees. It was very cloudy, and I needed to get very close to anything to see even shadows. Suddenly, the magnitude of sight hit me, and I began to tear up thinking about what my parents had been able to do for four people with their four eyes. What a gift.

CHAPTER 120
January 12, 2018, 10:07 A.M.

THE PAST COUPLE years had been hellish. I was rebuilding myself square inch by square inch, but I was broken still, and the darkness loomed. Guilt and Individuation were still present, though most of their interactions were now much more tolerable, and the more I came to understand Guilt's motivations, the less I viewed it as the enemy. Underneath its brash and bullying ways, Guilt wanted connection and acceptance. I wanted that too, and once I understood that, I wondered if we really were that different after all? Guilt was a powerful being, and only acting how it knew to do so for survival. If Individuation could befriend Guilt, I wondered what kind of existence that would be. If they understood each other's motivations rather than fought over them, what might change? I deemed to never stop trying with those two in service to curiosity. My new identity depended on it.

The parents-shaped hole in my being was still there, still sore, and I was still fragile. After learning of the death of my dad's brother, my Uncle Roger, in February 2017 and of Dr. Bob Witchel in May 2017, I had given up completely. My Uncle Rog had been fighting COPD for years, and it finally caught up to him. Dr. Witchel's death was a mysterious passing in his sleep, with no explanation. His words floated back to me now more than ever: "Death ends a life, not a relationship." I decided to adopt this philosophy—it was something I hadn't yet tried, and I was out of ideas of my own. His death was tragic and senseless, and no explanation could help me make sense of it. Or of the deaths of five people close to me occurring within nine months, two of whom were my parents.

My depression over all these deaths led me to seek additional support through a local program for grief and depression. I found myself there on my parents' one-year death anniversaries, and staff sat with me through my body's violent shaking as it remembered. My therapist explained that my body was holding memories just like my mind did, and both of them needed to process. I exhaled as she said this. It was no longer something I needed to fear, but something I could let happen in the service of healing. I began to realize how important self-restoration was for my future, no matter what my future looked like.

CHAPTER 121
March 14, 2018, 1:31 P.M.

IT WAS MY mom's birthday. She would have been sixty-seven, and she was on my mind. She, my dad, and I all had spring birthdays roughly two weeks apart, and my mom's was the first birthday domino. It was strange to celebrate without her, and my mind drifted to those who had received her corneas. They were the only tangible parts of her that remained in this realm. I had written letters to the recipients of my parents' corneas and received two letters back, one from a recipient of each parent's cornea. I became very curious about them and their lives.

So eager to connect with them and potentially share their stories, I sent off another round of letters, explaining this desire and hoping my hardest for more responses. I envisioned meeting them. We would connect, cry, hug, and bond over the whole journey, and they would enter into my family fold for life, Seven Pounds style. I hoped that it would hold the relief it already did in my mind, for which I was continually searching in reality.

CHAPTER 122
April 10, 2018, 5:56 P.M.

I HAD HEARD nothing from any of the recipients. It was another blow. I busied myself learning as much as I could about organ donation. The eye bank held annual fundraising events, where I volunteered, and Colton invited me to tell my folks' story at one of them. The eye bank did such good work, and I was truly captured by their vision (pun intended).

The concept of organ and tissue donation had captivated me throughout my experience, and it began to occupy copious amounts of real estate in my mind. I was grateful that my dad had made his wishes to donate his body to science clear to Mat and I throughout our lives, and that it had been a relatively easy process to follow postmortem. Not one without heartache, but one that tapped into a meaning and a purpose that joined the pain. My mom's body was too sick to donate, but her corneas were not, and were still very meaningful.

What an amazing eye-specific fact—that corneas were largely salvageable, no matter the greater issues with other systems or the eye itself. This was another facet of miraculous, and I could hear my dad's joking nature say,

"I want to give everything away that I can. I don't need any of it anymore; I'm dead! Why wouldn't I help someone else live?" To help or save another with your death was a completely redemptive concept, and redemption remained an underlying tenet of my faith system as I began to see its roots appear again. It was comforting.

I wondered how separate those organs or parts remained once they were donated. And to what degree would a melding of spirits occur? If at all? This seemed mystical and mysterious, just like the ethereal presence, and regardless of the answer, there was great solace to be taken in allowing my parents to continue on in this form of aid to another. It suddenly made the little organ donation heart on my license come to life. Beat. Pulsate. Including that heart on a license was such a seemingly easy box to check on the application, and a decision I had not given much thought to until it came to life before me. What a lens.

CHAPTER 123

April 17, 2018, 10:18 A.M.

MONTHS HAD NOW passed since my initial letters to the recipients of my parents' corneas, with no further replies. I was devastated but had no choice other than to turn over my disappointment to mystery. It didn't fail. I didn't know the answers. I had no idea why they didn't write back, why my parents died so young, why my mom suffered for so long, why my dad died suddenly, what I was supposed to do with all this grief, and especially who I was now. But Mystery did.

I felt the ethereal presence swirl around my heartbreak like a summer breeze as I realized that perhaps I was not meant to get it; rather, I was meant to see it. To witness what was and what is now. To see the joy that holds both the pain and the good, and to watch the Truth unfold all around me in every way I couldn't imagine. To truly see others with all their wildly murky and intoxicating layers. To see myself as I truly am, underneath all the filters and pretenses, assumptions, fears. To zoom out and see the world in all its magnificent facets. To zoom in and see the intricate details of a person, a story, a flower, a raindrop. To see the ethereal power of mystery and love and uncertainty and wonder and the universe and curiosity and space and the maybes and creativity and the I-don't-knows and the freedom that comes from Letting. It. All. Go. And to see that these are enough. And perhaps the Godiverse looked different than I once thought.

A sharp expanse of space rippled through my chest, releasing the knotted ways of what once was. The dogged pursuit of needing to understand, to be in control, to always know the next step of the plan, to only play by my rules. My rules felt useless compared to this freedom.

I began to cry happier tears. Watching my parents endure the events of the last five years had tilted my perspective into another dimension of the present. One I hadn't seen before. It was a rich layer that provided peace, calm, and rest even when I didn't know the "why." Even when I was struggling with crippling sadness and anger. Even when I wondered if the void I felt in their absences would ever heal, especially on important days like today. Especially when I didn't know the answers. Definitely when I was full of doubts about my own possibility of recovery from all of this.

This insight brought me new life. A life that now looked different in every way. My parents were dead, and nothing was ever going to change that. And when they died, the one thing they left was their sight. To help others truly see. Of course, they did. It's who they were. It's who I still am.

I let a single tear run all the way down my cheek without wiping it away as the date came into focus through this new lens. Six years ago, my dad's surprise party had taken a very different turn, and life had shifted in a way I could have never envisioned. I felt its weight.

I inhaled a breath that felt as if it reached my toes. And in that moment, I truly let go of everything I thought I knew. It wasn't mine to hold. I let mystery and love and wonder completely take over. My inner knowing returned. I didn't know where we were going, and I didn't need to. I knew they would show me. I just had to look.

Happy birthday, Dad.

ABOUT THE AUTHOR

ALISHA BASHAW IS a writer, musical theater enthusiast, and an equine and mental health therapist. While in graduate school across the country from her family in 2012, her parents suffered illnesses that took Alisha back and forth between duty and desire, mystery and the known, and pursuit of her own identity and caregiving for family. She began the long stint of learning to let go of the things she held dearest while completing grad school and eventually moving home to help care for her folks. After a five-year battle with death, Alisha's parents passed, and Alisha began to learn how to live life as a young adult orphan. With a front row seat to her parents' declines, and a battle between guilt and individuation of her own, Alisha sought meaning for herself and her parents through the healing world of organ donation. She sees life as a story, and couldn't get through hers without playing and singing music, hanging with her two beloved cats, Olive and Stinker (Pax), and reveling in the immense power of kindness. She fully embraces the belief that "I don't know" is a complete answer, and that love and mystery prevail. She resides in Aurora, Colorado.